THE COMPLETE
SALMON
FISHER

VOLUME TWO:
Salmon on the Fly

THE COMPLETE
SALMON
FISHER

VOLUME TWO:
Salmon on the Fly

MALCOLM GREENHALGH

BLANDFORD

From a book you cannot learn the whole art of salmon-fishing, but you can learn to avoid many disastrous mistakes, and you can learn endless 'wrinkles' which make your fishing more finished and much more effective than before.

A.H. CHAYTOR, *Letters to a Salmon Fisher's Sons*, 1910

....

A BLANDFORD BOOK

First published in the UK 1996 by Blandford
A Cassell Imprint
Cassell plc, Wellington House,
125 Strand, London WC2R 0BB

Distributed in the United States by Sterling Publishing Co., Inc.
387 Park Avenue South, New York, NY 10016-8810

British Library Cataloguing-in-Publication Data
A catalogue entry for this title is available from the British Library

ISBN 0-7137-2545-1

Printed and bound in Great Britain by Hartnolls Limited, Bodmin, Cornwall

CONTENTS

INTRODUCTION

Composure, patience, and perseverance are indispensable qualifications for all followers of this art, but more especially for the Salmon Angler. He must lay his account with frequently beating the waters in vain exertion; in being long wet and weary, ere he can (to use the fisher's expression) move a fin; and when he does, to be perhaps then only mocked with a wanton rise, or a false bite; or should he at last prevail in luring the Salmon to his fly, and after working and playing him through many streams, and through many pools, he brings him within reach, and then thinks he is to take possession of his prize, in a moment the tackle snaps, and all is gone.

Edinburgh Encyclopaedia, nineteenth century

Most of the books about salmon fishing that have been published have been written by anglers who were fortunate enough to fish the best waters when they were full of salmon. Making big bags of fish in the years up to 1970 was not particularly difficult. In recent years, however, things have changed: the timings of salmon runs have altered, the numbers of salmon running many rivers have declined, and the best fishing is now beyond the means of most of us. We have to work hard to catch one fish in a week, never mind a dozen in a day! However, fishing hard water with only a small head of fish and having to experiment in order to wheedle out the occasional fish probably teaches more than catching big bags every time one goes fishing.

I have been lucky. I am old enough to have witnessed the bonanza of the end of the 1960s, when every river was full of fish waiting to grab the fly. Since I gave up paid employment ten years ago, I have been fortunate enough to fish for salmon for up to 100 days each year in some of the top salmon rivers and lakes in Britain and Ireland, Scandinavia and North America and in some very difficult rivers, when there were very few fish about and when taking one salmon for ten days' fishing was a great success. I have had it easy – and I have found it difficult!

This book is about salmon flies, flies that will catch the occasional fish when there are few about. It is about fishing these flies, not in a mechanical manner that will take a crop from a fantastic run but in a variety of ways, one of which might work. If you are fortunate enough to fish a prolific river, these flies and methods might help you make an even bigger bag!

In many North American and Russian salmon rivers, and in an increasing number of British rivers, there is a growing move to restrict the numbers of salmon that an angler can kill. I support this restriction, for there is no excuse for killing the sorts of bags that were killed in past years. How can anglers make a valid protest about offshore and inshore netting if they are killing many salmon and selling their surplus? Only fishmongers sell fish! I kill about ten fish a year, which, smoked and fresh, are ample for my table.

I am not, however, in favour of enforced catch-and-release – hooking a salmon, playing it to exhaustion and then hoping that it will survive to spawning. I will put back any fish that is not pristine silver and big hen salmon (as distinct from grilse), but I spend time making sure that the fish have fully recovered before I release them. Having some restriction on bag limit, whether it be self-imposed or enforced by the fishery regulations, does encourage one to experiment. Why go through the same old routine if the deep freeze is not awaiting a supply of fish? Having caught one or two, the pressure is off! One can try things that one would never have dreamed of without those restrictions – for instance, trying a dry fly or nymph, dibbling the fly, working the fly, backing-up and using a host of different flies that one would not normally have considered in the past.

If you are new to salmon fly fishing I hope that this book will help you on your way, for you have taken up a super sport, despite the pessimistic view of the editors of the *Edinburgh Encyclopaedia*! Don't, whatever you do, become hidebound with the techniques of more experienced anglers. Try new methods and new flies, especially if things are a bit dour. If you are an experienced salmon angler, I hope that there will be a few points that you find worthy of consideration.

MALCOLM GREENHALGH
LOWTON, 1996

ACKNOWLEDGEMENTS

I would like to pay a compliment to all those fishery owners and fishery boards who have allowed me access to their waters, to various tourist boards who have given me the chance of fishing places that I would have had difficulty in reaching with my limited funds, and to the many friends with whom I have shared a beat or a boat. They are too many for me to name them all.

I must, however, formally acknowledge some special people. Thorbjorn Tufte and the Norwegian Federation of Hunters and Anglers most generously introduced me to Norway's salmon rivers. John Todd has shared many Irish rivers, lakes and bottles of Bushmills with me. Frank Elliott and his great friend Ted Browne have let me use their great beats on Mourne and Finn. Ken Walker, of Bruce & Walker, has offered much help with fly rods and with providing fishing on Scottish beats that I could otherwise not afford. Alan Bramley, of Partridge fame, is a great friend who has provided me with hooks and other items of equipment and also offered great support. Frank Casson has let me delve through his vast collection of ancient and classic flies from a bygone era. Those two great salmon fly dressers, Peter Canning and Frankie McPhillips, have donated their effective flies. So, too, did the late Michael and Rita Rogan in the years before their deaths.

It has been a privilege to talk to Hans Odegard, Mikael Frodin and Lars Berg about trends in Scandinavian salmon flies. Paul Morgan of Coch-y-Bonddu Books has been a great help in searching through the literature. Ann Parkinson of Sportsfish and Phil and Mary White of Lathkill have provided fly tying materials; Mary provided the best vice in the world (Dyna-king), and Ann the most superb magnifying lamp, which has enabled my ageing eyes to tie without strain. I must also acknowledge the assistance of David Goodchild, Roy Arris and Crawford Little, editors of *Salmon, Trout & Sea-Trout*, and of Mark Bowler, editor of *Fly-Fishing & Fly-Tying*, who let me air many of the points included in this book.

Anyone who puts his or her head on the block by writing a fishing book needs a lot of encouragement. My fishing club, Bowland Game Fishing Association, is a case in point. The committee keeps on acquiring new river beats, each offering a new challenge, and the members constantly raise my spirits with generous support. Among them, I must make particular mention of Brian Wells, Brian Hoggarth, Chris Heap, Roy Brierley, Chris Hosker and my regular fishing comrades Geoff Haslam, Dave Evans, Alan Davies, Keith Owen and Paul Stanton. Also to Bill and Marie Arnold and Kathleen Falkus, whose hospitality in Eskdale has been wonderful.

I also acknowledge my debt to Hugh Falkus, who has provided me with much friendship, discussion, encouragement and Scotch over the years.

Finally, I must say thank you to Yvonne, who has worked to pay the bills, spent her spare time in keeping the office tidy, cleared away my fly tying kit and always sent me away on my frequent fishing trips with a bag of clean clothes. And to my son Peter.

....

Conversion table

1 inch = 2.5cm
1 foot = 30.4cm
1 yard = 1 metre
1 mile = 1.6km
1 sq foot = 0.09 sq metre
1 sq yard = 0.8 sq metre
1 acre = 0.4 hectare
1 ounce = 28.3g
1 pound = 0.4kg
1 ton = 1.01 tonnes
$°F = (9 \times °C) \div 5 + 32$

PART ONE
The Salmon Fly

....

Inasmuch as the use of the fly surpasses every other mode of Angling, in the same ratio is the Angling for *Salmon* superior to common Trout fishing.

GEORGE C. BAINBRIDGE, *The Fly Fisher's Guide*, 1816

CHAPTER 1

THE EVOLUTION
OF THE SALMON FLY

The Samon is the moost stately fyssh
that only man maye angle to in fresshe water.

DAME JULYANA BERNERS, *The Treatyse of Fysshynge wyth an Angle*, 1496

It is generally accepted that the first book to deal fully with fly fishing and that referred to fishing for salmon was *The Treatyse of Fysshynge wyth an Angle*, which was published in 1496 by Wynkyn de Worde (who succeeded William Caxton at the Westminster Press). The *Treatyse* was a supplement to a second printing of an earlier work, *The Boke of St Albans*, first published in 1486, which described the essentials of the gentlemanly sports of hunting, hawking and heraldry, and it is likely that the contents of the *Treatyse* were collected together from a variety of contemporary sources. The salmon, the *Treatyse* tells us, is in season from 'March to Myghelmas' (Michaelmas, 29 September) and 'is seldom seen wyth a dubbe' (an artificial dubbed fly), although the angler should fish 'wyth a dubbe at such tyme as when he lepith'. Bait is the recommended method. 'Fyrst wyth a red worme . . . also wyth a bobbe that bredyth in a dunghill and specyally wyth a souerayn bayte that bredyth on a water docke.' Red worm? Maggot? Dock-grub? For salmon? One is led to suspect that the author was offering advice on how to catch smolts passing downstream rather than returning big salmon, although the line that she recommends suggests otherwise – 15 horsehairs plaited together, instead of the nine hairs used to catch big trout.

Twelve 'dubbes' or flies are recommended in the *Treatyse*, and although they were meant to imitate insects that immature salmon, trout, grayling, chub and other feeding fish would eat, they were also accepted as being suitable flies for catching salmon. In the fifteenth century the life history of the salmon and the fact that fish returning from the sea do not feed in fresh water were unknown. The 12 flies of the *Treatyse* are the foundation on which the development of the salmon fly is based. By modern standards, they were all simple flies, with a dubbed wool body (hence the name 'dubbe' for these flies) and wings composed of two, sometimes four, full feathers. I will list these as the good Dame did, in fifteenth-century English. The Plate section includes my interpretation of the first 'donne flye'. It is great fun interpreting the Dame's English and then tying her flies during long winter evenings!

Thyse ben the .xij. flyes wyth whyche ye shall angle . . . and dubbe lyke as ye shall now here me tell.

Marche

The donne flye of the donne woll & the wyngis of the pertryche. Another donne flye, the body of blacke wool: the wyngis of the blackyst drake: and the Iay vnder the wynge & vnder the tayle.

Apryll

The stone flye. the body of blacke wull: & yelow vnder the wynge. and vnder the tayle & the wynges of the drake. In the begynnynge of May a good fly. the body of roddyd wull and the lappid abowte wyth blacke silk: the wynges of the drake & of thre redde capons hakyll.

May

The yellow flye. the body of yelow wull: the wynges of the redde cocke hackyll & the drake lyttyd yelow. The black louper. the body of blacke wull & lappyd abowte wyth the herl of the pecok tayle: & the wynges of the redde capon wt a blew heed.

June

The donne cut: the body of blacke wull & yelowe lyste after eyther syde: the wybges of the bosarde biund on wyth barkyd hempe. The maure fly. the body of doke wull the wynges of the blackest mayle of the wylde drake. The tandy flye at saynt Wyllyans daye. the body of tandy wull & the wynges contrary eyther ayenst other of the whitest mayle of the wylde drake.

Iuyll

The waspe flye. the body of black wull and lappis abowte wt yelow threde: the wynges of the bosarde. The shell flye at saynt Thomas saye. the body of grene wull & lappyd abowte wyth the herl of the pecoks tayle: the wynges of the bosarde.

August

The drake flye. the body of black wull & lappyd abowte wythe blacke sylke: wynges of the mayle of the blacke drake wyth a black heed.

The simplicity and general drabness of these flies dominated fly fishing in

Britain for at least two hundred years, and their influence continued in salmon flies well into the nineteenth century. Compare, for instance, Bainbridge's Wasp Fly in the Plate section with the first Dun Fly recommended in the *Treatyse*.

Dame Julyana's flies were painstakingly copied, without acknowledgement, by several writers well into the seventeenth century, but in this long period few had anything new to offer on the subject of salmon fly fishing. At that time anglers faced almost insurmountable obstacles when it came to angling for the powerful salmon, as distinct from the parr and smolts that they did catch and eat. Fine horsehair lines, of fixed length and tied directly to the end of hazel or ash rods, did not allow salmon lies to be covered in any but the narrowest of streams, and when a salmon was hooked the fish would almost certainly smash the line on its first powerful run. Leonard Mascall noted, in *A booke of fishing with Hooke and Line* (1590), that: 'The Salmon is a gentle fish, but he is cumbrous to take.' In 1614, in *The Second Booke of the English Husbandman*, Gervase Markham advised:

> Now, lastly, as touching the angling for Salmon, albe he is a fish which in truth is unfit for your Travaile, both because hee is too huge and cumbersome, as also in that he naturally delighteth to lie in the bottomes of the great deepe Rivers, and as neare as may bee in the middst of the Channell.

For those determined to catch salmon, Markham repeated the flies given in the *Treatyse* but also recommended worm. He introduced double hooks to the angling world but stressed the need for skill when playing a salmon on the existing crude tackle: 'The danger is all in the running out of both Salmon and Trout, you must forecast to turn the fish as you do a wild horse.'

Some modern writers have suggested that in these early days of fixed, short lines, anglers hooking a salmon would throw their rod into the water and retrieve it later when the fish was played out. There is no evidence that this was common practice, and, as those who have dropped a long rod into a river will testify, the usual outcome would be a lost rod (and salmon).

It was early in the seventeenth century that several improvements of fly fishing tackle evolved that would help an angler play and land a salmon and that would encourage further use and development of the salmon fly. In the second edition of Thomas Barker's tiny book *Barker's Delight: The Art of Angling*, published in 1659, we find a description of a two-piece rod, the bottom section being 10ft in length, the top 6ft, that must be 'pretty stiffe'. A ring was fitted to the tip of the rod. This was the first mention of rod rings, although it was not until 1706 that Robert Howlett described, in *The Angler's Sure Guide*, rod-rings or 'loops' being fitted along the entire rod to guide the line. Barker also described the use of a 'winder' or reel, clipped to the rod butt, that could release or retrieve line by means of this single tip ring. The line was not now of fixed length, and Barker described one made by plaiting three lengths of silk with three lengths of horsehair (this silk/horsehair line continued well into the nineteenth century) that, though only 26 yards in length, would be strong enough and long enough for playing grilse and small salmon.

Barker wrote with authority, as someone who really did know about salmon fishing. His recommendation to use two worms and 'angle as nigh the bottom' still holds good today for those fishing bait, as does his description of 'trouling' (or spinning) with a dead gudgeon. As for the fly, Barker was the first to deviate from the dozen found in the *Treatyse*, and he gives advice of flies specially tied for salmon fishing: 'If you angle for him with a flie (which he will rise at like a Trout) the flie must be made of a large hook, which hook must carry six wings, or four at least.' He was the first to publish the adage: use a dark fly on a bright day and a bright fly on a dull day (another, contradictory, adage goes: bright day, bright fly; dull day, dull fly, but we will analyse these adages later, see page 45). Barker was also the first to describe how to dress a fly, including the wound hackle. This method of dressing a fly continued to be used for two hundred years, until the advent of the gaudy, so called 'classic' fully dressed fly (pages 25–33).

1. Cut a broad slip from a feather to make the wings; you will need two or three slips when dressing a salmon fly in Barker's style, for, as we have seen, he recommended two or three pairs of wings on salmon flies. Tie these on top of the hook shank with the tips pointing forwards, away from the hook bend.
2. Strip away the fibres from one side of a cock's hackle.
3. Take the tying silk to the hook bend and there tie in the hackle, tinsel rib bing and body material (usually fur dubbed on the silk).
4. Wind on the body, then the rib and bring the hackle forwards in open turns to give a palmered hackle. Tie these in.
5. Divide the wing slips into two wings with a needle, pull them back so that they now lie over the body and hackle and tie them down with turns of silk before finishing the fly with two or three half-hitches (the modern whip-finish was devised in the nineteenth century).

'There is judgement in making those flyes,' concluded Barker. The Plate section includes a salmon fly dressed according to Barker's recipe.

Angling literature in the third quarter of the seventeenth century was dominated by three authors. Izaak Walton, the most famous of the trio because of the literary value of *The Compleat Angler*, published in 1653, knew little, if anything, of salmon fishing. Charles Cotton, author of a supplement to the 5th edition (1676) of *The Compleat Angler* entitled 'How to Angle for Trout and Grayling in a Clear Stream', also was not a salmon angler. But the third, and least well known, Colonel Robert Venables, was a great salmon angler, and perhaps the first to deserve that description. His *The Experienc'd Angler, or Angling Improved* was first published in 1662.

Venables was a Roundhead, fighting for the Parliamentary forces against the Royalists in the English Civil War. He commanded a company of Lancashire foot-soldiers (forerunner of the Lancashire Regiment) and fought in the battle of Westhoughton Common in December 1642. In July 1649 Oliver Cromwell sent him to subdue the natives of Ireland, and from October 1649 to 1654 he was governor of Ulster. Here Venables took the opportunity to fish, with the fly, in Northern Ireland's magnificent salmon rivers. His book, published eight years after he left the Province, described salmon flies and fishing as practised in the mid-seventeenth century and provided several tips that are as valid today as they were three hundred and fifty years ago.

'The Salmon takes the artificial fly very well,' wrote Venables. 'But you must use a troll [reel], or he, being a strong fish, will hazard your line, except you give him length: his flies must be much larger than you use for other fish, the wings very long, two or four, behind one another with very long tails.' Very long wings and very long tails equal movement of the fly in the water. This movement is a highly important ingredient of successful salmon flies (see Chapter 2).

'Young salmon under a quarter of a yard long, have tender mouths, so as they are apt to break their hold,' Venables pointed out. Nine inches long, with tender mouths? Venables was clearly talking of sea trout herling, which abounded in Irish rivers. But he then described the merits of double hooks for soft-mouthed fish, which applies today during a run of summer grilse: 'fasten two hooks together . . . not with the points opposite to one another, but about a quarter of a circle, and on them they make their Flie, that if one Hook break hold, the other may not fail!'

River conditions and the correct choice of fly colour were important to Venables:

You must either fish in a river not fully cleared from some rain lately fallen, that had discoloured it. . . . If you angle in a river that is muddied by rain, or passing through mosses or bogs, you must use a larger bodied fly than ordinary, which argues, that in clear rivers the fly must be smaller. . . . If the water be clear and low, then use a small bodied fly with slender wings . . . when the water begins to clear after rain, and is a brownish colour, then use a red or orange fly. . . . If the day be clear, then a light coloured fly, with slender body and wings. . . . In dark weather, as well as dark waters, your fly must be dark. . . . If the water be of a whey colour, or whitish, then use a black or brown fly; yet these six last rules do not always hold, though usually they do, or else I had omitted them.

The choice of fly, especially as regards size, is vitally important today (see Chapter 2).

Let me also add three great hints from Venables that are still valid today.

First, the angler's position in relation to sun and moon.

Keep the sun, and moon, if night, before you, if your eyes will endure which I must question, at least be sure to have those planets on your side, for if they be on your back, your rod will with its shadow offend much, and the fish see further and clearer, when they look towards those lights, than the contrary; as you may experiment thus in a dark night, if a man come betwixt you and any light, you see him clearly, but not at all if the light come betwixt you and him.

How few anglers today are aware of this real problem, whether they be fishing in a bright day with the sun streaming down the river (from behind the angler) or at night with the moon casting flickering shadows over the fish.

Second, the care of fly hooks.

Have also a little whetstone about two inches long, and one quarter square; it's much better to sharpen your hooks than a file, which either will not touch a well-tempered hook, or leave it rough but not sharp.

Most modern anglers rarely examine the sharpness of their hooks, and even fewer carry a little carborundum stone.

Third, how deep is the pool?

Get a musquet or carbine bullet, make a hole through it, and put in a string twist, hang this on your hook to try the depth of a river or pond.

It is essential to have some idea of water depth, especially early and late in the year when the fly must be fished fairly deep. Yet many anglers still do not know how to plumb the depth of a salmon pool.

The Lancastrian James Chetham closely followed on the heels of Venables with *The Angler's Vade Mecum* (1681). Chetham listed such a vast array of materials that could be used in fly dressing that it is clear that anglers of the time were not hidebound about using standard patterns but experimented with new patterns. He also introduced the hackle pliers for producing the wound hackle, adding that: 'If pliars be wanting, a piece of silk fastened to the end of the feather will answer the purpose.'

Chetham was a firm believer in the creed that a salmon continues to feed when it returns from the sea, stating that, 'for Flies, he [the salmon] takes the same that the Trout generally doth, whether Natural or Artificial,' and he came up with the Horseleech Fly. Horseleech Flies, an old English name for the dragonfly, 'are of various colours,' wrote Richard Brookes in *The Art of Angling*, in 1766, and 'have great Heads, large Bodies, and very long Tails [abdomen], and two, some have three, Pair of Wings, placed behind each other'.

The entomological observations of these seventeenth- and eighteenth-century writers left something to be desired, for all dragonflies have two pairs of wings, never three. But their piscatorial observations were also somewhat astray, in that they believed that big fish, like pike and salmon, fed keenly on large natural flies, like dragonflies and damselflies, which were then known as devil's needles because it was believed that they could stitch up human mouths! They also called these insects 'salmon flies' and 'pike flies'. This ignorance spawned several salmon flies that imitated dragonflies. In *Northern Memoirs* (1694), for instance, Richard Franck described a 'glittering fly, the body composed of red twisted silk, intermingled with silver, and eye of gold'. The wing was a 'dappled feather of a teal'. The barred feather that we use today for a Teal & Red and Peter Ross is, in fact, a modification of Franck's glittering fly. Undoubtedly, the glittering fly was an imitation of a red-bodied damsel- or dragonfly (see Plate section).

Throughout the second half of the eighteenth century and first few years of the nineteenth century, the mistaken belief that salmon actively feed on insects, especially large ones, dominated the artificial salmon fly. Giles Jacob, in *Country Gentleman's Vade Mecum* (1717), recommended wet mayfly imitations, arguing that: 'A Salmon will likewise sometimes rise at the May-flies; when you are to manage your Matters very tenderly, to preserve your lines.' My late edition (1826) of Richard Bowkler's *The Art of Angling Improved in all its Parts* (edited by his son Charles) continued the dragonfly theme by recommending two artificial flies, the King's Fisher or Peacock Fly and the Dragon-Fly, each of which is a 'large gaudy artificial fly, which they [the salmon] probably mistake for a gay Libellula, or Dragon Fly'. Bowkler reinforced the theory that salmon feed after they have returned to fresh water from the sea and that salmon flies should imitate those foods by concluding that: 'The angler should imitate principally the natural flies found on such rivers where salmon abound.' As late as 1845 Cornelius O'Gorman noted (in *The Practice of Fishing, particularly as regards Ireland*) that: 'When natural trout-flies begin to appear on the rivers, your salmon-flies should be as nearly of their colour in the body as possible.' In other words, like trout, salmon eat natural flies, and so you should be fishing with trout flies but in a bigger hook size.

George C. Bainbridge's *The Fly Fisher's Guide* (1816) is an angling classic, for it gave reason for salmon fly design before the gaudy, fully dressed fly revolution that occurred shortly after that book was published. There is the continuation of the 'dragonfly as food' theory: 'Those made in imitation of the Dragon flies are the most to be depended upon, as these insects are constantly hovering over the water, consequently are more familiar to the view of the fish.' And among his recommended flies, Bainbridge included a wasp imitation of which he wrote:

No. 5. is a copy of the Common Wasp in the natural state, which has been selected as being a favourite with the salmon peal [sea trout herling], mort [adult sea trout] or grilse; and well grown fish will sometimes rise at this fly in preference to any other. It is to be made of the wool of the sheep or other animal dyed yellow, and a black hackle twisted at intervals over the body, or vice versa, or a black body and yellow hackle.

Bainbridge's Wasp is shown in the Plate section.

Then, suddenly, Bainbridge lets us into a little secret, which jettisons the food imitation that had prevailed for so long. 'They [salmon] are however so capricious, that they will not infrequently rise at an extremely gaudy fly, which bears no resemblance to nature, in preference even to a real Wasp or Dragon fly.'

It is clear from a thorough reading of late eighteenth- and early nineteenth-century literature that the fly that imitates food was slowly being ousted by flies that did not imitate food at all but that were great catchers of salmon. So we have the Tweed angler John Younger insisting, in *River Angling for Trout and Salmon* (1860), that salmon eat march browns and that 'they feed . . . exactly as the trout does'. By contrast, William Scrope, in his magnificent book *Days and Nights of Salmon Fishing in the Tweed* (1843), gave six flies that bore no relation to possible food items and that were chosen (as Venables urged almost two hundred years earlier) according to water conditions.

> My rule has been to adapt my fly, both as to colour and size, to the state of the water: a large fly with sober colours for deep and clear water, and a smaller equally unassuming, where it is shallower; in the throat of the cast [pool neck], as long as it continues rough, a large fly also; at the tail of it, where the water runs more quietly and evenly, a smaller one serves the purpose best. Thus you should change your fly in every stream once or twice.

This advice holds good today, over a century and a half later!

Scrope's six flies are important, for they are the definitive salmon wet flies of sober hue that were widely used but then ousted by the gaudy, fully dressed fly revolution. They evolved because they caught salmon, but not anglers. They were simple to dress (see below) and used the minimum of readily available materials. What is more, although Scrope stipulated what feathers to use in their construction, it is clear from other writers of the time that others could be used with equal effect. Tie these with a brown or black hairwing; they are still excellent flies.

Scrope's six flies

These are the definitive sombre salmon flies.

Kinmont Willie

Wing	underwing of drake teal (teal flank)
Head	yellow wool
Body	hare's ear
Tag	red wool
Tail	yellow wool
Hackle	black cock

The Lady of Mertoun

Wing	underwing of drake teal (teal flank)
Head	crimson wool
Body	water-rat fur
Tag	crimson wool
Tail	yellow wool
Hackle	red cock (red game, not dyed red)

Toppy

Wing	white tipped black turkey
Head	crimson wool
Body	black bullock hair*
Tag	crimson wool
Tail	yellow wool
Hackle	black cock

Michael Scott

Scrope described this as 'a most killing pattern'.

Wing	mottled feather from back of a drake (bronze mallard)
Head	yellow wool and a little hare's fur next to it
Body	black wool
Tag	hare's ear then crimson wool, with a small red gamecock hackle
Tail	yellow wool
Hackle	black cock
Rib	gold twist (oval gold tinsel)

Meg with the Muckle Mouth

Wing	brown turkey
Head	crimson wool
Body	yellow silk
Tag	crimson wool with red cock hackle
Tail	yellow or orange wool
Hackle	dark red cock

Meg in Her Brawes

Wing	light brown bittern
Head	yellow wool
Throat hackle	blue jay
Body	brown wool mixed with bullock fur
Tag	green wool then crimson wool
Tail	yellow wool
Hackle	furnace cock
Rib	gold twist (oval gold tinsel)

Scrope's flies are illustrated in the Plate section.

*A small, red gamecock hackle was often added to the end of the body.

Notes:

1. A yellow tail or tip to the body is acknowledged as a killing feature of many salmon flies: Scrope was the first to highlight this feature using wool. Today, golden pheasant crest is the most popular tailing material.

2. Note the use of readily available wool, bullock hair, and the common colours of gamecocks.

3. Meg in Her Brawes was the first to have a blue jay throat hackle, an essential ingredient in many modern salmon flies, such as Munro Killer, Connemara Black and the Bumbles.

4. Today, European fly dressers must buy white-tipped black and brown turkey quills, for modern farmed turkeys are white. This was not so in Scrope's day, for the wild-plumaged turkey had been imported into Britain from North America and was gaining in popularity as Christmas fare.

5. Bittern feathers! Today this species of heron is on the verge of extinction. But in the mid-nineteenth century no one cared about the extinction of rare birds. The red kite still occurred through much of the wilder parts of Britain and its tail (glede's tail) was much in demand for winging salmon flies. One anonymous Victorian writer even urged young anglers to go out immediately and shoot a kite before they became extinct!

6. Scrope referred to the tag as the end of the body.

7. All Scrope's patterns have virtually a Dee strip-wing style with the exception of Michael Scott. This, with its bronze mallard wing, is closer to a Spey fly.

Scrope was a robust gentleman, as were all anglers of that era. The Tweed is a mighty river, and he had no qualms about taking his 18–20ft rod and wading, fully clothed, to 'the fifth button of the waistcoat!' It reminds me of the late Rita Rogan of Ballyshannon (the last of the Rogans, page 28), who described to me how, when her husband Michael hooked a salmon on the Erne, she would tuck her dress into her knickers, throw off her shoes and enter the icy waters, armed with a landing-net! 'I took a spare dress and changed behind a stone wall before we walked home!'

That this style of drab flies dominated salmon angling in the early 1800s is clear from many writers. The anonymous author of *The North Country Angler* (1786) introduced a most killing fly that will catch salmon today, over two centuries later.

Wing	bronze mallard or dark turkey tail
Head	yellow and brown mixed pig's wool
Body	peacock herl

Tail	5–6 strands peacock herl
Hackle	black cock

This fly is shown in the Plate section.

Notes:

1. This is the first reference to pig's wool in a salmon fly. Seal fur later superseded the very coarse pig's wool.
2. It is surprising that more salmon flies have not been devised with a peacock herl body, for such bodies are very attractive to trout and sea trout.

Alexander MacIntosh added another pattern of the same style in his *The Driffield Angler* (1808), which he called the Black Dog. Again, note the simplicity of style. This was, once again, a fly that had proved itself among salmon, not fly dressers!

Black Dog

Wing	dark heron quill plus a few fibres of turkey tail
Head	dark green mohair
Body	lead-coloured pig's wool (later given as blue dun or grey seal fur)
Hackle	black cock
Rib	gold tinsel

How did they tie their salmon flies in the latter half of the eighteenth century and early years of the nineteenth century? The best description is by Samuel Taylor in *Angling in all its Branches* (1800). Incidentally, Taylor was the first to describe the use of the vice in fly-tying.

1. Take a broad slip of feather, and tie this in with waste to the rear and wing extending forwards over the front of the hook. MacIntosh recommended tying in two slips, to make the two wings.
2. Take the tying silk down the shank and, if the pattern demands it, tie in the tag (if there is a small hackle at the end of the body, this is tied in and wound). The tail is now tied in (if there is no tag or hackle at the rear of the body, the tail is tied directly at the end of the shank).
3. Tie in the hackle by its tip, directly in front of the tail.
4. If the pattern has a rib, tie this in front of the tail.
5. Dub the body fur on the silk, and wind this dubbed fur up the hook shank.
6. Wind the hackle forwards, in open turns, up the body (palmered) and tie off. Follow this with the ribbing material if appropriate to the pattern.

7. Bring the wing back over the body, and bind down with three or four turns of silk (some tiers used a little dubbing on the thread to help hold the wing back).
8. Dub a little head fur on the silk and wind to create a neat head.
9. Tie off the silk with three half-hitches between the front of the wing and head.
10. Take a needle and separate the one winging slip into two wings (unless using two slips from the start as recommended by MacIntosh).

In 1834 George Hansard published his *Trout and Salmon Fishing in Wales* and wrote of salmon fly patterns that they should be 'very sober in colour, and few in number'. Two of his flies lacked the currently popular palmered hackle, the hackle being just at the throat. They are quite simple flies and were highly recommended for the Welsh Dee.

Spring Fly

Body	orange silk
Rib	broad gold twist (oval tinsel)
Hackle	smoky-dun cock
Wing	dark mottled brown bittern

Summer Fly

Body	yellow silk
Rib	gold twist (oval tinsel)
Hackle	deep blood-red cock
Wing	brown turkey plus a few strands green peacock herl

These drab flies of the 1700s and early 1800s caught salmon, but they quickly lost favour. In his *The Angler's Guide* of 1808 Thomas Salter noted that:

The artificial flies, sold at fishing tackle shops, are principally made from the directions given by Bowkler of Shrewsbury; and, perhaps, have been but little improved during the last century.

By the end of the nineteenth century they had been ousted by the so-called 'classic', fully dressed gaudy style of fly. There were a few obstinate anglers who persevered with the sombre style, including A.H. Chaytor, whose only book, *Letters to a Salmon Fisher's Sons* (1910), showed him to have been a thoughtful and great angler.

Chaytor recommended just three simple flies (although one has eyes of jungle cock, one of the 'essential' ingredients of the gaudy fly era in which Chaytor found himself).

White & Silver

Body	oval silver tinsel
Hackle	two turns long white cock
Wing	dark turkey
Cheek	jungle cock

Claret

Body	rough claret wool or seal fur
Rib	broad silver tinsel
Hackle	claret cock
Wing	bronze mallard or brown turkey

Gipps

Body	half black and half orange-brown seal fur
Rib	narrow silver tinsel
Hackle	black
Wing	brown turkey

Few salmon fishers of Chaytor's era would have fished with these simple flies, for as Chaytor noted:

Still more salmon fishers, however, pin their faith to an endless variety of gorgeous flies with charming names – names that plainly speak their real use and object, that is, to catch the fisher, not the fish. These names are a comedy.... The conclusion is that I would feel as confident of success with the old type of [simple, drab] fly as with the new [complex, gaudy], or vice versa. The unromantic conclusion to which observant anglers have come is that the colour and materials of fly matter very little, if anything, while the size and movement thereof is all important.

Francis, Hale, Hardy, Kelson, Pryce-Tannatt and the gaudy fly

Several factors combined in the middle years of the nineteenth century to replace the simple-to-tie, sombre salmon flies, of which there were very few patterns and which required very few, easily obtained materials, with hundreds of patterns of more complex, gaudy flies.

The first was the growing availability of exotic, brightly coloured feathers.

In the Victorian era Britain had a vast Empire, 'on which the sun never set' and which covered the atlases of the time with red. The Victorians were great collectors, and they scoured their Empire for the rare and bright. This collecting mania included birds from all corners of the globe, and the demand for the brightest of plumages quickly grew as Victorian ladies embellished their hats with the feathers of flamingos, cock-of-the-rock, Indian crows, blue chatterers, birds of paradise, florican bustards, toucans, macaws and so on.

Professional fly dressers immediately adopted these materials and incorporated them into their salmon flies, and they started to make the ways in which these flies were tied ever more complex. There was a good reason for this – money! Flies that demanded few, easily obtained materials and that were easy to dress made little profit. A fly dresser would have to tie many each day to make a living. There was far greater profit in the new, gaudy, complex flies, even though it took much longer to tie them. At the same time, most amateur tiers would find the new flies so difficult to make that they would have to purchase them. With sufficient propaganda to create a demand, the new flies made some fly dressers both more famous and better off than they had formerly been.

The primary movement in this revolution came from Ireland, mainly around the River Erne in Co. Donegal (Rev. Henry Newland, *The Erne, Its Legends & Fly Fishing*, 1851) and the Shannon where Cornelius O'Gorman (author of *The Practice of Fishing*, 1845) was the leading fly dresser. In the nineteenth century these were among the world's most prolific salmon rivers (they were subsequently ruined by hydro-electric schemes), and on their banks lived other great fly dressers, who supplied a host of wealthy visiting anglers with essential flies. One Pat McKay had a business in Ballyshannon from about 1810. Another, James Rogan, founded the great Rogan fly tying dynasty at about the same time and opened his famous shop by the Erne at Ballyshannon in 1830. (Although the last of the Rogans, Rita, died in April 1991, Rogan's shop is preserved as a working shrine to these great fly dressers.) Alas, neither of these fly dressers published accounts of their flies and how they came to devise them. Two others did write books that included information on their fully dressed salmon flies, however. Thomas Ettingsall, author of *The Green Bank* (1850), dressed flies in his tackle shop in Dublin where, no doubt, many visitors having just arrived in Ireland would have purchased flies before heading west. William Blacker, author of *Art of Angling and Complete System of Fly Making and Dyeing of Colours* (1842) and *Blacker's Art of Fly Making* (1843), began his fly dressing career in Belfast but moved in 1840 to London where he could exploit the wealthy salmon anglers who lived in that city. The bright, gaudy flies, using the most exquisite of rare feathers, tied by these men commanded huge prices – anything up to half a guinea (52½ pence) each, at a time when the working man was earning little more than that sum for a full week's labour.

The rapid spread of the gaudy salmon fly depended on widespread publicity. This seems to have come in two forms. The first of these was probably through the export of flies from Ireland to Britain, and thence later to Scandinavia and North America. The rapidly increasing number of gaudy salmon fly patterns gave Victorian collectors something else to collect and admire. Then, realizing the demand, British fly dressers began to copy the Irish patterns and develop their own. Among these was James Wright, fly dresser on the Tweed at Kelso. (Wright later established a large fly dressing factory at Redditch in Worcestershire that was close to the leading hook manufacturers.) Wright is best known for his involvement in designing the famous Greenwell's Glory trout fly, but he also invented many gaudy fully dressed salmon flies for use on the Tweed in the mid-nineteenth century. Yet the great success of Wright's inventions was almost contemporary with Thomas Stoddart's note in the 1853 edition of *The Angler's Companion*:

Salmon were [a generation ago] of sober tastes and simple habits. They esteemed the speckled feather or white tip of some strutting turkey, the dun plume of the gledd [red kite] or buzzard, select filchings from the maldrake, teal, or widgeon, along with twitches of home-dyed wool, rough barn-fowl hackles, and thread from an old service-worn epaulette, better than the combined luxuries of Mexico, the Indies and New Holland . . . the salmon fishers of Tweedside not only held what is called, the Irish fly [gaudy flies, involving exotic feathers] in absolute ridicule.

The main form of propaganda came from the leading writers of the Victorian era, who scorned the simple, drab flies and extolled the virtues of the complex, gaudy flies. Chief among these was Francis Francis, editor of *The Field*, the most influential magazine for wealthy sportsmen, and author of *A Book on Angling* (1867). Born Francis Morgan, he had a wealthy uncle whose surname was Francis. His uncle's will left him the entire fortune on condition that he changed his surname to Francis. Having done this, Francis Francis had all his available time to encourage and publicize the development of the complex, gaudy fly. In his book, which included over 300 patterns, Francis actually argued that salmon had changed their taste in flies, from the old drab patterns to the new gaudy ones. Compare, for instance, what he had to say of the Tweed with what Stoddart had said only 14 years earlier: 'The fish have undergone a complete change in their tastes since I was there; for when I was there they preferred a sober-coloured fly, but of late years they prefer more showy ones.' He then produced extensive essential lists of complex, gaudy flies for all the major salmon rivers of Britain and Ireland. Only the brave would venture forth on an expedition to the Nith and Annan, or Wye, Spey or Blackwater, without the flies that Francis recommended for that river. And in a back-handed swipe at Tweedsdale's Scrope, he wrote:

> There are many persons who hold that half a dozen flies are enough to kill salmon on any river in the kingdom, and who despise the notion of such an extended list of flies. To such irreverent scoffers and heretical unbelievers I have nothing to say. Let them indulge in their repertoire of a bit of old Turkey carpet and a live barn-door rooster.

He then gave James Wright the accolade: 'Wright is one of the neatest and best tyers in Tweedside, his name being known far and wide.' In the 1862 World's Exhibition and 1882 Fisheries Exhibition Francis and his wealthy cronies made sure that Wright was awarded medals, prizes and diplomas for his salmon flies (Durham Ranger, Silver Grey, Black Doctor and Silver Wilkinson). Each year Francis and his associates took Michael Rogan, who had followed James in the business at Ballyshannon, to London for up to three months to dress his famous and gaudy flies for the now defunct London Salmon Fly-Fishers' Club. In 1883 Rogan was awarded the gold medal at the Fisheries Exhibition.

By the end of the century Francis and his associates had completed their task, for he could then write:

> From 1840 onward a rivalry was set up on many English and Scottish rivers between the old drab patterns and the new gaudy invaders from Ireland, the usual result of which was the defeat of the native flies or at least their partial suppression. On some rivers the revolution did not take place until much later – as late as 1890.

As late as 1890? On one of my home rivers, the Eden, drab flies were recommended up to 1890, but by 1900 they had vanished.

One other medium that should not be overlooked in any discussion of the propaganda of the new styles of salmon fly was the chief angling magazine of the time, *The Fishing Gazette*. Published in London, this magazine was taken by anglers throughout the world. By recording every new salmon fly as it was devised, the *Gazette* made sure that the gaudy salmon fly was adopted wherever there were salmon and anglers fishing for them.

Mary Orvis, who was born in Manchester, Vermont, USA, in 1856 was the daughter of Charles Orvis, founder of the famous fishing tackle company that still bears his name. In 1877 she married John Marbury and became Mary Orvis Marbury, the year after she had been given responsibility for managing the Orvis Company's fly manufacture. The business would grow only if she could provide her customers in North America with the most modern flies, and to this end she introduced into immediate manufacture those recommended to her by a host of correspondents and many that *The Fishing Gazette* had recently published. In 1892 she produced a book of flies, entitled *Favorite Flies & their Histories*. This book included many of the gaudy style of salmon flies, indicating that they were then well established on the Atlantic salmon rivers in North America, and it also contained an interesting insight into how she chose the flies that she sold to the American market.

Of that bright, fully dressed fly, Childers, she noted:

'The Fishing Gazette' wrote to a number of dealers in fishing tackle asking the following question: 'What six flies do you use most, consider best to have for the widest range, or sell the greatest number of for Scotch salmon angling?'

In answer to this enquiry the paper received lists of the salmon flies that were most largely sold, and in these lists the Childers was frequently included. It is well known to American fishermen. . . . In the nineteen lists of flies, the Jock Scott [see page 31] is included in every list except two, and the other seventeen lists are led by either the Jock Scott or the Silver Doctor, these two flies being without doubt the prime favorites with salmon anglers the world over.

In what was a relatively short space of time the gaudy fly had thus spread from Ireland to Britain and then through the entire range of Atlantic salmon fishing.

It is clear that many of Francis's contemporaries had some reservations about the extent of the propaganda given to the gaudy fly. Sir Herbert Maxwell, for example, in *Salmon and Sea Trout* (1898), noted that:

Bright flies are all the rage just now. . . . It is an extraordinary delusion that every river requires its particular combination of silk, wool, tinsel and feathers to take the salmon that frequent it. . . . In the whole range of angling there is no subject upon which such irreconcilable differences of opinion prevail as upon the need for variety with salmon flies and the respective merits of different patterns. . . . It does not matter what is the colour or material of the object called a salmon fly that one presents to the notice of a salmon, provided that it is not too large to excite suspicion, or too small to escape observation, and that it is given a lifelike motion.

Yet on the Tyne, Maxwell followed Francis by suggesting that the salmon had changed its tastes from grey, dun and brown flies to gaudy ones, such as the Jock Scott and Silver Wilkinson.

There was no holding back the complex, gaudy fly through the late Victorian and Edwardian periods, however. Apart from Francis, whose book was constantly in print well into the twentieth century, four writers guaranteed that. The first was Captain (later, when the 1919 enlarged edition of his book was published, Lieutenant-Colonel) J.H. Hale, author of *How to Tie Salmon Flies*, first published in 1892. Hale's book gives clear details on how to dress these complex flies and includes just 40 patterns. The second was George M. Kelson, whose monumental tome *The Salmon Fly* (1895) included 240 patterns – so much for Scope's six! Third came J.J. Hardy, a partner in the famous Hardy Brothers tackle company, now known as the House of Hardy. Hardy's book *Salmon Fishing* (1907) included an incredible 344 salmon fly dressings. These were later incorporated into the second edition (1919) of Hale's book, together with six new Scott Series flies and twelve 'Gem salmon flies with metallic celluloid bodies', which were devised by R.B. Marston, editor of *The Fishing Gazette* – one volume containing 402 different salmon fly patterns! Finally came T.E. Pryce-Tannatt, whose book *How to Dress Salmon Flies* (1914) gave 103 different dressings. Yet these are not the only ones. Less famous writers contributed their patterns in minor books and magazines, and others never saw print! I have located the names of 47 salmon fly patterns from this era in fishing records from Norway, Canada, Scotland and northern England that I have been unable to trace in the literature, and I have examined flies dressed in this era that do not match any published pattern. Such was the explosion of salmon fly patterns in the nineteenth and early twentieth centuries.

I would like to make five important points. First, I may have given the impression that I consider this huge array of flies to be something of a confidence trick. To some degree, I think that it was. These flies were certainly devised to catch anglers, and the fact that they also caught salmon demonstrates just how stupid salmon can sometimes be. In the main, no real thought was given to the salmon in their design. Many were based on whim and the

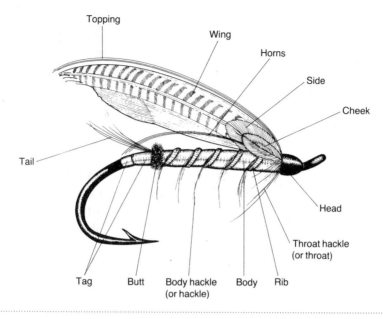

Fig. 1 – The parts of a classic salmon fly

appear for private sale, after being discovered in a Victorian collection of fly dressing materials. Such a fly, with authentic materials, is worth a lot of money and is far too valuable to get wet or chewed by a salmon! Most of those who tie these classic flies have to make do with substitutes – Poul Jorgensen suggests some excellent substitutes in his book – but substitutes are never quite like the real thing.

Finally, the parts of the salmon fly became standardized in the Victorian era, as shown in Fig. 1, although no modern fly has all these components.

Except for fly-fishing competition or for decorative purposes, the gaudy, 'classic' salmon fly has been abandoned by anglers in favour of the simple fly. The confidence trick is over! We have come full circle, back to the simple approach of Scrope and Chaytor – to flies that catch salmon.

The development of the modern fly

'It is no accident', wrote Colonel Esmond Drury in the *Journal of the Fly Fisher's Club* (1960), 'that the majority of the more ornate flies were devised in the latter quarter of the last century, which may be described as the Mrs Beaton era. The remarkable fact is that these Victorian relics have survived so long. The more particularly is this the case when one considers that they were, in the main, the product of ignorance and lack of scientific knowledge.'

When Drury wrote this, and well into the late 1970s, many suppliers of fishing flies still offered a wide range of the complex, gaudy salmon flies, albeit with substitute materials for those no longer available, for fishing. Yet by this time it had been discovered that much simpler flies were as effective as most of the complex flies, and often more so. Slowly, the salmon fly was changing back to a simple thing, whose aim was to catch salmon.

Recent developments – and by recent I mean the last fifty years – have followed four distinct lines.

The first is the development of new hooks, for in former times single and double hooks were dominant. We now have long-shank treble fly hooks, pioneered by Esmond Drury, one pattern in manufacture still bearing his name. We have wire shanks, to which a small treble is attached, that bear the name of the inventor, Richard Waddington. And we have tubes in plastic, aluminium, copper and brass for tying 'tube flies'. I will discuss these further in Chapter 2.

The second development has been in shrimp- and prawn-flies. These are described on pages 60, 71–6.

The third development has been in the use of hair for wings, and the fourth has been the use of dry flies and 'nymphs' for salmon fishing. I will conclude this chapter by describing how these evolved.

The evolution of the hair-winged fly

Hair-winged flies have a modern ring about them, for their development and widespread use dates from the early 1900s in the Atlantic salmon range in North America and from the late 1940s in Europe. However, in *Atlantic Salmon Flies & Fishing* (1970) J.D. Bates cited evidence that hair-wings were possibly being used to catch salmon in Newfoundland as long ago as 1795:

> He has seen a family Bible which belonged to a Newfoundland family named Stirling in which were handwritten entries dating between the years of 1720 and 1896. One of these entries, dated 1795, described a hair-wing fly called the Red Cow Fly and says that salmon were caught on it.

This simple pattern had a body of dubbed underfur from a red Hereford cow and was winged with hairs from the same cow.

Bates's research in North America demonstrated that in 1911 the hair-winged salmon fly became firmly established in North America when Roy Angus Thomson (R.A.T.) devised the first of the Rat series, which is still an outstanding set of flies for salmon fishing (see page 69). He also noted that bucktail-winged flies by A.S. Trude, initially designed for trout fishing, were fished successfully by Colonel L.S. Thompson on the Restigouche in the late 1920s, certainly before 1928.

In Britain and Europe the origin of the hair-winged fly is obscured by the ascendancy of the classic feather wing. The first published pattern (the Yellow or Garry Dog), which is still a great catcher of salmon, was devised by John Wright. In this case the wing was composed of yellow hairs from the tail of the minister's dog, Garry. That this pattern was not published in the major books about salmon flies in the first half of the twentieth century indicates that the authors of this time considered such simple flies to be irrelevant, compared with the more complex patterns of the day.

That some other fly dressers were experimenting with hair wings as early as the 1850s is borne out by the now forgotten Erris series of flies. These were devised by Pat Herne of Ballina, a small town on the banks of the River Moy in Co. Mayo, Ireland, and had a mane of mohair strands tied (in what we now call Matuka style) along the top of the body. There was, however, a feather wing over the top of them.

The major leap forward in hair-winged fly development was the conversion of the old, complex feather-winged flies to hair wings. So there arrived on the scene hair-winged Jock Scotts, Thunder & Lightnings, Dusty Millers and so on, the different colours of hair used to make up the wings being chosen and mixed to resemble the wings of the classic flies from which they took their name. The next step was a simplification of the rest of the fly, with the abandonment of complex tails, veilings, butts and body hackles. Even jungle cock eyes, which were considered so vital in attracting salmon, began to disappear as it became illegal to import them into Europe and North America, although the recent availability of home-bred jungle cocks enables many fly tiers to continue using them, if at high cost. Finally, we have seen a trend towards the abandonment of the original name, linking the modern hair wing with the old classic. One simple hair wing tying of the Thunder & Lightning, devised by the late J. Munro, tackle dealer from Aberlour on the Spey, became Munro Killer. Another hair wing Thunder & Lightning, purchased from a tackle shop on Brora, caught its purchaser so many salmon that it now bears his name, Willie Gunn. Yet another, the Blue Charm, has become the Hairy Mary, although I have not discovered the identity of the hirsute heroine! These are outstanding flies, especially when given the latest treatment (see page 65).

Many types of hair have been used for hair-winged flies. One of the first to gain notoriety in Europe was the dark tips of the tail of the stoat, hence the Stoat's Tail flies. It is likely that this series (which vary in body and hackle colours) originated on the Aberdeenshire Dee, for in this river small flies are supreme. The hairs on a stoat's tail are quite short and suitable only for winging flies in size 12 (perhaps 10) and smaller. Other species, with longer black hairs, are essential for dressing larger flies. In medium-sized flies – up to about size 2 or 4 – black squirrel tail has become the norm. In larger sizes, including big tubes and Waddington shanks, black bucktail is used. Nevertheless, these flies are widely referred to as 'Stoat's Tails'. Across the Atlantic, however, salmon anglers were using hairs from black bears in similar flies and calling them 'Black Bear'. In Canada I have even seen the Black Bear series of flies, tied in biggish sizes, with black bucktail wings. Yet another series of flies, the Collie Dogs, were initially tied with the long black hairs from the legs of collie sheep-dogs. First catch your dog! Today most tiers use black goat hair, which allows much longer Collie Dog wings and, when dyed goat hair is used, colours other than black.

Different species of hairs have different merits when it comes to tying and fishing flies. A Collie Dog tied with real collie hair or goat hair, for instance, is far more effective as a catcher of salmon than one tied with black bear hair. And on a small Stoat's Tail, Munroe Killer or Willie Gunn, Arctic fox seems more effective than black bear, which seems more effective than squirrel and stoat. I will have more to say on this point when it comes to discussing effective modern hair-winged patterns (page 64), but it is worth pointing out that we are in danger of giving a confusing host of names to what is, basically, one fly series – black hair wings.

The evolution of the dry fly and nymph

Accident, perhaps combined with a modicum of design – 'I have tried every-thing, why not this!' – has made several important contributions to angling progress, and dry fly fishing for salmon is one instance. Almost certainly seventeenth- and eighteenth-century anglers took salmon from the top of the water with their simple tackle. Franck, for instance, urged anglers to 'dibble but lightly on the surface, you will infallibly raise him'. And Gervaise Markham made his flies float by fixing 'a fine peece of Cork' to the hook shank. This was, however, more akin to dapping, as practised on lakes (see page 177), and dibbling and riffling a fly across the surface (see page 157). A dry fly floats down a river passively, without drag. It does not skate across the surface.

The first certain instance of the modern dry fly and dry fly technique catching salmon comes from Canada, in a letter dated 12 April 1906 from Theodore Gordon to the great English trout angler G.E.M. Skues:

> A friend of mine took a 14 pound salmon on a dry fly tied like a Coachman but dry fly style on a big Pennell hook. The line was slack [i.e., the fly was not dragging on a taut line], but he broke his rod in striking the fish and was a long time killing it. This was on the Restigouche and he got two more, a grilse and a small salmon in the same way out of the same pools in three days.

In 1924 George M.L. La Branche recorded in *The Salmon and the Dry Fly* that his friend Colonel Ambrose Monell

> calmly announced that he had killed a fifteen-pound salmon two years before on a dry fly, and assumed that it was not an accident. He had seen the fish rising just as a trout would rise and, having failed to interest the fish with any of the wet flies in his box, had deliberately cast across and upstream with a No. 12 Whirling Dun, floating it down over the fish, which took it at once. It was the taking of this fish, and the rising of six or seven others which he did not hook, that convinced him it would be possible to kill fish with the dry fly when the water was low.

That too was in North America. And writing is his book *The Atlantic Salmon* (1958), the great American angler Lee Wulff wrote how:

> In the early 'thirties it was unusual to meet a dry-fly angler and it was quite common when moving to a new river to find guides and fishermen who had never seen a dry fly fished and who were frankly doubtful that a floating fly would have attraction for salmon.

Yet Wulff persevered with the dry fly and, more than anybody, promoted the dry fly as an effective way of catching big salmon.

While standard trout dry flies have caught many salmon, some have been devised specially for salmon fishing (see page 92). So far, however, dry fly fishing for salmon has been slow to spread away from the North American rivers. Yet enough salmon have been caught, by accident or design, in British and Scandinavian rivers to make the method a realistic proposition. This is one area in which we will certainly see the continued evolution of salmon flies.

Another area is weighted nymphs designed to catch salmon. Strictly speaking, a nymph is a weighted wet fly that imitates the immature stages of things like stoneflies and mayflies, but here I take it to mean any weighted, simple fly that looks good to eat.

Perhaps the first salmon ever caught deliberately on nymph on the eastern side of the Atlantic (I stress deliberately, for there may have been some accidental captures earlier) was taken by the great Frank Sawyer on the Hampshire Avon in about 1955. In Chapter 12 of his classic *Nymphs and the Trout* Sawyer describes seeing three salmon lying under a bridge, casting an 'outsize' Killer Bug to them, making the bug rise through the water just in front of the fish, and

> As I lifted so all three fish came to life, so to speak. As it so happened the bug was nearest to the middle one and like an outsize grayling she took. The view was perfect. I saw the mouth open and close, as I have many thousands of times with trout and grayling. As it closed so I tightened, and home went the hook.

That fish weighed 15lb. The next chance Sawyer had of trying nymph for salmon was also on the lower Avon, near Ringwood, Hampshire. He tells us a little more about his nymph and tackle – a Killer Bug on a size 12 hook, a 10ft 6in rod, a no. 4 line and leader tapering to 4lb test. The first salmon took on about the twentieth cast and, of seven salmon in the pool, Sawyer hooked five of them.

At the same time, in the 1950s, on the western side of the Atlantic, Keith Fulsher and Charlie de Foe were pioneering nymphs for salmon and, rather than basing their nymphs on those that were proven trout catchers, they simplified traditional salmon flies by removing the wing.

Since these pioneers, relatively little development has occurred in nymph fishing for salmon, mainly I suspect because most anglers are completely lacking in faith! And yet there are enough 'accidental' captures of salmon on nymphs to suggest that, when conditions are right, nymph fishing may be a most effective method. As with the dry fly, this is an area where the salmon fly should continue to evolve.

Chapter 4 gives a full account of dry flies and nymphs for salmon and Chapter 8 describes how to fish them.

CHAPTER 2

EFFECTIVE SALMON RIVER WET FLIES

The salmon fly, however, imitates Heaven alone knows what,
and if it does in certain instances bear a remote (and rather glorified)
resemblance to some insect, the circumstance is the result of accident and
not intention. . . . It has been suggested as a convenient compromise that
salmon flies should be called 'lures'.

T.E. PRYCE-TANNATT, *How to Dress Salmon Flies*, 1914

It is all too easy, when writing a book about salmon fly fishing, to search the literature and then give a vast list of flies that have caught salmon in the past. Tie just about anything to a hook and eventually it will catch a salmon and merit the name 'salmon fly'. What every angler needs are the best flies for catching salmon – flies that will, when conditions are appropriate for each fly, catch salmon when others will not; flies that have the edge over others; something special that will winkle out the odd fish when conditions are very difficult or, when there is a good run of fish, will catch more than others. This chapter includes such flies – some, rightly, firm favourites, others of recent design – that have proved themselves repeatedly in a range of rivers. All the flies included in this chapter are proven killers. Notes are given for each, when appropriate, on their virtues and when and where to fish them.

Before we start, however, we must decide on the features that make up a good salmon fly. In doing this we must ignore our own, human, foolish whims and consider fly design from the point of view of the fish. As we saw in the last chapter, fly fishers in the Victorian era became bogged down in making vast numbers of irrelevant patterns for anglers but not for the salmon. If we, like Francis Francis and his contemporaries, have hundreds of 'essential' flies, then we have one great problem when we arrive at the waterside. It will take a long time to choose which fly to tie on our leader from the vast suitcase of these so-called essential patterns.

Some very experienced anglers will argue that such a problem can be avoided by the minimalist approach of carrying just one fly. I know, for example, two anglers who use, almost exclusively, the Willie Gunn. They carry and use these in a vast range of sizes from 3in tubes to size 12 doubles. I know one angler who uses only the black-hackled Silver Stoat's Tail in exactly the same way. And another who, from late April to the end of the season, uses only the Munro Killer, again in a range of sizes. Yet I suspect – though I cannot prove it – that there are occasions when and places where these flies will not work and a careful change of fly would catch fish. For instance, a fly with more blue in it would catch more in Iceland, while one with far more orange would fare better in the many peaty rivers of Ireland or in coloured water in a falling spate in Scandinavia, northern England and Scotland. There is also the advantage in carrying more than one pattern that is a proven catcher of fish that after a couple of hours of casting or after working down a long pool without an offer, there is something uplifting in changing fly pattern. It raises morale and encourages us to fish hard and well rather than simply go through the motions of casting.

The design of salmon flies

In Volume One, *The Life of the Salmon*, I argued that salmon take the fly primarily out of aggression and perhaps also out of curiosity and fear. There may also be an element of the reawakening of lost feeding instinct. It follows, therefore, that our flies should be specially designed to exploit these traits.

The most important factor in the equation is not in the design of the fly, but in making the fly work properly, through the water, so that it entices the salmon to take hold. This is an angling, not a fly tying, matter and it is dealt with in depth in Chapter 4. However, it is clear that many anglers take far more pains in choosing or dressing their flies than in making sure that the flies are fished properly, and I have met several anglers who blamed their flies and not their angling limitations for a failure to catch fish. I recall one incident some years ago, when I was chatting to another angler at the car park by the Spey. My companion, whom I had just met, had a couple of fish and I had one. Two other English anglers arrived and examined our catches. They asked what flies we had used, and we showed them our boxes, each containing a different array of flies. They asked where they could buy them, but both of us tied our own. They protested that the local tackle shop did not have these flies for sale (yet their own boxes contained flies that would catch salmon), and one of them concluded by saying, 'We must learn to tie our own flies!' The following day I watched one of them fishing. He would have done far better going for some casting lessons! I know another angler who is a great fly tier and technically far better than me, but so far he has not caught a salmon. I watched him fish his immaculate flies. He whipped the water surface so heavily that every salmon in the pool would have needed a dose of paracetamol!

Size of fly

Atlantic salmon that have returned to the river from the sea to spawn and that have completely ceased feeding respond to different sizes and types of lure depending on water temperature and water height/flow rate.

First, water temperature. In some rivers that are not frozen through the winter, fish fresh from the sea may run in January, February and March when water temperatures are close to 32°F. Similar temperatures prevail in the rivers of eastern Canada and Scandinavia during the spring thaw. Then, through late spring and summer, water temperatures rise, sometimes reaching close to 68°F. Finally, during autumn, water temperatures decline and, in rivers that have a run of fresh fish during late October and November, water temperatures as low as 41°F may be experienced.

All fish are poikilothermic – cold-blooded – which means that the body temperature of the fish is about that of the surrounding water and that, as water temperature rises or falls, so too does the body temperature of the fish. In all poikilothermic animals the energy available to the animal is related to body temperature, which is, of course, related to environmental temperature. In cold conditions the fish are very sluggish; in warmer conditions, when they have more energy, they are more active. It is, for example, well known that salmon are unable to ascend even small waterfalls or some particularly long stretches of white water unless the water temperature is above, say, 42°F – at such low temperatures they lack sufficient energy. Most experienced salmon anglers would also agree that a salmon hooked in very cold water fights much more dourly, lacking acrobatics and fast, forging runs, than one hooked in warmer water.

Just as the energy available for muscular activity varies with temperature, so too does the energy available for observation, analysis by the brain and a corresponding response to lures. In very cold water the lure must be big enough and be fished slowly enough and close enough to the fish to evoke a response. This may mean a fairly heavily dressed lure tied on a 3in brass or aluminium tube with treble hook behind, used in conjunction with a fast-sinking fly line that will help take the big lure deep, between midwater and the bottom. As temperature rises, progressively smaller lures are more effective, perhaps because at higher temperatures, when the fish have more energy and are more 'alert', bigger lures may have too strong an impact. It is a common experience to have a salmon move to, but not take, a big fly when the water is fairly warm. Should this happen, standard practice is to change the big fly for a smaller one straight away and to cast over the fish, which will often obligingly take this smaller fly. It is not just size that needs to be reduced as the water warms. So too should be the weight of the lure and the way the lure is fished. In very warm water salmon are often receptive to a wet fly, with a very sparse dressing and fished on a floating, sink tip or intermediate fly line, close to the surface. In such warm conditions they may also take forms of surface 'dry flies' (see Chapter 4).

The following table summarizes effective salmon wet fly length and water temperatures. It is clear that a salmon angler who will fish through an entire season must prepare by tying a wide range of lure sizes.

Water temperature	Fly size
Less than 43°F	2–4in tube fly or weighted Waddington shank
43–50°F	hook size 2–6 or 1–1½ in tube or Waddington shank
50–55°F	hook size 6–8 or ¾–1in tube or Waddington shank
55–59°F	hook size 8–10 or ½–¾ in tube or Waddington shank
59–64°F	hook size 10–12 or ¼–½ in tube
above 64°F	hook size 12–16

I once asked Alan Bramley, Managing Director of the hook manufacturer Partridge of Redditch, what was the commonest size of low-water salmon hooks – hooks for fishing between late spring and autumn – sold in the British Isles. He replied, 'Size 6.' This is far too large for most rivers in the British Isles when, through the period when these flies are being used, water temperature is commonly above 55°F. In a typical warm British and Irish summer size 10 and smaller are far more appropriate. Likewise, sometimes in Scandinavian and Canadian rivers when water temperature exceeds 59°F, flies tied on size 10–16 are sometimes more effective than size 8 and bigger. Geoff Haslam tells the tale of fishing that mighty Lapland river, the Tana, when, after failing to catch on a range of quite large flies, he turned to a Goldie (see page 68) tied on a size 14 treble and started to catch fish with it. Alas, many anglers seem frightened of fishing tiny flies, and this fear is promoted by many tackle shops, which do not stock tiny salmon flies.

The table gives a range of hook sizes and tube and shank fly length for each temperature range. If the temperature is in the lower end of the range, start with the larger size. But another set of factors is also involved in determining size: water conditions in terms of water height, flow rate and colour.

When the river is high, perhaps following a spate, it may be necessary to move to one or two sizes of fly larger than that suggested by the water temperature/hook size table or to use a fly with a slightly heavier dressing. When the water has some colour in it, such as a peat tinge or clay suspension following a spate, a slightly larger lure with a heavier dressing may again be better at evoking a response from the fish. When fishing through one pool it is often essential to start with a bigger fly in the fast water of the pool neck and to change to a smaller, more sparsely dressed fly when the slower body of the pool has been reached.

In addition to varying size, I have suggested varying the amount of dressing in the lure. Some should be tied sparsely, others a little more thickly. How sparsely? Many amateur fly dressers dress their salmon flies too heavily and most shop-bought salmon flies are dressed on the heavy side (simply because anglers would feel cheated if the flies had less material in them). The Plate section shows a straightforward Stoat's Tail dressed heavily and sparsely. The sparse dressing is for clear, less turbulent stream water; the heavier dressing is for slightly coloured or very fast water in which a stronger image might better bring the fly to the attention of the fish.

The illustration also shows flies dressed 'short' and dressed 'long'. Short dressing, designed for fishing in warm water with a floating line, allows for a small fly to be tied on to a hook that is too big for it (in this case, a fly that would normally be tied on a size 10 hook is tied on a size 6). The fly is tied on the front of the hook shank, well in front of the bend and point. By contrast a long dressing is where the entire hook shank is used in tying the fly. There are, it is said, two advantages of the short-dressed fly. A much larger hook can be used than would be dictated by the fly size/water temperature table, and the bigger hook (it is said) will hold a salmon better than a small one. Also, if the salmon takes the fly that is dressed on the front of the hook shank, the point and bend of the hook will be well inside its mouth. The problem with this argument, as far as I see it, is that a short-dressed fly tends to be dominated by the over-large hook and there is a reduction of mobility of the fly. If you are restricted to flies dressed on single hooks, the short dressing may have some merit, but modern small treble and double fly hooks take such a firm hold that a fly dressed long on these has the edge in mobility in the water. Furthermore, the hooking advantage probably does not exist. A salmon that is determined to take the fly into its mouth does not nip at the fly; it sucks it well into its huge mouth. If it did not, then we would never catch salmon on things like Collie Dogs and General Practitioners.

The amount of dressing or bulk of the lure – especially the thickness of the body – can also be varied to some extent by varying the type of hook being used. Because different hook types have different weights, this also varies the weight of the fly. So, in late spring, when water temperature is 55°F and a lure tied on a size 8 hook is called for, according to the table, this may be achieved as follows:

size 8 heavyweight single salmon hook
size 8 low-water single salmon hook
size 8 Wilson single salmon hook
size 8 heavyweight double salmon hook
size 8 low-water salmon hook
size 8 Wilson double salmon hook
size 8 Edmond Drury (long-shank) treble hook
¼ in Waddington shank with size 12 treble
¼ in plastic tube with size 12 treble
¼ in aluminium tube with size 12 treble

Notes:
1. In some regions weighted flies or treble hooks are not permitted, so check regulations before you start fishing.
2. Details of salmon fly hooks are given on pages 53–6.

Of course, few anglers would carry this full range. I would carry the low-water double, the Wilson double, the Esmond Drury treble and the aluminium tube. The bigger, the faster and the more coloured the water, the heavier the fly I would use, with the aluminium tube and Drury treble being the heaviest and the Wilson double being lightest.

The importance of colour

What colours or materials are best in salmon flies? What patterns are best? This is an area that the novice salmon angler or dresser of salmon lures finds most confusing. You may go to fish one of the big Norwegian rivers and be told that the best lure is a Green Highlander (a lure exported to Norway from Scotland), yet I have never used this lure in Norway and have always had splendid sport. You may go to Scotland's River Nith and be told that you will do little without a Brown Turkey, yet I and several of my friends have caught many salmon from this river on much simpler lures. Pattern is pretty irrelevant, but some colours are relevant simply because they are easily seen by the salmon.

Many writers have attempted to argue that certain patterns are better than others under certain conditions. There is the 'bright day, bright fly; dull day, dark fly' theory, which suggests that on a sunny day a fly of the Silver Blue type (page 62) would be ideal, while on a dull day an all-black pattern of the Stoat's Tail type (page 65) would be the thing to use. By complete contrast there is a theory that argues the opposite: 'bright day, dark fly; dull day, bright fly'. Another theory, expounded in great depth by R.V. Righyni in his books *Salmon Taking Times* (1965) and *Advanced Salmon Fishing* (1973), puts fly patterns into six categories.

1. Silhouette flies that are all black (e.g., Stoat's Tail and Blue Charm), for use in clear water in bright dazzling conditions or for dusk and at night when the sky is overcast.
2. Translucent illusion flies that have a silver body and pale or yellow wing (e.g., Silver Blue and Silver Grey), for use in clear water in strong but not dazzling light (i.e., bright day, bright fly).
3. Normal image flies that are medium in tone (e.g., March Brown and Logie), for medium light and when there is a slight tinge to the water.
4. Flashing illusion flies with a silver body and dense bright colours (e.g., Bloody Butcher and Silver Wilkinson), for deep, rocky small pools and pots where the fly suddenly appears in front of the fish.
5. Normal image/silhouette flies with black bodies and bright colours in hackle and wing (e.g., Jock Scott and Thunder & Lightning), for conditions where a stronger image is needed than the normal image.
6. Translucent illusion/normal image flies with slightly denser colours than the translucent image (e.g., Lemon Grey), in shallow, streamy lies and bright conditions.

This categorization makes things needlessly complicated, however. There are certain conditions in which particular colours of flies or colours in flies seem to have the edge on others. When we look at fly patterns later in this chapter such properties will be noted. But it is the presence of colour in a fly, not the pattern of the fly, that is important.

Black, although not strictly speaking a colour, is visible to the salmon in all conditions, either directly or as a silhouette. For this reason some black is found in most salmon flies, either in body or wing or hackle.

Yellow has proved to be an effective colour component in salmon flies. Small amounts, either as tail or tag, seem more effective in clear water. Far more yellow, as wing, is effective in flies that are fished deep in cold water or in flies fished in coloured water. An Irish friend, Ted Browne, fishes the Yellow Dog the entire season in the peat-tinged waters of the Rivers Finn and Mourne; in 1994 he caught 78 salmon on it.

Blue, usually the light blue sometimes called 'teal blue', is an effective colour in very clear waters. It is an almost essential component, usually as a hackle, in flies for use in some Canadian and Icelandic rivers.

Orange or orange-red is an indispensable colour series in peaty waters or in highly coloured water following a spate or in flies being fished deep in cold water. The success of the range of shrimp- and prawn-flies is certainly because of the dressing being dominated by some shade of orange or orange-red.

Pink and purple have been little exploited by fly dressers. However, both colours are effectively used by bait anglers who dye their shrimps and prawns these colours.

Brown, as a wing, is often considered synonymous with black by salmon anglers, some tying their hair wings with black squirrel, others with dark brown. As a silhouette there is perhaps little to choose between them, although black possibly gives the stronger image to the salmon's eye.

Greens and olives, though an important colour range for imitative trout anglers, are less important for salmon. It has been said that salmon in parts of Scandinavia and Canada find the green of the Green Highlander the essential ingredient, but I doubt it. I may be wrong, though.

Flash and sparkle

Salmon flies have long had some flash and sparkle, primarily from tinsel ribs and, sometimes, tinsel bodies. It is possible, however, that the flash and sparkle that we see in the tinsel of a salmon fly that we hold up in the air may be subdued when the fly is in the water, for the tinsel will reflect the colour of light in the water. In the dark there will be little or no flash, for there is little or no light. At the bottom of a deep pool in early spring there will be little flash, for there is little light. In a peat-tinged or slightly coloured water the flash from a silver tinsel will be a dull peaty-orange colour. You can see this effect if you examine a large silver object, such as a toby spoon, in different water conditions.

It is worth using tinsels as ribs or bodies, because the flash may help to bring the fly to the attention of the fish. Modern non-metallic synthetic tinsels are far better than the old metallic varieties because they do not tarnish. Silver and gold are the most commonly used, although copper is very effective, especially in coloured water.

During the last 10 years I have been investigating the effectiveness of bright fluorescent materials and flashy materials – especially Crystal Hair and Mobile by Lureflash – in salmon flies. And although my trials of the same flies tied with and without these materials have not yielded enough data to demonstrate statistical significance either way, I am wholly convinced that salmon flies tied with fluorescent and flashy materials are more effective than those tied without. In fact, I am so convinced that I shall not be continuing my trials, for I cannot now bring myself to use a salmon wet fly that lacks these materials. It is all a question of confidence, and I am far more confident with flies having these two additions. One evening recently, for example, having just caught a grilse, I found it necessary to put on a fresh fly. The successful one had been my 'flashy variant' Munro Killer, tied on a size 12 Wilson double. I opened my fly box and discovered to my horror that I had only the plain ordinary tyings. I just could not tie one of these on the leader, even though in years past I had taken many salmon on them! Instead, I tied on a size 12 'flashy variant' Silver Stoat and within five minutes had another fish on the bank. Would a plain Munroe or Silver Stoat have caught this second fish? Possibly. But possibly not. I might not have fished it properly because I did not feel confident, but the traditional dressing, without the flash, might not have attracted the salmon to take.

I am not alone in this belief, for all the innovative salmon fly dressers and anglers I know – and that includes some from the USA, Canada, Norway and Sweden as well as the British Isles – insist on adding small amounts of these materials to their flies.

It is essential not to overdo the use of fluorescent materials when modifying salmon flies. I restrict their use to small tags of fluorescent floss, two or three turns wide, immediately behind the tail or, in tail-less flies, at the end of the body. Another way of using fluorescent materials in wingless, hackled flies is by adding a little 'thorax' of fluorescent fur or chenille at the front of the fly, immediately behind the hackle. This holds the hackle out and enhances its movement in the water. The Hackle Orange Shrimp (page 60) is an example of this. I have tried putting strands of fluorescent material in the wing and tail, but feel that this is too much. The little tip at the end of the body or behind the hackle perhaps adds a little focal point that catches the salmon's eye, although what the salmon really thinks is open to question.

Four colours of the Glo Bright range seem most effective: no. 1 neon magenta, no. 2 pink, no. 5 fire orange and no. 9 chrome yellow. Tips of these can be profitably added to any salmon fly, with numbers 1, 2 and 5 perhaps being best in coloured water or in dull light and no. 9 best in clear water or bright conditions. For some reason yellow has always been a great body-tip colour in salmon flies.

When it comes to flashy additions to salmon flies, many old, successful, fully dressed salmon flies had horns, made, usually, from fibres of macaw tail tied alongside, but standing out from, the wing. When the fly was fished, these fibres flickered in the water, emitting blue and orange or yellow flashes. Many of the old successful flies also incorporated flashy rare feathers from now protected species, such as the blue chatterer, toucan and cock-of-the-rock. Natural seal fur has a similar sparkle, and many of the old fly dressers, such as the late Michael Rogan of Ballyshannon, enhanced this sparkle by picking out strands of seal fur from the body of the fly so that the strands had movement as well as sparkle when the fly was being fished.

Many of today's salmon flies lack this life-simulating mobility, flash and sparkle. They are tied with neat, tight bodies of floss or tinsel, have dyed hackles and often straight-fibred hair wings, which do not move in the water as much as we might imagine. The addition of a few strands of Lureflash Crystal Hair or, in bigger flies, Mobile to the wing or tail of the fly gives flash and movement, creating flickering shafts of light. I stress, a few strands. If salmon could speak I reckon they would tell us that they find between three and six strands far more seductive than 15–30 strands. Do not over-egg the pudding by over-flashing the fly or you will lose the subtle illusion that only a few strands imparts to the fly.

In winged patterns incorporate these materials into the wing, with the fibres extending back beyond the end of the wing. In unwinged, hackled patterns, tie them in with the tail, cutting them a little longer than the tail. In both styles, the flash and mobility thus extend backwards behind the more solid structure of the fly.

Lureflash produces a large range of colours of Crystal Hair and Mobile, and also Twinkle and Flashibou, which might be used in the largest of flies. Most of the flies I have tied and tested thus far have incorporated a limited number of colours: gold, silver, hot orange, hot yellow, pink-pearl, red and smolt blue. Gold and silver are excellent on big flies, such as 1½–3in aluminium tubes, fished deep on sinking lines. Incidentally, the silver is a great addition to sea trout flies for night fishing. Hot orange and red seem to be very effective in coloured water or in the early morning or at sunset. Pink-pearl and smolt blue seem effective in very clear water with overcast skies. And hot yellow is effective under most conditions (why do salmon fall so well for the colour yellow?) but, like the Yellow Dog, is great for autumn fish.

Essential movement

The flash of Crystal Hair, Mobile, Twinkle and Flashibou also adds movement, one of the main ingredients in any salmon fly. As the fly works through the water, these few strands sparkle and move. One of the greatest criticisms of the old slip-wing, mixed-wing and built-wing classic salmon flies is that they lack essential movement in the water. It was in an attempt to add movement that Rogan picked out the seal fur of bodies and separated the wing fibres of his fully dressed flies, but this became unpopular because it spoilt the neatness of the fly. Certainly, any competitor in a fully dressed classic salmon fly competition who did this to increase the movement of the fly would stand little chance of winning a prize! The Dee and Spey flies, with their long, flowing hackles, had, by contrast, great movement. So, too, had some of the Victorian grub patterns, such as the Brown Shrimp.

Other features of a salmon fly that may add to this essential movement or mobility in the water are the tails, hackle and wings. Did not Venables, as long ago as 1662, extol the virtues of salmon flies 'with very long tails'? Many modern salmon flies continue the Victorian theme of having a relatively short tail of golden pheasant topping. This feather has two merits: it is yellow, which is, as has been noted, a great attractor for salmon, and it has some flash. However, it is lacking in movement. Longer tails composed of mobile hair, perhaps up to three or four times the length of the hook, will add movement. So too will feathers, such as red or yellow golden pheasant body feathers, which can be tied in as a tail or, to enhance movement, be wound at the end of the hook shank as a tail hackle.

Wound hackles (as distinct from tightly bunched false hackles) add movement as each fibre flickers in the water. Plain hackled flies, such as the Mallard Shrimps (page 63) or Hackle Orange Shrimp (page 60), utilize both colour and mobility of the hackles used. Although they look really scruffy objects out of the water, they flicker with life when being fished – and they catch salmon. Mobile heron hackles are now difficult to obtain, because herons are protected throughout much of Europe and North America, but it is well worth experimenting with other large, mobile hackles – large chicken feathers, capercaillie (which is hunted in great numbers in Europe), a host of wild duck and goose species, and so on.

Hair wings move far better in the water than feather slip wings, but the choice of hair is all-important. In big flies or in very fast, turbulent water, bucktail is fine, but in smaller flies or less turbulent water it is less mobile. For the long-winged Collie Dogs and Tadpoles nothing beats the softness of goat hair, unless you have a collie dog. For most small to medium-sized flies (tubes and Waddington shanks to 2in and hooks of size 4 and smaller) most fly dressers use squirrel tail. Squirrel is, however, somewhat lacking in mobility, and far better are (in brown and black) bear, or (for very small flies) calf tail, or (best of all) Arctic fox tail. This last, which can be dyed in all colours, is becoming more readily available since several Norwegian and Swedish tiers introduced it to the angling world in the 1980s.

When tying or buying salmon flies for fishing, therefore, or when choosing which fly to use, start by getting the size right. The next thing to consider is its mobility – how the fly will move in the water. Linking mobility to colour is flash and sparkle. Make sure that the fly has some sparkle in it. The first thing to look for as far as colour is concerned is, I believe, a small point of strong colour that the salmon might notice – a touch of bright fluorescent material. The rest is up to you, but note especially the merits of black (or dark brown), yellow, orange-reds and blue.

The paramount factor in fly design being size, it is now necessary to consider wet fly hooks, for they are important in determining the size of fly that is tied on them.

Hooks for salmon river wet flies

Then buy your Hookes the finest and the best
That may be had of such as use to sell,
And from the greatest to the very least
Of every sort pick out and chuse them well
That Hooke I love that is in compasse round
Like to the print that Pegassus did make.
JOHN DENNYS, *Secrets of Angling*, 1613

The salmon fly hook has three important functions: it is the foundation on which the fly is built; it is the only part of the angler's tackle to which the salmon becomes attached when it takes the fly; and it is the one part of the angler's tackle that holds on to the salmon between the moment the fish is hooked and when the fish has been successfully landed. The latter two functions are the most important because we do not really need a hook for fly tying, for we can tie a fly equally well on a straight piece of wire. To fulfil the functions of hooking and holding a salmon the hook must be sharp, with a good, short point, a small barb, forged at the bend for added strength, and ideally a shank length that is two or two and a half times hook gape. Hook holds, when hooks with a significantly longer shank than that are used, frequently fail because the extra-long shank levers the hook point out of the jaw of the fish. Those hooks, sold as 'outpoints', are a potential disaster when it comes to playing and landing big fish, for the 'outpoint' is actually the beginning of the hook being opened out. It would be inaccurate to say that either an inpoint or outpoint hook increases hooking potential. Neither does. The optimum for hooking and holding salmon is a point that is parallel to the hook shank. Check hooks carefully before you buy them, as John Dennys suggested almost four centuries ago. An apparently expensive hook is not expensive when it lands a salmon; a cheap hook is very expensive when it breaks or opens out and loses a salmon.

The perfect salmon fly hook is shown in Fig. 2. Note the following points.

1. Check that the eye is in line with the hook shank and has no rough edges chaff the leader.
2. The hook shank should be straight and 2½ times gape. In doubles and trebles, check that the brazing binding the two or three shanks is neat   and secure.
3. Check that the hook bend is smooth and not kinked, and that it is forged – i.e., flattened slightly side to side – for extra strength. In doubles and trebles check that the bends are perfectly in line (this is a common fault in double and treble fly hooks).
4. Check that the point is short and sharp and parallel to the hook shank. You will recall that as long ago as the seventeenth century, Robert Venables recommended the use of a small stone to keep the point sharp (page 17).Carry a piece of carborundum stone for this purpose.
5. A barb of any sort impedes hook penetration, so make sure that the barb is small. Besides impeding penetration, a large, deeply cut barb is a weak point on a hook, increasing the chances of the point of the hook breaking off at the barb when put under pressure.
6. In some hooks the gape is relatively small in relation to the length of the hook shank. These hooks do not hook and hold fish as well as hooks with proportionally larger gapes. Ideally the hook shank should be two or two and a half times, at most three times, the gape.

Finally, consider the finish or colour of the hook. Most salmon hooks are black, but this black is simply a varnish over the bare metal and is no different from the bronze varnish used in most other hooks. Check that the finish is uniformly smooth, with no blemishes where rust may set in. It is worth adding extra protection, before tying a fly, by giving the hook shank a coat of fly tying cement. Partridge offers a different finish on some patterns of hooks – the grey Niflor finish of the Grey Shadow GRS range – and this offers maximum protection against corrosion and gives extra protection to the hook point. This finish is quite slippery and also seems to enhance the penetration of the hook. Although more expensive than the plain black finish, it is highly recommended.

The variety of hooks

In the nineteenth century and early years of the twentieth century almost all salmon flies were tied on single hooks, although double hooks became

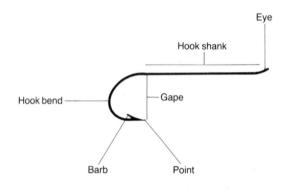

Fig. 2 – The perfect salmon hook

increasingly popular through this era. Initially, these hooks were 'blind' or eyeless, so an eye had to be added, made of strong gut and whipped to the tapering hook shank. Even today, many fly dressers who demonstrate the art of tying 'classic' salmon flies prefer to use the old blind hooks and gut eyes, for they are contemporary with, and therefore the authentic medium on which to tie these exotic flies. The gut eye is a weak link, however, for it rots easily. So there quickly developed the traditional up-turned metal loop eye that we still use today. Why a loop and not the sort of ring eye that is used in other hooks? The advantage of the loop was that the double length of wire immediately behind the eye of the hook provided a useful foundation on which to build the complex, often many-layered, wing of the classic fly. Today there is no advantage. Why up-eyed? As far as fly tying and hooking and playing the salmon are concerned, there is no real advantage in up-eyed, down-eyed or straight-eyed hooks. It is purely tradition. However, if you wish to tie the fly to the leader with a double turle knot, the up-eyed hook is essential (see page 128).

Choice of salmon fly hooks

Single salmon fly hooks are still made and their use is essential in some regions and some river beats where the rule is 'single hook only'. However, few anglers use a single hook today unless forced to do so by fishery rules, for most argue that a double or treble fly hook holds much better than a single (this is not completely true; see below). Where catch-and-release of salmon is imposed by fishery regulations, single hooks ought to be mandatory, for it is much easier to unhook a salmon on a single than on a double or treble hook. As well as the alleged attribute of double and treble hooks in holding on to salmon, they always fish better, and a badly tied fly on a single hook will often fish on its side.

There are, however, two occasions when a single hook may have the advantage. The first is in autumn, when there may be a mass of leaves floating downstream. A single hook picks up leaves far less than a double or treble. The second is when biggish hooks are being used. I have found that double and treble fly hooks in sizes larger than 6–8 do not hook or hold a salmon as well as a single of the same size. I discussed this in Sweden with that great salmon angler Mikael Frodin. He agreed and suggested that a size 6 is the largest safe size of double or treble fly hooks. That the hook hold is poor on these moderately large doubles and trebles is borne out by the fact that of the salmon that I have landed on them, the hook fell out of the jaw of 28 per cent of them. Had those fish been given a little slack line, I would have lost them. The problem with biggish doubles and trebles seems to be that they do not slide around the mouth of the salmon when it takes the fly. They have too much bulk. When a salmon takes a big single, on the other hand, it slides around the mouth of the fish and usually takes a good hold in the corner of the jaw (the scissors).

When we anglers talk of the big flies today, we usually mean tubes and Waddington shanks tied with a small treble at the rear (see below). The problem is that if the fish is very big, the wee treble opens out and the fish is lost. Fine wire trebles are great for most salmon, say up to the 20lb+ class. But where there is a chance of a real whopper – in the Tay in autumn, for example – a big single is probably far better. One Eden springer, which weighed only 17lb, was a hair's breadth from being lost on a size 8 treble, one of the hooks having been opened up completely and the other, to which the fish just remained attached, being nearly half straightened out. Had that fish been a bit bigger or taken an extra few minutes to bring in, I would have lost it.

Recommended salmon fly hooks are illustrated in Fig. 3.

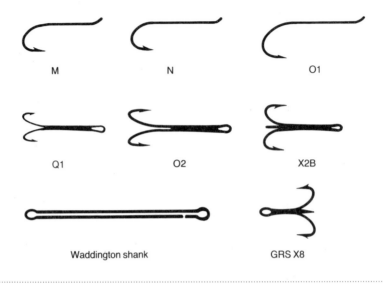

Fig. 3 – Salmon fly hooks. All hooks shown are size 6.

- Partridge single salmon code M – available in sizes 10–5/0; these are recommended in sizes 1–5/0 wherever there is a chance of a 30lb+ salmon or in very cold water conditions.
- Partridge single low-water salmon code N – available in sizes 10–8/0, these are recommended in sizes 1–8/0 wherever there is a chance of a 30lb+ salmon or in very cold water conditions; also for rivers where doubles and trebles are prohibited or for those wishing to release the salmon they catch. These are a little lighter in the wire than code M.
- Partridge single Wilson code 01 – available in sizes 16–2, they were designed for salmon dry flies (see page 92). They are, however, also ideal for summer salmon fishing where one is obliged to use a single, and for tandem mounts. Although quite fine in the wire, they do hold fish very well (the biggest salmon that I know of that was landed on one of these hooks weighed 34lb).
- Partridge double low-water salmon code Q1 – available in sizes 12–3/0, they are recommended in sizes 6–12 for summer salmon fishing. In larger sizes, use singles or tubes/Waddington shanks. A Grey Shadow version of these, with a grey Niflor finish instead of the usual black one, is superb. Code GRSQ2 comes only in sizes 6, 8 and 10.
- Partridge double Wilson code 02 – available in sizes 2–16, these are also

great for flies for summer fishing in sizes 8–16. They are also recommended for tandem mounts. They are a little lighter in the wire than code Q1.

- Partridge salmon fly treble code X2B and the Esmond Drury treble – available in sizes 16–2, they are recommended for small flies in sizes 8–16. The Partridge version has a smaller point and barb than the Drury hook.

Small treble hooks, sizes 10–16, are excellent for hooking and holding salmon (but see the problem with very big salmon, above). Sometimes the hook will be embedded so deeply that it must be cut from the jaw of the fish. This attribute has contributed to the popularity of Waddington shanks and tube flies, where a fly up to 3–3½ in long – equivalent to the biggest of standard sizes singles and doubles – is used with a small treble.

Initially Waddington shanks were made from one length of wire, with an up-turned loop-eye at one end and a ring to take the treble at the rear end. Later, following the advice of the late Steve Riding, Partridge redesigned Waddington shanks to produce a shank of double wire. Many anglers make their own shanks out of stout wire, such as paperclips. One problem with using the Waddington shank was fixing the hook on to the shank so that it always fished in line with the shank. This problem is overcome by holding the hook in place with a piece of fine silicone rubber that extends from the rear of the shank to over the eye of the treble. A second problem is one of leverage, especially in the larger sizes of shanks. When a salmon is played, the stiff wire shank is pulled against the side of the fish's head and thereby exerts great force on the hook hold, which can pull out the hook easily. (The same problem exists for those who spin for salmon with the popular toby spoon.)

Waddington shanks have an advantage over the popular tube flies (see below) in that, with their fine diameter, they sink very quickly. To make them sink even more quickly, they can be weighted by binding a length of lead wire in the grooves between the two lengths of wire that make up the shank.

Waddington shanks code V1B, made by Partridge, are available in lengths ⅖–3½ in.

The tube is an alternative to the Waddington shank, over which it has two advantages. First, it is easy to change the treble hook, should the one in use become damaged. Second, there is no problem in leverage when playing a fish for, when the salmon takes the fly, the tube slips up the fly line and out of the way. The problem with tube flies is their bulk, so very slender flies cannot be tied on them. This bulk also slows down sinking rate, compared with Waddington shanks.

Tubes come in three weights: lightweight (plastic), medium weight (aluminium) and heavyweight (brass). The aluminium and brass tubes by Slipstream are lined with plastic to prevent the metal tube chaffing the line. Many anglers use brass tubes in very cold water to get down to the fish. Far better is a lighter tube (aluminium) fished on a very fast sink fly line (see page 135) – it is easier to cast and fishes better. Brass tubes are ideal for very deep, turbulent lies fished from a boat or for harling in spring (page 165). In addition to the commercially produced tubes, light plastic tubes can easily be made from the ink tubes from ball-point pens, the outer sleeves of electricity wire and from 'shrink tubing' used by the medical profession.

Slipstream tubes, marketed by Veniard Ltd, are available in lengths ½–3in.

The size of treble to use with Waddington shanks and tubes is shown in the following table.

Length of shank/tube	Size of treble
up to ½in	10–14
½–1in	6–10
1–2in	4–6
2–3in	2–4

Relatively few salmon anglers use tandem mounts, even though they are very effective for flies 2–4in in length. The mount enables very slender flies to be tied, the two hooks enhance hooking power, and the flexibility of the mount prevents hooks being levered out, which is a problem with Waddington shanks. Of course, these must be made. One method of making a tandem mount was published by Hugh Falkus in *Sea Trout Fishing* (1964). An equally effective modern method is by joining the two hooks with stiff braided nylon fly line backing. The hooks are whipped in place, and the whippings given a coat of superglue and then three coats of fly tying cement.

I make my mounts in lengths of 2, 2½, 3 and 3½in. Some have two size 8–10 Wilson low-water single hooks (lightweight); some have two size 10 and 12 Wilson low-water doubles (middleweight); and some have a size 10 Wilson low-water double at the front and a size 12 treble at the rear (heavyweight).

River wet flies

Bearing in mind what was discussed earlier in this chapter, we will now examine the range of effective river wet fly patterns. I stress the word 'effective' – this section does not include all flies that have caught salmon or flies that were tied on the whims of fly dressers. Nor is this section an encyclopedia of salmon fly patterns. Other books serve this purpose, including recently *A Guide to Salmon Flies* by John Buckland and Arthur Oglesby (1990) and *Flies for Atlantic Salmon* by Dick Stewart and Farrow Allen (1991). The flies described here are great catchers of salmon, provided that they are fished in the right place at the right time, and properly.

There is a problem when it comes to fly 'patterns' and names. Consider the following fly:

Tag	fine oval gold or silver tinsel, and yellow floss, or none
Tail	golden pheasant crest or none
Body	black floss silk
Rib	oval gold or silver tinsel
Throat hackle	black
Wing	black hair
Cheeks	jungle cock or none

This basically single fly could be called Black Bear (if black bear hair is used, but Stewart and Allen accept black squirrel as a substitute for bear), Black Fitchtail (black fitch as wing) and Stoat's Tail (no matter what sort of hair is used!). And as soon as the tag or hackle or tail is changed, or the wing is made of dark brown hairs, or the body is wool or dubbed fur instead of floss, the number of names proliferates: Blue Charm, Thunder Stoat, Hairy Mary, Black Cosseboom, Black Bomber, Black Coltrin, Black Conrad, Black Wulff, Black Sheep, Blue Sapphire, Tosh, Haggis, Black Maria, Munro Killer, Oglebug, Atherton Mink Tail, different colours of butted Black Bear, Restigouche Black Dose, Black Silver Tip, Black Fly, Half Stone, Hot Orange, Interceptor, Irritator, Margot, Preacher . . . and there will be some that I have missed.

These are, in fact, all variants on the black fly – tinsel-ribbed black body and black or dark hair wing – and if you want to tie one of these named varieties consult the books to which I have just referred. But when it comes to tying the most effective flies and then fishing them, we need to know: 'Do we fish a predominantly black fly?' and 'Are there minor points to add to the predominantly black fly that will help us catch more salmon?' A predominantly black salmon fly is, in most circumstances, the fly that is most visible to the salmon, especially when it is being fished above the level where the salmon is lying, because it makes a strong silhouette against the sky. It is for the opposite reason that sea birds are white underneath – their fish prey are less likely to see them from below. Most experienced anglers carry many predominantly black flies, simply because they are so effective, especially in clear or clearing rivers, early in the morning and late in the evening, in overcast conditions or at night. But they add other materials to increase the visibility or mobility of the fly or to add a flash of colour that will catch the eye of the fish. From the practical angling point of view, this seems a better line of attack than being bothered with huge numbers of named patterns that vary only in additions. It is the variety of these additions that has spawned the large and confusing number of names given to predominantly black flies.

The patterns included below allow you to make a choice of fly for all water conditions you are likely to encounter. If, for instance, you are going to fish very clear Icelandic rivers, choose flies with blue in the dressing; in Irish waters use orange and red. Notes are given after each fly or series of flies to help in your choice. Have alternatives with you so that after an hour or so you can change fly. This might simply raise your morale, but it might produce a fish! You might decide that you will fish a Flashy Stoat's Tail; try the plain Stoat's Tail first and then change to a Silver Stoat's Tail. You may, on the other hand, decide to start with a Yellow Fox and, if that is unsuccessful, change to a Yellow Dog. Be prepared also to try something that may seem outrageous. Water conditions may suggest that one of the Irish shrimp patterns or a General Practitioner would be the best bet. If one or two of these have been tried but failed to catch, try a Collie Dog or Tadpole. You never know – salmon know not the rules written in books about salmon fishing!

Beware of those who say, 'This fly always works!', or 'If nothing else works, this one will!' No fly *always* works. If someone suggests that one fly catches fish when others do not, that person is a fool.

In the descriptions of the flies, I have suggested the conditions when each fly or variant of a fly might be more successful. This is a guide, nothing more. To attempt to fix rules in this subject would be foolish, for there are always some salmon that disobey every rule we make.

Most salmon flies used today have a tag, a tail, a ribbed body, a hackle and wing (a wing usually of hair), but there are much simpler flies, lacking a wing, that the novice fly tier will find easier to dress. We will begin with simple hackled patterns and progress with increasingly complex patterns.

Simple hackled spiders

In these flies the hackle should be sparse, no more than three full turns.

Black and Peacock
Thread   black

Tag	very short, fluorescent yellow, orange or red floss
Tail	three strands Crystal Hair and wool (optional) in yellow, orange or red
Body	bronze peacock herl
Rib	fine oval silver tinsel
Hackle	black henny-cock

This is a great clear-water, high-water-temperature, black summer fly and is best dressed on sizes 8–14 single or treble fly hooks. It is also effective when dressed on a 2in tandem mount, the dressing being repeated on each hook. As such this is a variation of the Worm-fly.

Black Pennell

Thread	black
Tail	golden pheasant tippets
Body	black floss silk*
Rib	narrow flat silver or oval silver tinsel
Hackle	long-fibred (at least twice the gape width) black henny-cock

Pete Hemmings, the great Spey Valley angler of Angus Stuart's tackle shop at Grantown, demonstrated the effectiveness of this simple, ancient fly some years ago on the Nith, Lune, Ribble and Hodder. He caught salmon with this fly when anglers fishing larger, more conventional salmon flies failed to catch. It is a super summer, low-water pattern and is also effective when the river has almost reached summer level after a spate, especially for grilse. It is tied on small, single hooks, sizes 10–14. The Black Pennell is also a great lake fly (page 79).

The Silver Pennell is identical, except that it has a body of silver tinsel. Traditionally, flat silver tinsel is used, but it is improved with a body wound of oval silver tinsel. In small sizes, tied on treble fly hooks, sizes 10–14, it is a great fly in bright summer conditions.

Black and Purple

Thread	black
Tag	fluorescent pink floss
Tail	three strands pink Crystal Hair

*This can perhaps be improved with a very short tip of yellow or red fluorescent floss.

Body	purple floss silk
Rib	oval silver tinsel
Hackle	long-fibred black henny-cock

We now substitute black with purple in the body of these very simple initial patterns to produce a most useful pattern. Purple and black is a very effective colour scheme in my home rivers – Lune, Ribble, Eden and Nith – where there is a slight grey tinge in the water at the last stage of a spate. Tie this on treble fly hooks in sizes 8–14, and on tubes and Waddington shanks up to 1in long.

Partridge & Orange

Thread	red
Tail	three fibres orange Crystal Hair (optional)
Body	hot orange or fluorescent orange floss
Rib	fine gold wire
Hackle	brown speckled partridge
Head	red

The P&O is an ancient spider trout fly, and this is a modified dressing for salmon. Tie it on size 12–14 single or treble fly hook. Over the years many trout anglers fishing the conventional P&O have found a salmon attached to their line. I could quote the capture in recent years of fish weighing 14lb, 11lb, 8lb, two at 6lb, 4½lb and 3½lb that had been taken accidentally on the P&O – but I won't. This is usually considered accidental, but it isn't. It simply indicates that salmon find sparsely dressed, simple flies very attractive. It is the angler who feels that these simple flies are not good enough for the salmon. To my knowledge, this fly has caught fish in rivers as large as the Spey and as small as the Ribble and Hodder from March to August, in clear low water and in a falling spate.

The Endrick Spider is of the same school as the P&O, but it has a body of ruddy cock pheasant tail herls. Like the P&O, although it is superficially a food-imitating trout fly, it is also an excellent lure for Atlantic salmon and sea trout.

Hackle Orange Shrimp

Thread	red
Tail	orange bucktail, three times the hook length, plus three

	strands orange Crystal Hair
Body	orange floss, ribbed oval gold tinsel, with, at the front, a 'thorax' of fluorescent, hot orange fur
Hackle	hot orange cock
Head	red

Tied on size 8–14 treble fly hooks, this is a great fly for the peat-tinged water that is found in many Irish rivers or for coloured water in a falling spate or fishing in autumn. In Sweden it has caught salmon to over 40lb and sea trout to over 20lb, and it has caught fish on the Spey when other patterns failed to score. It is also a great fly for the peaty Irish loughs (page 174) – only recently a spring salmon took this fly in Lough Fern, Co. Donegal.

Two other patterns based on the Hackle Orange Shrimp are worth trying – the Hackle Pink Shrimp and the Hackle Purple Shrimp. To dress these, simply change colour of hackle, body and fluorescent fur and Crystal Hair to pink or purple. The pink variety succeeds in water that is only slightly coloured, while the purple variety is best in clear water. All three are as simple a shrimp pattern as one can find. Yet so very effective.

Double-hackled patterns

The following patterns have two hackles. Tie in and wind the rear hackle first, leaving sufficient room at the front for the second hackle plus head of the fly. After completing that first hackle, tie and wind the front hackle before completing the lure.

Dark Hackles

Thread	black
Tag	fluorescent yellow or orange or red floss
Tail	golden pheasant crest or yellow hackle fibres plus three strands yellow, orange or red Crystal Hair
Body	black floss
Rib	oval silver tinsel
Hackles	rear: black or blue or orange or crimson henny-cock
	front: bronze mallard or cock capercaillie feather
Head	black

These excellent summer salmon patterns are best tied on short tubes or Waddington shanks (up to 1in) or, even better, on size 8–14 treble fly hooks.

Use the orange or red variants in slightly coloured water and the yellow, black or blue ones in clear water. These are, in effect, hackled forms of a wide range of flies including Blue Charm, Hairy Mary, Thunder Stoat and Stinchair Stoat. The dark bronze mallard, commonly used in traditional slip-winged flies, adds great movement to the fly when it is tied as a hackle instead of a slip-wing.

Teal, Blue and Silver Hackle

Thread	red
Tag	tiny red or yellow fluorescent floss
Body	flat silver tinsel
Rib	fine oval silver tinsel
Hackles	first, tie in three to four strands smolt blue Crystal Hair, then
	rear: teal blue henny-cock
	front: teal breast feather
Head	red

A hackled version of the many flies based on the teal, blue and silver theme, this is a summer fly for both salmon and sea trout in fine, clear water and bright conditions. Tie on treble fly hooks (sizes 8–14) or short (½–1in) tubes or Waddington shanks.

Yellow and Blue Hackle

Thread	black
Tail	yellow hackle fibres or golden pheasant crest plus three strands
	yellow Crystal Hair
Body	rear half: yellow floss
	front half: black floss
Rib	oval silver tinsel
Hackles	rear: blue henny-cock
	front: mallard breast dyed bright yellow
Head	black

A good autumn fly, based on the colour scheme of the popular Yellow Dog but in which the hackles give great mobility in the water. Tie on treble fly hooks (sizes 8–12) and tubes or Waddington shanks to 2in long. It is my first choice on the Lune in autumn when there is a foot or more on the gauge and falling.

I called the next three patterns 'shrimps' when they were first devised, and, because this name has been used in magazines, it is retained here. In essence, however, they are grey/purple, orange and pink double-hackled salmon flies.

These are flies to use from spring to autumn (April to September) when floating or intermediate line tactics are being employed. The feathers do not allow for big tubes or Waddington shanks, and although they can be dressed on singles and doubles, I prefer treble fly hooks in sizes 8–14.

Capercaillie Shrimp

Thread	black
Tail	three strands yellow or red or orange Crystal Hair or Twinkle
Tail hackle	two turns yellow golden pheasant body feather
Body	rear half: fluorescent red or yellow floss
	front half: purple floss
Rib	oval silver tinsel
Hackle	rear: purple henny-cock
	front: cock capercaillie*
Head	black

This pattern will catch salmon in most water conditions including the clearest of water. To date it has caught fish in four Irish, eleven British and five Scandinavian rivers.

Orange Mallard Shrimp

Thread	black
Tail	three strands orange Crystal Hair or Twinkle
Tail hackle	two turns red golden pheasant body feather
Body	rear half: fluorescent red floss
	front half: black floss
Rib	oval silver tinsel
Hackle	rear: three turns of grey (silver) mallard flank feather dyed in hot orange
	front: one turn bronze mallard
Head	black

This is a fly for coloured water or water that has a permanent peat tinge of the kind so often found in Ireland and western Scotland. It has caught salmon in seven Irish, five British and two Scandinavian rivers. In difficult low-water summer conditions on the River Mourne, it recently hooked six fish on its first

*It is difficult to get cock capercaillie hackles in Britain and North America. Instead, use grey (silver) mallard flank dyed dark iron blue dun.

go down one drought-shrunken pool. Then, so that I could take a few photographs, I let the gillie have a few casts, and he caught a fish on his fourteenth cast. I returned to the Mourne in September and gave a fly to Ted Browne, a local angler. On the first evening he had, I believe, three fish on it.

Pink Mallard Shrimp

Thread	black
Tail	three strands pearl Crystal Hair or Twinkle
Tail hackle	two turns red golden pheasant body feather
Body	rear half: fluorescent pink floss*
	front half: black floss
Rib	oval silver tinsel
Hackle	rear: three turns of grey (silver) mallard flank feather dyed pink
	front: one turn bronze mallard
Head	black

This pattern seems to catch fish better than the orange shrimp in clear water or in water lacking a peat tinge. It is, therefore, a 'light' pattern alternative to the 'dark' Capercaillie Shrimp, which is very effective in bright, low-water conditions. On the Aberdeenshire Dee or Spey in summer, for instance, when there are lots of grilse about, I would bet on this pattern in the bright late morning and afternoon and on the Capercaillie Shrimp in the early morning and evening. The Pink Mallard Shrimp has caught fish in four Irish and eight British rivers; the purple-bodied variety (see note above) in another two Irish, five British and three Scandinavian rivers. It has also proved itself as a reasonable sea trout fly in 'half-light' early morning and evening.

All three patterns have proved themselves as catchers of salmon in the most dreadful conditions, when there are few fish about or when the rivers are low and the weather is sub-tropical. When fished on a two-fly cast in conjunction with a more traditional fly, including Stoat's Tail/Munro variations and varieties of GP shrimp/prawn flies, these have attracted far more salmon. I put this down almost entirely to the life and movement of the long hackles.

Hair wings

There is no doubt that hair-winged salmon flies are the most popular of all the flies that are used to catch salmon throughout the entire range of *Salmo salar* – hence the number of named patterns, many of which are very similar.

---

*Initially I used purple floss with some success, but the fluorescent pink seems better.

Flashy Munroe

Thread	black
Tag	Glo Bright pink or fire orange floss
Tail	golden pheasant crest
Body	black floss
Rib	fine oval gold tinsel
Hackles	hot orange cock, mixed with blue jay
Wing	underwing: three strands hot yellow Crystal Hair plus a few yellow squirrel or Arctic fox hairs overwing: natural black or dark brown squirrel tail or Arctic fox tail
Head	black

The Munroe Killer is a great modern variety of Thunder & Lightning. The suggested modification will catch fish anywhere on floating/intermediate line tactics. Tie this on single, double or treble fly hooks, sizes 8–14.

Flashy Stoat's Tail

Thread	black
Tag	Glo Bright neon magenta or pink or fire orange or chrome yellow floss
Body	black floss or flat silver tinsel*
Rib	fine oval silver tinsel
Hackle	black or orange or crimson or blue cock
Wing	black hair (use stoat if you want smallest sizes, but squirrel or bear are better and Arctic fox even better still), plus three to six strands of Crystal Hair or Mobile in silver, or hot orange, or hot yellow, or pink-pearl, or red, or smolt blue
Cheeks	jungle cock (optional)**

This is one fly series, with a range of alternative fluorescent and flashy colour additions and with alternative bodies, that will kill fish throughout the season in any river that has a run of Atlantic salmon. In coloured water go for the

*With the silver body this becomes a Silver Stoat's Tail, with the black floss body simply a Stoat's Tail.

**You can tie jungle cock cheeks to any salmon wet fly, including those tied on the largest tubes. They certainly look good on the salmon fly, although whether the salmon notice them is open to question. Jungle cock is available, though expensive, from companies that breed them for the fly dressing market.

orange and red additions; in very clear water choose the blue. These can be tied on a wide range of fly hooks, from size 14 single, double and treble fly to 3in tubes, Waddington shanks and tandem mounts.

Yellow Calftail

Thread	black
Tag	fluorescent yellow floss
Tail	bunch yellow calftail plus three strands yellow Crystal Hair
Body	flat copper tinsel
Hackle	bunch yellow calftail
Wing	black calftail
Cheeks	jungle cock (optional)

There are two alternatives to this pattern: the Orange Calftail (change the yellow calftail and Crystal Hair for hot orange) and the Blue Calftail (retain the yellow tail, but give the fly a silver body and hackle of blue calftail).

These three hair-winged flies are useful for the novice salmon fly dresser to start with. Tie on single, double or treble fly hooks, size 6 or smaller, and fish the Blue Calftail in very clear water (it is a useful Icelandic fly), the Orange Calftail in coloured or peat-stained water (a useful west of Scotland and Irish fly), and the Yellow Calftail in water between these two extremes of clarity.

Black, Orange and Yellow (Willie Gunn)

Thread	black
Tip	Glo Bright neon magenta floss
Body	black floss
Rib	oval gold tinsel
Wing	sparse mix of hot orange, yellow and black hair, with three to six strands of gold Crystal Hair or Mobile
Head	black

Many angling fly dressers vary the proportions of the three colours of hair depending on water clarity. In clear water increase the black and yellow; in peaty or coloured water in a falling spate, increase the orange and yellow and reduce the black (see Yellow & Red and Yellow & Orange, below). The old Willie Gunn was mainly used for early-season and autumn fishing, and it was tied on a big tube or Waddington shank. It is, however, also an excellent late spring to mid-autumn pattern for floating line tactics, tied very sparsely on size 8–12 single, double or treble fly hooks. For many years this has been my first choice for sunk line, spring or late autumn fishing, although having seen two fish come from the Nith on a size 10 version of this fly in dreadfully low, clear water and bright conditions, I now find myself using it throughout the season.

One version, the Gold Willie Gunn, has a flat gold tinsel body.

Yellow Fox

Thread	black
Tip	Glo Bright chrome yellow floss
Body	black floss
Rib	fine or medium oval silver tinsel
Wing	Arctic fox tail dyed yellow, with a few strands dyed hot orange, plus three to six strands of hot yellow Crystal Hair
Head	black

Tied on sizes 8–10 double or treble fly hooks or on 1–2in tubes, this is a fly for floating or intermediate line fishing, close to the surface, in a clearing spate or in autumn. Tied on a 2in+ tube or Waddington shank and fished on a sinking line, it is a fine cold-water spring or autumn pattern. In 1994 it caught two big springers for Bob Bell on the Tyne. Arctic fox tail is the most soft and mobile of natural hairs, adding movement that most other hairs lack.

The Yellow Fox is similar to the very ancient Yellow Dog, but the latter fly has a blue hackle (I find dyed gallina preferable to the usual farmyard fowl). In the Yellow Dog the winging hair initially used was from a 'yellow dog' (perhaps a yellow labrador), but squirrel and bucktail are more commonly used today. Arctic fox is even better.

Yellow & Orange and *Yellow & Red*

Thread	red
Body	flat gold or copper tinsel
Rib	oval gold or (if you can get it) copper tinsel
Wing	equal mix of yellow and orange, or yellow and red, hair*

*A pair of flies devised for the peaty waters of Ireland, these can be tied on big tubes or Waddington shanks for cold-water spring fishing (bucktail is usually used for the wing), or, on treble fly hooks, size 6 and smaller, for warmer-water conditions (squirrel is usually used but I now prefer Arctic fox). Outside of Ireland these are effective in the larger sizes for early spring and autumn sunk-line fishing and in coloured water in a falling spate in the smaller sizes.

Goldie

Thread	black or red
Body	oval gold tinsel
Hackle	five or six yellow bucktail hair tips plus five or six fibres of orange bucktail hair tips plus two fibres of gold Crystal Hair tied short, no longer than the hook bend

This very sparsely dressed fly should be tied on size 12–16 treble fly hooks. Geoff Haslam introduced me to this fly after his experiences with it in Norway. The Tana was high and, after trying a range of larger, more conventional flies, the Goldie (nameless at the time) was tried. In addition to attracting a big salmon, estimated at 30lb+, which eventually broke free, it accounted for several other, lesser fish. Like the simple hackled patterns with which we started this section, the Goldie suggests that we often use flies that are far too big.

Blue, with a touch of yellow, is almost essential in Icelandic rivers and well worth trying in any cold, clear river. Among many flies of this nature, the following is now my first choice.

Blue & Yellow

Thread	black
Tag	fluorescent yellow floss
Tail	yellow calftail
Body	black floss
Body hackle	deep blue henny-cock, palmered
Rib	oval silver tinsel
Wing	mix of 45:45:10 deep blue, grey and yellow hairs (squirrel, calf, Arctic fox, etc.) plus three strands smolt blue Crystal
Hair	(keep it sparse)

Pink has never been a popular colour in Atlantic salmon flies, but Philip White's Brown & Pink Shrimp is a great hair-winged pattern, having caught many fish in Russia, Scandinavia, Scotland and Canada. I modify Philip's tying a little.

Brown & Pink Shrimp

Thread	black
Tag	fluorescent pink floss
Tail	pink bucktail plus three strands pink Crystal Hair
Body	purple floss

Body hackle	pink henny-cock, palmered
Rib	oval silver tinsel
Wing	brown bucktail hairs taken from a tail, dyed pink
Head	black

Silver Blue

Thread	red
Tag	fluorescent red floss
Tail	golden pheasant crest
Body	flat silver tinsel
Rib	fine oval silver tinsel
Hackle	blue henny-cock
Wing	grey squirrel tail plus three strands smolt blue Crystal Hair

As an alternative to the squirrel tail, try grey wolf or polar bear or any other light grey or cream hair.

The combination of blue, silver and squirrel (formerly barred teal feather slips) is a killer at times, in the entire range of sizes from big tubes and Waddington shanks – you will need a longer hair, such as wolf – to the tiniest double and treble fly hooks. I find it best in bright conditions and very clear water, and at night, when fishing for sea trout, in sizes 1/0–4 single fly hooks, it will also take summer grilse in the dark. In its large size, this is a hair-winged Medicine.

Grey and silver, with additions of other colours, have been popular among hair-winged flies since the invention of the Rat series by R.A. Thompson. The Silver Rat is, I consider, the greatest of these, working wherever there are salmon. I have modified this dressing as follows.

Silver Rat

Thread	red
Tag	fluorescent red or yellow floss
Tail	fibres gizzle cock hackle
Body	flat silver tinsel
Rib	fine oval silver tinsel
Wing	grey fox or wolf or squirrel plus three or four fibres of pearl Crystal Hair
Collar hackle	grizzle henny-cock
Head	red

This is a great salmon fly, which is also very effective at night for sea trout.

Peter Ross

Thread	black
Body	rear half: flat tinsel*
	front half: red seal fur
Rib	fine oval tinsel*
Hackle	black
Wing	grey squirrel tail plus two or three strands pearl Crystal Hair
Head	black

The original Peter Ross is a great lake fly and river sea trout fly (page 84). This hair-winged variation, in its three tinsel colours, was devised by Geoff Haslam, influenced by the late Jimmy Berry. It is a great salmon pattern, especially in its gold and copper forms. I was fishing some years ago with Geoff on the Bjora when he hooked a fish upstream of me. What a submarine that was. It zoomed downstream within a yard of me and I reckoned that it was over the 40lb mark. Alas, the hook hold gave way. A few minutes later Geoff landed a fish on this fly, and this hooked me on to the Peter Ross as a salmon fly. It really does work, tied on big single hooks, also on size 6 or smaller double and treble fly hooks. Incidentally, in big sizes it is also a great sea trout fly and, like the Silver Blue, will take grilse in the dark.

Collie Dog

Thread	black or red
Body	¾–1in aluminium tube
Wing	bunch of long goat hairs, up to 9in long**
Head	black or red

Tadpole

Thread	red
Tail	yellow goat hairs, tied long (up to 6in)
Body	rear half: yellow floss
	front half: crimson floss
Rib	flat silver tinsel

*The original has silver tinsel, but also tie with gold and copper.
**Originally hairs from the feathering on the hind legs of black collie dogs were used, but most of us do not have access to such an ideal pet. In coloured water I add a few hairs of goat dyed hot orange or yellow, together with two or three strands of the same colour of Crystal Hair. See also the comments on Tadpole, below.

70

Wing	black goat hair, extending back to the end of the tail*
Head	red

Both the Collie Dog and the Tadpole were popularized by the late Neil Graesser. Both highlight the point that has been a recurring theme throughout this chapter: the importance of movement in the fly so that it appears as a living thing to the salmon and not just an inert lump of fur and feather tied on a hook. Whichever flies you select to tie and take to the river, always include a few of these. In coloured or cold water try the Tadpole; in clearer water try the Collie Dog.

Shrimp- and prawn-flies

Natural shrimps and prawns, either in the boiled orange-pink state or dyed in red or purple, have long been used as bait for salmon. Their use, however, is becoming ever more restricted as they are banned from an increasing number of rivers. Artificial flies that look like shrimps and prawns are the modern fly-fisher's alternative, and because they catch a lot of salmon, shrimp- and prawn-flies are very popular.

The idea behind the use of natural or artificial shrimps and prawns comes from the fact that these crustaceans are a major class of food for sea-feeding salmon. I do not believe that the resemblance of these flies to real shrimps and prawns has anything to do with their success, however. The shrimps and prawns that salmon eat in the Atlantic are not garish pink, red or purple. They are a subdued sandy-grey or pink-grey. Furthermore, feeding salmon almost certainly cannot distinguish the colour of the shrimps and prawns they are eating in the poor light in the sea. Here, they are more likely to see silhouettes and movement, and possibly to detect their quarry by scent. The virtues of effective shrimp- and prawn-flies are, I believe, the same virtues as for all other effective salmon wet flies. These virtues are based on choosing the right size for the particular water conditions, on having movement and 'life' in the fly and on the basic colour. The orange-red range of colours is very effective for attracting salmon, especially in peat-stained rivers and in rivers that are slightly coloured or falling from a high spate. It is this range of orange-red that makes shrimp- and prawn-flies so very popular in Ireland, where vast peat bogs

---

*Originally collie dog was used as wing. I add three strands of yellow Crystal Hair to the tail and use fluorescent yellow floss for the rear half of the body. Tie on big single fly hooks, size 4 or bigger, for cold-water fishing, and on size 6 or smaller singles or doubles for warmer conditions.

drain into rivers and lakes giving a permanent peat tinge. If you go into any Irish tackle shop and look at the array of salmon flies tied by local experts or look into the fly boxes of a great Irish salmon angler, you will find that the overwhelming bulk of the flies could be classed as shrimp- and prawn-flies and that they glow with a range of reds, oranges and yellows. It is worth stressing the importance of movement. Many fly dressers have invented flies that are based on lifeless materials such as plastic, latex and rubber, but although these look remarkably like real shrimps and prawns, they are lifeless in the water and poor takers of salmon.

I have already described my own hackled shrimp patterns (page 60 and page 63). This section includes great Irish patterns, which will work throughout the range of the Atlantic salmon, as well as some outstanding patterns that have been devised elsewhere.

When it comes to selecting hooks for shrimp- and prawn-flies, treble fly hooks are preferable in the smaller sizes 10–16, while in sizes 6–10 (the most common sizes used) either treble or double fly hooks are to be preferred. Single fly hooks are best for larger sizes.

Curry's Red Shrimp

Thread	red
Tag	fine oval silver tinsel
Tail hackle	two turns golden pheasant red body feather
Body	rear half: red floss or seal fur
	front half: black floss or seal fur
Rib	fine oval silver tinsel
Middle hackle	badger cock
Rib	fine oval silver tinsel
Front hackle	long badger cock
Wing	jungle cock, tied in flat*
Head	red

This salmon fly, although invented early in the twentieth century, is still a great catcher of salmon, especially in peaty waters. It has spawned many similar patterns, based on the three-hackle, split-body system of tying.

*Originally two were tied in, but today some Irish professional tiers use just one jungle cock feather. Some omit the jungle cock, and the salmon seem not to notice. The same applies with other shrimp and prawn patterns given below. The original Red Shrimp of Patrick Curry also had veilings of Indian crow over the body. Nobody ties it this way today and, again, the salmon seem not to mind!

Bann Special Shrimp

Thread	black
Tag	fine oval silver tinsel
Tail hackle	two turns golden pheasant red body feather
Body	rear half: light yellow floss
	front half: black floss
Rib	fine oval silver tinsel
Middle hackle	orange cock
Rib	fine oval silver tinsel
Front hackle	long badger cock
Head	black

Apache

Thread	black
Tag	fine oval silver tinsel
Tail hackle	two turns golden pheasant red body feather
Body	rear half: yellow floss
	front half: crimson floss
Rib	fine oval silver tinsel
Middle hackle	yellow cock
Rib	fine oval silver tinsel
Front hackle	crimson cock
Head	black

Gold Foxford Shrimp

Thread	black
Body	rear half: fine oval gold tinsel
	front half: black floss
Middle hackle	two turns golden pheasant red body feather
Rib	fine oval gold tinsel
Front hackle	orange cock
Wing	jungle cock
Head	black

Purple & Gold Shrimp

Thread	black
Body	rear half: fine oval gold tinsel
	front half: black floss
Middle hackle	two turns golden pheasant red body feather

Rib	fine oval gold tinsel
Front hackle	purple cock
Wing	jungle cock
Head	black

Orange & Gold Shrimp

Thread	red
Tag	fine oval gold tinsel
Tail hackle	two turns golden pheasant red body feather
Body	rear half: flat gold tinsel
	front half: flat gold tinsel
Rib	fine oval gold tinsel
Middle hackle	orange cock
Rib	fine oval gold tinsel
Front hackle	orange cock
Wing	jungle cock
Head	red

Blue & Purple Shrimp

Thread	black
Tag	fine oval silver tinsel
Tail hackle	two turns golden pheasant red body feather
Body	rear half: broad oval silver tinsel
	front half: broad oval silver tinsel
Middle hackle	purple cock
Front hackle	blue cock
Wing	jungle cock
Head	black

Red & Yellow Shrimp

Thread	red
Tag	fine oval silver tinsel
Tail hackle	two turns golden pheasant red body feather
Body	rear half: red floss or seal fur
	front half: black floss or seal fur
Rib	fine oval silver tinsel
Middle hackle	red cock
Rib	fine oval silver tinsel
Front hackle	yellow cock

Wing	jungle cock
Head	red

Anyone going to fish the prolific Irish salmon rivers and loughs should take with them a box of these patterns, but several Irish friends have taken these elsewhere and caught fish. John Todd, for example, had several salmon on them from the Tay and Lyon in almost impossible low-water conditions.

General Practitioner

Whiskers (tail)	bunch of 10 orange bucktail hairs, long
Head (tail, above whiskers)	a pair of golden pheasant red body feathers, tied in concave side to concave side
Body	orange seal fur
Body hackle	orange cock
Rib	oval gold tinsel
Wing	in four sections (each section lying flat over the body with concave side of feather tied down)
	rear: golden pheasant red body feather
	next: golden pheasant tippet with centre snipped out to give a V-shaped, black-tipped pair of eyes
	next: golden pheasant red body feather
	front: golden pheasant red body feather
Head	red

The General Practitioner (or GP for short) was invented in the early 1950s by the great angler Colonel Esmond Drury for fishing on the Test, where using the natural prawn as bait was prohibited. It is one of the best 'prawn' patterns: the long tail, seal fur body and body hackle have movement, and the combination of materials gives the fly an orange glow in the water. It has spawned several offspring, one of which uses a wing of three or four golden pheasant tippets dyed scarlet, and another where all the materials used in the dressing are dyed purple (i.e., a purple prawn or Purple GP).

Krabla

Thread	red
Whiskers (tail)	two white and two pink hackle stalks, three times the length of the hook, tied so that they flare outwards; then a bunch of white marabou, half the length of the hackle stalks
Body	two deep pink and one white cock saddle hackles, wound in

	touching turns up the hook shank and then trimmed into shape
Rib	fine oval silver tinsel
Head	red

This Icelandic prawn fly is best tied on a single fly hook in sizes 2–6. I suspect that a orange-red alternative would be very successful in coloured water. Why not give it a go?

Chilimps

Thread	red or orange
Whiskers (tail)	two hot orange hackle points tied back-to-back with two or three strands of hot orange Crystal Hair between
Body	hot orange seal fur
Body hackle	hot orange cock, palmered in open turns
Rib	flat gold tinsel
Front hackle	long-fibred hot orange cock
Head	red

This is a modification of a Swedish pattern (the original had a red body, only one hackle point tail, and no Crystal Hair). A simple-to-tie palmer fly, it is nevertheless a very effective shrimp-cum-prawn pattern in a wide range of sizes.

Ally's Shrimp

Thread	red
Tail	sparse bunch of long hot orange bucktail
Body	rear half: red floss
	front half: black floss
Rib	oval silver tinsel
Wing	bunch grey squirrel tail under golden pheasant tippet
Hackles	bunch grey squirrel tail tied in as a 'beard', then in front as a collar hackle a long-fibred, hot orange henny-cock hackle
Head	red

Alastair Gowan's shrimp is one of the most popular salmon flies in use today in the British Isles. Ask almost anyone what they have taken their summer salmon on, and the answer is likely to be 'Ally's Shrimp!' I modify this fly by adding between two and four strands of hot orange Crystal Hair to the tail. Tie the fly on size 6–12 double fly hooks.

Tandems for night fishing or for estuaries

Too many salmon are caught at night for this to be accidental or exceptional. Yet most are caught inadvertently in the summer months, when sea trout are the intended quarry. Big Silver Blues and Peter Rosses are very effective, but in the early hours of the morning a much bigger fly, fished close to the bottom on a sinking line, has the edge. I have even had salmon, as well as sea trout, on such a rig at twilight on the Spey. The same is also true of tidal waters. Some years ago on the Ythan estuary these tandem lures took sea trout and salmon when smaller flies failed to score.

In bygone years tandem flies were known as Terrors and Demons, but after Hugh Falkus popularized them in his book *Sea Trout Fishing* (1964), they became known as Sunk Lures. I give Hugh's great pattern together with two of my own. Both have caught a lot of nocturnal salmon and sea trout.

Tie these on a two-hook tandem mount (see page 56), 2–3½in long.

Paint the mounts of the Falkus Sunk Lure and the Grizzle Lure at least three days before completing the fly; metallic paints are very slow-drying.

Falkus Sunk Lure

Thread	red
Body	metallic silver paint
Wing	two pairs of blue cock hackles* plus four to eight strands of bronze peacock herl
Head	red

Grizzle Lure

Thread	red
Body	metallic silver paint
Wing	two pairs of grizzle cock hackles** plus four to eight strands of bronze peacock herl, plus two to four strands of silver Crystal Hair or Mobile
Head	red

Why give these a red head? It is not for the salmon, for they cannot see red in the dark. It is our own little whim – they look nicer in the fly box!

---

*See note to Grizzle Lure.
**The two pairs of hackles should be tied back-to-back so that they flare out. This looks relatively untidy (they would be much neater if they were tied concave surface to concave surface to produce a single straight wing), but it increases movement in the fly.

Deer hair dibbling and riffling flies

Most wet flies can be dibbled and riffled across the water surface (see page 157). In turbulent water, however, there is an advantage in having more buoyant flies, which will be fished on the dropper of a two fly cast, with a conventional wet fly on the point. The ideal medium is deer hair, and the ideal hook is a ½–1in plastic tube. For dibbling, flies are tied on the plain tube. For riffling, a hole is burnt in the tube about a quarter of the way back from the front of the tube. The dropper is threaded through this hole and out of the back of the tube, where a small treble is tied to complete the rig.

Deer Hair Dibbler and Riffler

Thread	red or black
Tail	about six strands of bucktail plus three strands of Crystal Hair
Body	none
Head	deer hair spun muddler fashion and trimmed to shape, with a collar of unclipped hair tips pointing to the rear
Colours	black with pearl or silver Crystal Hair; orange with hot orange Crystal Hair; yellow with hot yellow Crystal Hair; white with hot orange tail and Crystal Hair

Muddler Heads

Thread	brown or black
Underbody	¼ –½ in plastic tube
Body (head)	deer hair spun and trimmed to shape on the entire tube

This is one way of adding extra buoyancy to any conventional wet fly to help it dibble or riffle on the surface. Slide one of these Muddler Heads on to the leader, and then tie on the fly. Slide the Muddler Head over the eye of the fly.

CHAPTER 3

LOCH AND LOUGH FLIES

. . . the light found its way through the ragged wings, trickled in and out of
the gleaming seal's fur, was reflected back from the hidden tinsel,
and turned the whole body into a haze of colour.

T.C. KINGSMILL MOORE, *A Man may Fish*, 1960

Because lake fishing for salmon is primarily carried out in the lochs of Scotland and loughs of Ireland, it is to there that I have turned to seek personal experience and to gain help and advice from local anglers and leading professional fly dressers in producing a series of effective salmon lake flies. In these great lakes – Melvin, Corrib, Conn, Fern and Glen in Ireland, and the wonderful lochs of Lewis and Harris and Wester Ross, for example – years of experience by many anglers have produced a selection of simple but traditional flies that catch a lot of salmon. The simplicity and effectiveness of these flies largely stem from the days before complex, gaudily dressed salmon flies invaded the rivers, and perhaps even Colonel Robert Venables would have acknowledged them in the seventeenth century. The gaudy fly did reach some salmon lakes in both Britain and Ireland, but it never ousted the much simpler flies, and many flies invented in the present century, such as the Bumbles, Dabblers and Goat's Toe, owe more to the simple old drab flies than they do to the days of Victorian splendour.

There are two main forms of salmon fly for lake fishing, each requiring different techniques: wet fly fishing and dapping. The techniques are dealt with in Chapter 7. Here we look at the flies and begin with wet flies.

Lake wet flies

Many of the comments that I made in Chapter 2 apply as much to lake salmon wet flies as they do to river flies.

Size is of paramount importance, but, because of the relative constancy of the lake compared with the river, size does not vary as widely. A lake is never in violent spate, although inflowing streams or high winds may colour the water and through the year its level may slowly rise and fall by several feet. Temperature may vary widely in the shallow salmon lies, from as low as 41–43°F at the beginning of the season on an Irish spring salmon lough to 64°F or higher in late summer. Yet this does not seem to have major consequences for the size of an effective fly. I have had spring fish take flies in sizes 8–10 in water with a temperature of only 43–46°F. In a river a big fly would have been necessary in such cold water (see pages 41–3).

Lake water is still, or almost so, so we do not have to consider changing to a larger fly in very fast flows and back to a smaller fly in slower water, as we do in rivers. What does dictate size of wet fly in salmon lakes is the roughness of the water – that is, the size of the waves. So, unless otherwise stated, salmon wet flies for lake fishing should be dressed on sizes 6–10 trout wet fly hooks – for example, Partridge Captain Hamilton Code L3B – or low-water double or treble salmon fly hooks. In rough weather, with a big wave or when the water is a little coloured, fish a size 6 or 8. In overcast weather with a slight wave use size 8–10. In calm, bright weather, with a slight ripple, fish size 10.

Because the lake's water is still, life is imparted to the wet fly by us, as we fish out a cast. This is a matter of angling technique. However, the use of certain materials, most notably seal fur in the body, a fully wound henny-cock hackle and fragile feather fibre wings, add mobility and life to the fly. Alas, many fly dressers who are perfectionists tie these flies too 'tightly'. Instead of being loose and straggling, seal fur bodies are dubbed and wound tightly and stray fibres are snipped away. Some fly dressers have recently taken to tidying up their feather fibre slip-wings by using fly-tying cement so that the wing stays solid without one fibre awry. Such tidy tricks are wrong. Note how Kingsmill Moore, in the quotation at the head of this chapter, referred to 'ragged wings' and the light trickling 'in and out of the gleaming seal's fur'. How can light trickle 'in and out of the gleaming seal's fur' if the body is dubbed so tightly that the light cannot penetrate? Kingsmill Moore was a great fly dresser and an expert lough angler.

Colour is important in lake wet flies, perhaps more so than in river wet flies, especially, it seems, in the multitude of Irish salmon loughs. Here, the careful selection of the precise shade of seal fur for the body, or the combination of two or three hackles of different colours, and the addition of tiny tags that may catch the eye of the fish are not anglers' whims. They are the result of generations of anglers testing and evaluating the merits of different shades and different materials. The successful combination of colour and shade in these old lake flies is not measured in tens or hundreds of salmon. Each of these flies has been responsible for the downfall of thousands of salmon.

It is normal practice to fish two wet flies on the leader; some fish three, but as far as salmon fishing is concerned I consider two to be far easier to handle and just as effective in catch rate. The fly at the end of the leader is the point fly. This will fish from a few inches to perhaps a foot or so depending on whether a floating or sink tip/intermediate fly line is being used (page 170). The second fly, tied to a dropper 3–4ft above the point fly, is the bob fly. This will fish just below, in or on the surface film.

Unless otherwise stated, the thread and head colour are black.

Point flies

Because we want these to fish more deeply than bob flies, they are usually of slimmer build, with softer, sparser hackling.

Connemara Black

Tag	fine silver wire and yellow floss*
Tail	golden pheasant crest
Body	black seal fur
Rib	oval silver tinsel
Hackles	black henny-cock and blue jay
Wing	bronze mallard

This is an outstanding pattern in any salmon lake. Although it is really a point fly, some Irish anglers fish this in very shallow salmon lies – less than 6ft – as a bob fly with a shrimp pattern on the point. Recently, in late March in very cold conditions, a size 10 Connemara Black accounted for a 10½lb springer from Glen Lough, Co. Donegal. What a great day that was!

Kingsmill

Thread	black
Tag	blue floss (optional)
Tail	golden pheasant crest
Body	black ostrich herl
Rib	oval silver tinsel
Hackle	black henny-cock
Wing	rolled rook or crow quill slip, with a topping over of golden pheasant crest (this should meet the tip of the tail, enclosing the fly in a golden halo)
Cheeks	jungle cock

*I now prefer fluorescent yellow.

Invented for Irish loughs by the late T.C. Kingsmill Moore, this fly has caught salmon on many lakes in its native country and the Scottish islands. It is an alternative black point fly to the Connemara Black.

Mallard & Claret

Tag	fine gold wire and red floss*
Tail	golden pheasant tippets
Body	very dark claret seal fur
Rib	oval gold tinsel
Hackle	very dark claret henny-cock
Wing	bronze mallard

Most fly dressers tie this with a lighter claret, but Peter Canning recommends a claret so dark that it appears almost black unless it is held up against the light. To distinguish it from the lighter claret version, this second version is sometimes called the Black Claret. An outstanding lake fly, it is usually fished on the point.

Sooty Olive

Tag	fine gold wire or oval tinsel
Tail	golden pheasant tippet
Body	sooty olive seal fur
Rib	oval gold tinsel
Hackle	sooty olive henny-cock
Wing	bronze mallard

The Sooty Olive appears to be black unless it is held up against the light, when it appears a very dark olive. One of the greatest Irish lough flies, it is usually fished on the point for salmon.

Golden Olive

Tag	fine gold wire
Tail	golden pheasant tippets
Body	golden olive seal fur
Rib	oval gold tinsel
Hackle	golden olive henny-cock
Wing	bronze mallard

This lighter version of the Sooty Olive is an excellent summer grilse point fly.

*I now prefer fluorescent red floss.

This is a great bob fly. On my visit to the Soval Estate lochs in the Outer Hebrides the 'keeper, Iain McLeod, recommended: 'If you have a Butcher on the point and Blue Zulu on the top dropper you can't go wrong!' He was right. I had run out of Blue Zulus by the end of my second week there, and I had taken a dozen. The ordinary Zulu has a black cock hackle at the front instead of the blue one. It, too, is a good bob fly.

Bibio

Tag	oval silver tinsel
Body	in three equal parts, black seal fur to front and rear with a band of red or orange seal fur in the middle
Body hackle	black cock
Rib	oval silver tinsel
Front hackle	black cock

An excellent alternative to the Zulus.

Following are three of T.C. Kingsmill Moore's bumble patterns. They are outstanding top-dropper bob flies.

Claret Bumble

Tail	four fibres of golden pheasant tippet
Body	medium claret seal fur
Body hackles	medium claret cock and black cock, wound together
Rib	oval gold tinsel
Front hackle	blue jay

A great sea trout lure, this is also a good salmon lake fly.

Golden Olive Bumble

Thread	olive or brown
Tail	golden pheasant crest
Body	golden olive seal fur
Body hackles	golden olive* cock and natural red (light brown) cock, wound together
Rib	oval gold tinsel
Front hackle	blue jay

The Golden Olive Bumble is a great brown trout, sea trout and salmon lure in lakes. A few years ago I tied some of these for a couple of members of the English fly fishing team who were taking part in an international on Lough

*Frankie McPhillips of Enniskillen recommends a yellow hackle in place of the golden olive.

Conn. They caught salmon as well as trout with them. One afternoon, in Victoria Bay on the same lake, I had nine grilse to this fly.

The Dabblers are a relatively new breed of lake flies. Two effective salmon patterns are given below.

Claret Dabbler

Tail	three or four fibres of cock pheasant tail
Body	claret seal fur
Body hackle	claret cock
Rib	oval gold tinsel
Front hackle	bronze mallard feather

Orange Dabbler

Tag	fluorescent hot orange floss
Tail	three or four fibres of cock pheasant tail plus two fibres of hot orange Crystal Hair
Body	orange seal fur
Body hackle	orange cock
Rib	oval gold tinsel
Front hackle	bronze mallard feather

I fish the Claret Dabbler in clear lakes, and the Orange Dabbler, which is, to all intents and purposes, a shrimp-fly, in peaty lakes.

The Goat's Toe is a great Scottish loch fly, which is best fished on the bob.

Goat's Toe 1

Tail	red wool (can be fluorescent)
Body	black floss silk
Rib	oval silver tinsel
Hackle	blue feather from peacock neck

Goat's Toe 2

As pattern 1, but with a red seal fur body and a bronze peacock herl rib.

Goat's Toe 3

As pattern 1, but with a tip of flat gold lurex, a body of bronze peacock herl and a rib of flat gold lurex.

Goat's Toes are usually tied on long-shank bucktail/streamer hooks in sizes 8–12. They are excellent flies.

Like Arthur Ransome's Elver, these bob flies are usually much larger than the point fly when used on Scottish lochs. They are excellent flies (usually fished on top dropper) for salmon and sea trout. The long fibres of the peacock neck hackle flicker with life in the water.

Elver

Hook	low-water salmon size 6–8
Thread	red
Body	black floss silk
Rib	oval gold tinsel
Wings	two vulturine gallina, tied long
Sides	jungle cock
Collar hackle	cobalt blue vulturine gallina

A popular bob fly on the wild Scottish salmon lochs.

Green Peter

Tag	oval gold tinsel
Body	light green seal fur
Body hackle	natural red henny-cock
Rib	oval gold tinsel
Wing	grey squirrel tail
Collar hackle	natural red henny-cock

This modification of a sedge-imitating trout fly can be fished on point or dropper for salmon. It is an especially great grilse pattern.

Black Pennell and Silver Pennell
Both these simple hackled flies were described on page 59. They are commonly used, especially in Scottish lochs, as bob flies.

Dapping flies

Dapping flies are huge, palmer-hackled lures commonly used in lakes in some regions – Scotland and Ireland, for example – but curiously not others, to catch primarily trout and sea trout but also salmon. The aim is to have a virtually unsinkable lure that can, with a very long dapping rod and light floss line, be fished so that it bounces across the water surface from wave to wave (see page 177). Lightness and action in dapping flies come from winding many hackles in touching turns down all or part of the hook shank, supported by tails and sometimes wings. Colour in dapping flies seems to be fairly irrelevant; action on the water counts for more. Take the four patterns given below and tie them in a range of sizes, and you have all the dapping flies you will need on any big salmon loch.

Suitable hooks are the Wilson or low-water salmon hook in sizes 6–10. Use black thread for all these flies.

Badger and Red

Tail	bunch of grey squirrel tail or badger hairs, or long badger cock hackle fibres
Body	none
Hackles	rear two-thirds of shank: crimson or scarlet cock
	front third of shank: badger cock

Bivisible

Tail	bunch of brown bucktail, squirrel tail or cock pheasant tail herls
Body	none
Hackles	rear two-thirds of shank: brown (natural red) cock
	front third of shank: cream or badger cock

Black and White Dap

Tail	bunch of black squirrel hair
Body	none
Hackles	rear three-quarters of shank: black cock
	front quarter of shank: white cock

Black Pennell Dap

Tail	long bunch of golden pheasant tippets
Body	black stout floss silk
Rib	medium oval silver tinsel
Hackle	black cock, palmered over front half of body

This popular dapping lure is simply a large, over-dressed version of the Black Pennell.

Those going to dap should also take advantage of dapping with real insects, something that takes us back to the primeval days of fly fishing. Ireland is the home of dapping with real insects, and usually two are fixed on a size 8 hook. In May and early June big mayflies are used, but through the summer and autumn either two daddy-long-legs or two grasshoppers, or one daddy-long-legs and one grasshopper, are fished on the same hook. It is said, by some sages, that a grasshopper dap is improved by adding a gorse flower between the two insects. A good Irish gillie will always have a supply of the appropriate insect for dapping. You can, of course, catch your own, and if you are going out fishing from a lakeside village, the local children are sure to pester you into purchasing theirs. 'Would ya like to buy sum mayflies, sir, an' they're only ten pee each, an' they're good 'uns sir?'

May on Conn or Corrib. Mayflies hatching. Trout rising. And a big silver grilse takes your dap. Now that is heaven!

CHAPTER 4

DRY FLIES AND
WEIGHTED NYMPHS

Memories of my first dry-fly salmon are still vivid. He rose
almost vertically in the clear waters of the Hut Pool on the Margaree.

LEE WULFF, *The Atlantic Salmon*, 1958

Dry fly and nymph fishing are the least used of all fly fishing methods
for catching salmon, but before we continue we must define some terms.
A fly floats on the water surface passively, drifting downstream on
the flow as though it were not attached to the line. This is precisely what trout
anglers mean by dry fly fishing. In their case, the dry fly behaves just like a real
insect. Dry fly fishing should not be confused with:

- Dibbled fly, when the fly is dibbled on the surface. This can be carried out
  in rivers (see page 157) and in lakes (see page 175), where the top fly in a
  two- or three-wet fly cast is worked on and in the surface. Flies for dibbling
  are described in Chapters 2 and 3. Dibbling is a very old fly fishing method,
  going back to the days of Dame Julyana Berners.
- Riffled or wake fly, when the fly is worked across the surface and against the
  current, either by allowing the fly to drag down and across the stream on a
  tight line, or worked across the flow on a short cast by manipulating the rod
  and retrieving line (see page 157). Many wet flies can be made to riffle
  across the surface by tying them in place on the leader with a special riffling
  knot (see page 159). Three special patterns are included in this chapter that
  are designed to float and to skate across the surface. They are, to some
  extent, dry flies; to no extent are they wet flies.
- Dapping fly is a fly used on lakes, which is bounced and spluttered from
  wave crest to wave crest by the wind. Dapping flies are described in Chapter 3.

In trout fishing terms a nymph is the immature stage of insects such as stoneflies, mayflies and dragonflies. Salmon feed rarely, if at all, on such creatures,

however. Indeed, many 'nymphs' that have caught salmon barely imitate insect nymphs. I use this term to differentiate standard wet flies, described in Chapter 2, from weighted wet flies or, in trout anglers' parlance, weighted nymphs and other buggy creations. But – and this marks the difference between nymph and wet fly – the fishing techniques are different. Trout fishers' nymph techniques are used to catch salmon on these weighted nymphs.

Dry fly fishing is fairly popular in some Canadian rivers, where the technique was largely pioneered. It has spread to some rivers of Scandinavia, although it is practised there by only a minority of anglers. In the British Isles its use has been restricted to a very few rivers, and more salmon have been hooked accidentally by dry fly trout anglers than deliberately by dry fly salmon anglers. Nymph fishing for salmon is in its infancy. Again, a few devotees have succeeded in taking salmon on nymph deliberately, such as Frank Sawyer and Keith Fulscher and Charlie de Foe (see page 98), but over most of the salmon's range more have been hooked accidentally on nymph by trout anglers than have been hooked deliberately by salmon anglers.

Why are dry fly and nymph fishing for salmon such a minority sport? First, because most anglers are not prepared to experiment. Why try something new if the old and trusted wet fly will work? Surely it is wasting time trying things such as dry flies and weighted nymphs. After all, salmon are generally hard enough to catch as it is.

There is some logic in these arguments, and I, for one, would not waste time fishing dry flies and weighted nymphs if the more usual wet fly gave me the best chance of catching a fish. However, with the increased trend to bag limits and catch-and-release, the pressure to catch as many salmon as possible has been eased. The next time I fish on the Aberdeenshire Dee, where the estate has imposed a 'no kill' rule for all salmon, I will not fish standard wet flies there for salmon but take the opportunity to experiment by fishing only dry fly and nymph. The river will, happily, also be full of sea trout, which will also take my dry flies and nymphs, so that the experiment as far as the salmon is concerned will catch this other species.

The second reason dry fly and nymph are not popular is that they appear to be successful only in special circumstances, circumstances, incidentally, that will probably prevail when I am next on the Dee and that will make me happy to experiment further with them there. To catch salmon on dry fly or weighted nymph you must know precisely where the fish are lying. In Canadian rivers it is often possible to see them through the crystal clear water, which is why that country has been a pioneer in these techniques. Because Frank Sawyer could see the salmon, he found them relatively simple to catch in the Test on his

Killer Bugs (see page 98), but what a pity it is that in the forty years since Sawyer's time no one has repeated the experiment in the clear chalkstreams. In most rivers you must fish 'blind' but have precisely worked out lies in which salmon are lying. This is impossible when the river is in a spate, but when the river is very low, the lies are often quite discrete.

Dry fly and, as far as I can tell from the information I have gleaned, nymph attract salmon best when the water temperature is fairly high, between about 59°F and 70°F, and this often coincides with a summer drought and a shrunken river. Needless to say, success with these rather special techniques also requires there to be a good head of fresh fish in the river.

Such a combination of factors is not a common event in the British Isles, but it does often occur in rivers such as the Dee and Spey in summer, when, despite low flows and high water temperatures, fresh fish can run easily. It also occurs in some chalkstreams, where the water level falls only slightly during a summer drought, and in some Irish rivers, especially those delightful short rivers of northern and western Ireland, where prolific runs of grilse occur from late June to August no matter what the height of the river. In many British rivers high temperature is linked to such low water levels that there will not be any fresh fish in the river, and under such conditions even standard wet fly fishing is largely a waste of time. I have also come across ideal conditions for dry fly and nymph in September when an Indian summer has closely followed a wet spell and brought in shoals of silver salmon. Such conditions offer the chance to try dry fly and nymph on rivers where fresh-run salmon would be rarely encountered in a summer drought.

If you find yourself on a river when conditions seem ideal, try dry fly and nymph. Find some fish and give it a go. Catch a fish and you too will be a pioneer.

Dry flies

Bear in mind that dry fly hooks for salmon fishing should be strong in the wire, otherwise they are likely to open out when the fish is hooked or while you are playing the fish. For size 8 and smaller, Partridge L3A Captain Hamilton or GRS3A Grey Shadow are ideal, while for bigger flies and for all deer hair patterns – Bombers, for example – Partridge Wilson salmon fly hooks are the ones to use. All are single hooks.

In the late 1920s Lee Wulff, aided by Dan Bailey, developed the famous series of dry flies that are named after him. These are still outstanding salmon dry flies.

Grey Wulff

Tail	natural brown bucktail or calf
Body	blue-grey wool or dubbing (e.g., muskrat or beaver)
Wings	natural brown bucktail or calf
Hackle	two blue-grey (medium dun) cock

White Wulff

Tail	white bucktail or calf
Body	cream wool
Wings	white bucktail or calf
Hackle	two light badger cock

Brown Wulff

Tail	brown hairs (impala in the original)
Body	cream angora
Wings	white bucktail or calf
Hackle	two badger cock

Black Wulff

Tail	black moose hair or calf
Body	pink floss silk, lacquered
Wings	black moose hairs or calf
Hackle	two furnace cock

Grizzly Wulff

Tail	brown bucktail or calf
Body	light yellow floss silk, lacquered
Wings	brown bucktail or calf
Hackle	one brown and one grizzle cock, wound together

Royal Wulff

Tail	white bucktail or calf
Body	rear quarter: peacock herl
	central section: scarlet wool
	front quarter: peacock herl
Wings	white bucktail or calf
Hackle	two brown cock

This series, tied in hook sizes 6–10, allows the angler to offer the fish relatively subtle changes of size or pattern. Having covered a salmon several times with one fly, go up or down a size or change to a different pattern in the same size. The white-winged Wulffs are ideal in dark or dappled water because they are easy to see. In dry fly fishing it is essential that the fly is constantly in view.

The Bivisible series of dry flies has the same advantages as the Wulffs: great visibility for the angler because of the white front hackle and a colour range that allows the angler to change pattern but retain the style of fly. The subtle change may trigger off a rise in the salmon. Bivisibles are also very simple flies, with great floatability, having just a tail of cock hackle fibres, a body of closely wound cock hackles (three to six to a fly) and a white cock hackle wound at the front. The ideal sizes of Bivisibles are 6–10.

	Black Bivisible	Brown Bivisible	Ginger Bivisible	Grey Bivisible	Grizzly Bivisible
Tail (hackle fibres)	black	brown	ginger	blue dun	grizzle
Body (cock hackle)	black	brown	ginger	blue dun	grizzle
Front hackle	white	white	white	white	white

The Bivisibles, which were devised by E.R. Hewitt in the 1930s, are very similar to many conventional palmer-hackled sedge patterns used in trout dry fly fishing, and such sedges will also catch salmon. One on which I have taken salmon and sea trout is a modified Great Red Sedge, as used on Irish loughs for trout.

Salmon Sedge

Hook	8–10 Wilson or Mayfly hook
Body	olive fur (synthetic or a soft natural such as dyed beaver or rabbit)
Body hackle	brown cock (e.g., Metz or Hoffman)
Wing	slips of cinnamon turkey or bleached elk hair
Front hackle	brown cock

Another salmon (and sea trout) dry fly taken from the world of imitative trout fishing is the Daddy-long-legs.

Deer Hair Daddy

Hook	size 10 Wilson or size 12 Partridge Caddisfly K12ST (you need a hook with a wide gape)
Extended body	natural deer hair, bound (i.e., ribbed) black thread; this is

formed by binding the deer hairs along a needle with the black thread, removing the needle after the body has been formed and securing the thread at each end with flexible cement; the body is then fixed in place on the hook shank

Thorax	brown fur
Legs	eight cock pheasant tail fibres, knotted twice
Wings	two pairs of blue dun cock hackle points

Deer hair, a highly buoyant material, has been incorporated into many salmon dry flies. Most famous of these are the Bombers, which were pioneered by the Rev. Elmer Smith of New Brunswick in the 1950s and 1960s. They are now tied in a wide range of colours, but the essential ingredients are common to them all: a tail and wing of calftail or bucktail, a spun deer hair body, which is trimmed to cigar shape, and a hackle palmered through the trimmed body. I prefer a tail and wing, which is tied forwards over the eye of the hook, of white calftail, as this makes it easier to see the fly on a riffled water surface. Bombers are tied in quite large sizes; Wilson salmon hooks sizes 4–8 are ideal, while a size 10 can also be used for sea trout.

	Brown Bomber	Black Bomber	Orange Bomber	White Bomber	Green Bomber
Tail and wing	brown	white	white	white	white
Body deer hair	natural	black	orange	white	green
Hackle (cock)	brown or grizzle	ginger	white or red	orange or grizzle	brown

In the 1970s the clipped deer hair bodied Bombers spawned much smaller dry flies known as Buck Bugs or Salmon Bugs. These are tied on sizes 8–10 trout hooks, such as the Partridge Captain Hamilton L2A. (I prefer wet fly hooks because the extra weight is unnecessary with the deer hair body and they are stronger than dry fly hooks.) As with the Bombers, there are now many colours of Buck Bug, some of which have been given names by their inventors that do not make it clear that they are, in fact, Buck Bugs.

Some Buck Bugs have tails, some have a butt of one or more fluorescent flosses, but all have the spun and trimmed deer hair body with a cock hackle palmered through it as in the Bombers. None has a wing.

	Brown Buck Bug	Black Buck Bug	Green Buck Bug	Orange Buck Bug	White Buck Bug
Tail	0 or brown hair	0	0	0 or white hair	0 or white hair
Butt (fluoro-floss)	0 or red or green	red	green and red	red	0 or red
Body (deer hair)	natural	black	green	orange	white
Hackle (cock)	brown or grizzle	black or grizzle	brown or grizzle	white or red	orange or grizzle

A grizzle-hackled Brown Buck Bug is shown in the Plate section.

The Irresistible series of salmon dry flies combines the floatability of the trimmed deer hair body and the heavy hackling of the Bivisibles. They are outstanding patterns, as they are for sea trout. A Wilson salmon hook, sizes 4–10, is preferable. The deer hair for the body is spun on the rear half of the hook and then trimmed to a cone shape. The hackles are wound on the front half of the hook.

	Irresistible	White Irresistible	Orange Irresistible
Tail	brown bucktail	white calftail	white calftail
Body	natural deer hair	white deer hair	orange deer hair
Wings	brown bucktail or grizzle hackle points*	white calftail	white calftail
Hackles	brown cock	blue dun cock	grizzle cock

Harry Darbee's Rat-faced McDougal is very similar to the Irresistible and concludes our selection of very effective salmon dry flies.

Rat-faced McDougal
Tail	brown deer hair
Body	natural deer hair, spun and trimmed
Wings	grizzle hackle points
Hackles	ginger

*When it has grizzle hackle point wings, this is known as the Adams Irresistible.

Surface wake lures

Many of the dry flies described above can be used as wake lures. If they are pulled across the flow, either by stripping in line or by allowing them to skate round on a tight line, they create a wake in the surface of the water. The Bombers and Salmon Bugs are ideal, but three other patterns are suggested below, purely as wake lures and not as dry flies.

Muddler Minnow

Thread	brown
Tail	slip of oak turkey quill
Body	flat gold tinsel
Rib	fine gold wire or oval tinsel
Wing	a sparse bunch of grey squirrel under two slips of oak turkey
Head and collar	spun and clipped deer hair, leaving a collar of deer hair tips extending to the rear

This is Don Gapen's original tying; today Muddler Minnows are tied in all colours using dyed deer hair. This is also a great wake lure for sea trout.

Yellow Dolly

Thread	black
Body	red plastic tube, $\frac{1}{4}$ – $\frac{5}{8}$ in long
'Skirt'	yellow deer hair at rear of tube, tied on a ridge foundation of tying thread
'Shawl'	black deer hair at front of tube, tied on a ridge foundation of tying thread
Head	black

The Yellow Dolly was invented by Derek Knowles and described in detail in *Salmon on a Dry Fly* (1987). Derek suggested fallow deer hair, but eastern white-tail seems easier to use. This is, of course, a small tube fly and it is fished with a tiny treble at the rear. (Derek uses these down to size 20.) Although Derek refers to these as dry flies, it is clear from reading his book that the Yellow Dolly is rarely allowed to float down the flow passively. It is allowed, and some-times encouraged, to move on the surface contrary to the river's flow. Thus, by the definitions given earlier, it is a wake fly and not a dry fly. Fished correctly, this pattern will score on rivers far removed from its native north of Scotland.

Skitterbug

Thread	brown
Body and hackle	natural or dyed deer hair

A fly that is easy to tie but difficult to describe. Take a bunch of deer hair and spin it on to the middle of the hook shank with the butts to the rear. The tips will flare out as a hackle. Pull these out at right angles to the hook shank, then tie them in and spin a second bunch of deer hair, but this time the other way round, with butts to the front and tips to the rear. This time the 'hackle' of deer hair tips will be against the hackle formed by the rear bunch. Push both hackles tightly together in the middle of the hook shank and tie off the thread. Trim the rear butts and forward-facing butts into tiny muddler-style 'heads' on either side of the long deer hair hackle.

This excellent wake fly was devised by the great American fly dresser Dick Stewart in the 1970s and first shown to me by Terry Ruane in 1989. Tie it in a range of colours on Captain Hamilton hooks, sizes 10–8.

Nymphs

I have thoroughly investigated the literature, and the following selection of weighted nymphs and bugs is offered as a starting point for those who wish to investigate further the catching of salmon on nymphs. More work needs to be done on this fascinating aspect of our sport.

First, it is possible to convert most wet flies into weighted flies that could be loosely called nymphs or bugs. One way of doing this is by adding a flashy gold head or silver head behind the eye of a single low-water salmon hook and tying the wet fly sparsely behind this. One very effective pattern is the Flashy Stoat's Tail (page 65). Tied on a size 8 single hook (the actual Stoat's Tail dressing is equal to a 10–12 because the gold head takes up room at the front of the shank) this is a good way for those wishing to start nymph-style fishing for salmon.

Killer Bug (Sawyer)

Hook	sizes 10–12 Partridge L2A Captain Hamilton wet fly
Thread	fine copper wire
Underbody	fine copper wire built up into rugby ball shape
Overbody	pink-buff wool wound over the underbody

This was the pattern used by Frank Sawyer to catch salmon in the Hampshire Avon (see page 38). The wool that Sawyer used was a brand for darning socks called Chadwick's 477, which is now not available – a card was sold at auction for £35 in 1992 – although tackle dealers offer a substitute. The Killer Bug is also an excellent sea trout nymph.

Pheasant Tail Nymph (Sawyer)

Hook	sizes 10–12 Partridge L2A Captain Hamilton wet fly
Thread	fine copper wire
Underbody	a double winding of copper wire down the hook shank and then a build-up behind the eye of the hook to create a thorax
Tails and overbody	cock pheasant tail herls; create tails with the herl tips; then twist herls and wire together and wind the body; then create two layers on top of the thorax

Why did Sawyer not try this for salmon? It is certainly a very effective nymph for sea trout, and I have three records of its having caught summer grilse.

Hare's Ear Gold Head

Hook	sizes 8–10 Partridge L2A Captain Hamilton wet fly
Thread	brown
Behind eye	a gold-plated brass bead
Underbody	fine lead wire (optional, for very fast or deep water)
Body	hare's ear
Rib	fine oval gold tinsel

Oliver Edwards hooked a salmon on a Gold Head when he was fishing a chalk-stream for trout. Alas, the fish broke free. This fly has accounted for at least three salmon on the Eden, when trout were the intended quarry, and also one on the Ribble and one (lost) on the Hodder.

B&P Silver Head

Hook	sizes 8–10 Partridge L2A Captain Hamilton wet fly
Thread	black
Behind eye	a silver-plated brass bead
Underbody	fine lead wire (optional, for very fast or deep water)
Body	bronze peacock herl
Rib	fine oval silver tinsel
Hackle	black henny-cock

A black and silver alternative to the Hare's Ear Gold Head, the B&P Silver Head can claim one salmon to its credit.

Salmon Fur Nymph

Thread	brown
Tail	three cock pheasant tail fibre tips

Body	light brown, brown or black-brown seal fur (substitute)
Rib	medium oval gold tinsel
Thorax and legs	guard hairs and fur from dark brown, light brown and natural rabbit, spun on dubbing loop
Wing cases	latex strip, coloured brown with waterproof pen
Head	butt of latex thorax

This pattern was devised by the great American tier Poul Jorgensen. I have never fished it, but Poul told me that it has taken several salmon on the western side of the Atlantic.

Twinkle Bugs

Thread	brown
Underbody	fine lead wire wound in close turns along hook shank
Body	rear two-thirds: mix of seal fur and chopped Twinkle*
	front third: hare's ear, straggly (I use a dubbing twirler)

Tied on wet fly hook sizes 8–12, these are great buggy catchers of many fish species. The straggly appearance and the mixture of colour and movement in the water are their prime attributes, and the more chewed they become, the better.

*The following mixes are recommended:
1. 40% orange + 30% yellow + 25% pink seal fur + 5% chopped pearl Twinkle
2. 40% blue dun + 30% medium olive + 25% yellow seal fur + 5% chopped pearl Twinkle
3. 40% black + 30% red + 25% yellow seal fur + 5% chopped pearl Twinkle

PART TWO
Fishing the Fly

....

. . . salmon fishing is both a science and an art. A science can be set out in so many words and learnt; an art can only be hinted at. . . . The artistry of fishing is a thing that grows, moulded by the thousand unheeded influences of long days beside the river, till a man catches fish without knowing why he does so.

ANTONY BRIDGES, *Modern Salmon Fishing*, 1939

CHAPTER 5

THE WHY, WHEN AND WHERE OF FLY FISHING FOR SALMON

High-water running conditions seem to really bring out the
predatory instinct in salmon. There is seldom anything tentative about
the take, with fish often taking in a broad sweeping arc that sets the reel
screaming from the word go! A long Collie Dog fly can be
tremendously productive at such times.

CRAWFORD LITTLE, *Success with Salmon*, 1988

In Volume One of this book, I spent some considerable time discussing why salmon take the angler's fly or bait, when they are more likely to take the fly or bait and where they lie in rivers and lakes. It is, I think, necessary to summarize what was said there, partly because there may be some who have not yet read that book and partly because the three questions of Why?, When? and Where? are of paramount importance in catching salmon. Visit the greatest salmon beat in the world, and if there are no salmon in the water you are fishing or if they are not in a taking mood, you are scuppered. It is rather like one London surgeon, who spent two weeks each year on a great Tweed beat. After several fishless years he asked an experienced angler what he was doing wrong.

'When do you fish that beat?' he was asked.

'The last two weeks of July!' he replied.

'That's why you don't catch anything. There are no fish in that beat in July!'

Only an idiot, even an intelligent idiot, would not check first that there was a good chance of fresh fish running the river or lake when planning a visit. This information is available, if you ask. Private beats should be prepared to let you see catch returns, by month, over several years. Search also fishing reports and articles in magazines. Ask friends who have fished there. And remember that when the river is at its best, the price will be at its highest!

Even if you go to a river or lake that is holding fish, it is important to remember that the fish are not evenly spread through the water. Salmon have lies, and it is on these lies that we should concentrate. Simply to start drifting across the wide expanse of a lake or to start at the top of a river beat and finish at the bottom, wastes much time. The greatest time and effort should be concentrated on the known lies, because that is where you will catch the fish. If you do not know where the fish are lying then the first thing you must do is to find out: ask a gillie if there is one, or someone who has fished the water before, or follow the tips given later that will enable you to work out to some extent the likely holding places.

Why and when do salmon take the fly?

What is the salmon doing and thinking when it is lying in the river? The first thing that it is *not* doing is looking for food. The salmon does not feed after it has left the sea and is waiting to spawn. The salmon does not take our fly because it wants to devour it.

Some people would disagree with this statement. However, it must be borne in mind that the gut of the salmon is atrophied when it returns to the river, so that it is incapable of digesting food, and rarely are any items found in the stomach of a salmon caught in a river or lake. Any items that are found are just as likely to be inanimate objects, such as tiny pebbles, bits of leaf or twig, as well as tiny animals, such as insects or crustaceans.

In the sea the salmon selects fairly large foods, such as lesser fish, large shrimps and prawns. If the salmon fed in the river or lake we would expect similar foods to be taken, and we would also expect salmon to take large flies all the time. They do not, and in fact they will often refuse anything bigger than a size 12–16 fly. Some authors have tried to explain this by suggesting that this preference for tiny flies is a throw-back to their days in the river as parr, when they ate insects. But if this were true, we would catch far more salmon on trout flies than we do; we would find them rising more to take flies from the water than we do; and we would find more insects in their guts than we do. Furthermore, in the sea the salmon is an opportunistic feeder, taking whatever is available. This is not so in rivers or lakes. I have watched salmon parr, small trout and shoals of small dace swimming close to salmon lying in the river and never seen a salmon respond to their presence. Indeed, as has been said so many times, if salmon or big sea trout did feed in the river, the river stocks of small fish would quickly become depleted. After all, why do salmon smolts go to sea? To feed. Why do they return? To spawn.

That is not to say that salmon will not occasionally use their mouths to take hold of something that may, to our eyes, suggest food and that they are feeding. Salmon have been very occasionally recorded taking grasshoppers, adult sedges, daddy-long-legs and mayflies, but that does not mean to say they were feeding on them. As we saw in Chapter 1, the old fly dressers actually thought that salmon ate dragonflies and butterflies and designed their flies accordingly. But salmon in rivers do not feed on dragonflies, wasps and butterflies, any more than they feed on shrimps, prawns, earthworms or tiny insects. They may take them into their mouths, but they are not feeding on them. The fact that anglers have taken salmon on flies that look like real insects and baits such as small fish, worms and shrimps does not mean that the salmon were after a quick snack when they seized the fly. If they wanted to eat it they would take such a fly or bait the first time they saw it. Often they do not. With a dry Salmon Sedge, a Daddy-long-legs or a wet shrimp- or prawn-fly, you might fish over a salmon a hundred or more times before it takes the fly. Did the salmon feel hungry only after the fly had passed over it umpteen times? No, the salmon got so annoyed at the pesty thing disturbing it that it grabbed the fly.

The point is that because salmon take our fly or bait into their mouth, we automatically associate this with feeding. After all, that is what we are usually doing when we pop something into our mouth. Or, as T.C. Kingsmill Moore put it in his classic book *A Man may Fish* (1960):

Modern man uses his mouth only for eating (apart from talking and kissing which have no interest for fish) and he assumes that when a fish takes something into his mouth the reason is that he wants to eat. This overlooks the cardinal anatomical fact that a fish has no hands. Everything that a man does with his hands, or other animals do with their paws, a fish must do with its mouth if it does it at all.

In Volume One, *The Life of the Salmon*, I noted many responses of salmon to baits that could not be construed as feeding.

This range of responses from a predatory fish indicates that, if it were intending to take and swallow the fly as food, it could intercept a fly perfectly with great precision. The fact that in only one of these responses is the fly firmly taken into the salmon's mouth indicates that most reactions are not feeding responses. Furthermore, that the salmon does (too rarely!) take our fly into its mouth properly does not mean that the salmon takes it as a food item.

I have no reason to think, when I have caught salmon on fly, spinner, shrimp, prawn or worm but not been able to see the fish take, any of the salmon took because they were feeding. But this begs the question, why does the salmon take our fly or bait?

T.C. Kingsmill Moore suggested that, apart from feeding, there are three reasons why a fish may take something into its mouth: fear of the object, anger at the object's presence, and curiosity about the object. Hugh Falkus took this a stage further by suggesting six reasons a salmon might take our fly or bait, and Gary Anderson concurred with Falkus's reasons for Atlantic salmon on the western side of the Atlantic in his book *Atlantic Salmon: Fact and Fantasy* (1990). These six reasons or motives, given by Falkus and then Anderson, for a salmon to take the fly or bait are:

- the sudden reawakening of the feeding habit
- aggression (the fly invades the territory of the salmon)
- irritation (the, often repeated, appearance of the fly irritates the fish)
- inducement (the fish is induced to chase and grab a fleeing fly)
- curiosity (what is it?)
- playfulness

Falkus considered that the typical take that results in the fish being hooked is indicative of the feeding habit response, and that the aggressive response is indicated by a violent, positive 'crunch' take. In both of these the salmon is usually well hooked. It is also usually well hooked if it takes by inducement, although, as I have just described, the fish may follow the fly and turn away without taking. Curiosity, irritation and playfulness may result in a variety of 'takes' from one that the angler may not be aware of to a gentle tweak, a knock or pull. These rarely result in a well-hooked fish.

Before re-analysing these reactions, I feel that it is first essential to remind ourselves that not all salmon will respond to our fly and that there are times when salmon will respond better than at other times. The clue to why a salmon will take – and also how it takes – our fly or bait is when it takes.

Salmon will not take our fly consistently well throughout the day. There are times when they may take keenly, times when the occasional fish may take, and periods when the fish seem completely uninterested in our fly. It would be quite useful if there were hard-and-fast rules about salmon taking times. There are not, but there are pointers that might be useful.

First, salmon take well when the river begins to rise during or immediately after heavy rain. They do not take well when the river has become coloured and is in flood, but when the river begins to fall and clear the salmon take well right through to the river reaching summer level (see Fig. 4).

Second, in spring (January to late April) and late autumn (mid-October to

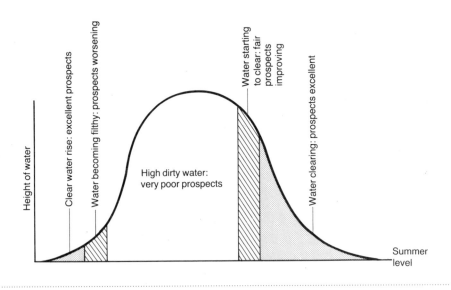

Fig. 4 – Taking times through a spate

the end of November), late morning and the afternoon through until dark are good taking periods. Note, however, that in late autumn I have had the occasional fish right through the day from dawn through to dark.

Between late spring and autumn (late April to mid-October), between dawn and mid- to late morning and in the late afternoon through to dark are always great salmon taking times. In very bright weather and low or warm water summer conditions, late afternoon to midnight and around dawn are the main taking times, with the possibility of a fish or two through the early hours of the morning and in the three or four hours after sun-up.

Actual timings seem to vary from river to river, and from year to year.

I am sure that these times coincide with the times of the day when salmon are preparing to run, when they are resting in between bouts of running and when they have just completed a run. They may be silver fish, fresh from the sea, which are creeping slowly or running quickly upstream to where they will rest before spawning, or they may be fish that have been in the river some while, resting in a pool for weeks, perhaps months, and have just started or completed a run, perhaps to their spawning redds. Recently John Todd had a fish in this last category from Glen Lough. It had obviously been in fresh water for some time, for it had lost its bright silver for a drab pewter colour, but it had only just arrived in the lough – its underside had raw, red patches where it had scraped its belly scrambling up the shallow rocky rapids in the Lackagh

106

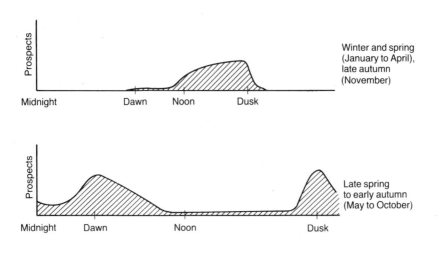

Fig. 5 – Taking times through the day

River, just before the outfall from the lough. So it had spent a long time resting in the short river before making its run and being caught.

Many earlier angling writers have suggested other pointers for good and bad taking times: the river is too high or low; it is too warm or too cold; it is rising; the wind is from the north, the south, the east or the west; the river is rimmed with ice; the air temperature is colder than water temperature – and so on. Some of these may be valid reasons in that they affect the timing of salmon runs and thus whether there are catchable (i.e., taking) salmon in the water. If just one salmon runs into a lie and your fly covers it, however, the chances are that the fish will take hold. No matter what the weather or river conditions, if you can, go salmon fishing. You may find a fish that has not read all the reasons why you will not catch it.

In his book *Salmon Fishing* (1959), Richard Waddington proposed the oxygen theory of salmon taking times, and this was later expanded by R.V. Righyni in two books, *Salmon Taking Times* (1965) and *Advanced Salmon Fishing* (1973). The theory suggests that taking times are related to changes in the oxygen levels in the river or lake, which are themselves affected by climatic variation. The theory is based on the fact that the amount of oxygen that can dissolve in the water depends on water temperature, being at maximum when water temperature is 40°F and declining as temperature rises. Any factor that causes a sudden rise in temperature in the day will reduce the amount of oxygen that the water can

107

hold in terms of volume of the gas, whereas any factor that causes a sudden drop in water temperature will increase the amount of oxygen that the water can hold. If a climatic factor causes a sudden cooling or warming of the air, the concentration of oxygen will either decrease or increase, and this will put the salmon into a taking mood by making them become alert and more likely to take the fly.

It is a great theory, and I would recommend salmon anglers to read the three books that describe it. However, the theory simply does not work because, as long as the water temperature is within the normal range of 36–68°F and the water is clean, the sensory system of the salmon is no more likely to notice the small and sudden change of oxygen level produced by changes of the intensity of sunlight, atmospheric pressure, relative humidity and so on than we might notice a slight rise or fall in the oxygen level in the air we breathe.

There are, I think, two physiological reasons why the theory does not work. First, it is the amount of oxygen carried by the blood around the body that is important to the salmon, not the subtle changes in the amount of oxygen held in the water. The sort of subtle changes envisaged by the oxygen theory would have no significant effect on the amount of oxygen carried by the blood of the salmon, so the salmon would not notice the change. Second, the breathing response in the salmon is controlled, not by oxygen levels, but by the carbon dioxide levels in the blood. The brain of the salmon is therefore unable to monitor slight changes in oxygen levels in its body when it is living in clean, well-oxygenated water. Hence the salmon is not going to respond to our flies because of slight changes in oxygen levels in the water.

Earlier I suggested that taking salmon are those that have just finished running or those that are running and are resting momentarily or those that are preparing to run. I would also add to these groups those fish that are maturing rapidly and are ready for spawning. I believe that the taking behaviour is affected by hormones that reach their peak at these times – hormones that prepare a salmon for migrating or for breeding.

The hormonal hypothesis of salmon taking times

I am not the first to come up with the idea that hormones have a part to play in the behaviour of salmon. Dr David Goldsborough proposed a theory that was first described by Hugh Falkus in his book *Salmon Fishing* (1981) under the title the Goldsborough hypothesis. This hypothesis states that when they return to fresh water the feeding drive of salmon is suppressed and the sex drive increased. These changes, which are both physiological and behavioural, are controlled by hormones produced in a tiny part of the brain known as the pituitary–hypothalamus axis. Among the effects of these hormones are the development of the reproductive organs, secondary sexual characteristics, such as skin colour changes and the kype of the male, and sexual behaviour. Other effects are the suppression of appetite so that the salmon do not feel hungry and are reluctant to swallow food – they become anorexic – in the river or lake, and the aggression that readies the salmon for obtaining a mate and territory and for fighting off intruders. The effects of these hormones might affect the salmon's response to our flies – the aggressive trait, for instance – but I believe that there is another step in the hormonal theory of when and why a salmon takes.

The pituitary gland also regulates the production of the hormone thyroxine by the thyroid gland. Increased thyroxine causes increased energy production (or increases the metabolic rate) in muscles, alertness in nerve cells, brain and sensory organs, an increased heart rate and an increase in restlessness. It is the main hormone, or one of the main hormones, that encourages a salmon to migrate, whether over long distances or merely from one pool to the next. Studies have shown a great increase of thyroxine in the blood of salmon that are migrating upstream and very low levels in salmon that not migrating – i.e., those salmon that are settled, for long periods, in pools and that ignore our fly.

We can now look at answers to our two questions of why and when salmon take our fly.

Although some salmon may take a fly because they have had a temporary return of the feeding habit (see below), the primary reason is from alertness linked to aggression. Salmon that are starting to move upstream or are resting (perhaps for a few seconds or a few hours) in a bout of running or have just finished running have a high thyroxine level. They are alert. They will respond to anything that threatens them or to which they are unaccustomed. They are prone to taking the fly. When they stop migrating upstream, the longer they stop the lower their thyroxine level and state of alertness become. They become increasingly less likely to take the fly. When they have become settled in one lie after their initial run, their thyroxine level becomes minimal and they are at their least alert and almost impossible to catch.

We can see this from the general pattern of taking times, which matches running times, which match variations in thyroxine levels. The first rise of water in a spate, before the water colours, is a potentially good taking time. Fish caught then are probably those that have been in the pool but dour, with low thyroxine levels. The initial rise in water, which will later encourage them to run, perhaps results in an increase of thyroxine, which increases alertness and thereby turns them into taking fish. The fish that we catch as the water clears after a spate are running fish or fish that have just completed their run and still have high thyroxine levels. Even in low water in small rivers salmon may try to run in a summer's evening. They will move to the neck of a pool and perhaps be unable to go further. These fish have a high thyroxine level, and they are, therefore, potentially taking fish. Earlier in the day or during the following day when they have dropped back into deeper-water lies and their thyroxine levels are low, they are not taking fish.

Two other observations support the alertness/high thyroxine level theory of why and when salmon will take the fly. If a pool is full of dour salmon, one trick has been to arouse them by throwing stones into the water or sending the dog in for a swim. Twice I have caught dour fish which had been turned on by a flotilla of canoes. The disturbance raised the hormone level and increased the alertness of the fish.

Many anglers will have noticed that a quite high proportion of the fish that we catch have been injured by encounters with nets, seals, sometimes lampreys, otters, cormorants and herons. In fact, 23 per cent of 430 rod-caught fish examined over a 10-year period exhibited some sort of damage, even though it was sometimes very slight. I think that this incidence of damaged fish is higher than that occurring in the entire population of salmon, and I suggest that it is related to slightly higher hormone levels in these salmon making them more likely to take the fly. Injuries are traumatic and result in raised hormone levels. The healing process also results in raised hormone levels. It is likely, therefore, that an injured salmon has a higher state of alertness than an uninjured fish, and this makes it more likely to take the fly.

Salmon will, therefore, take only when they are at their most alert, when thyroxine levels are high, during or either side of movements upstream.

Alertness may be closely linked, through the pituitary–hypothalamus axis, to aggression and fear in the salmon. The salmon are preparing to spawn and this requires alertness and, to compete for mates and redds, aggression. A salmon that sees a fly may respond violently or it may simply chase the fly or it may even flee from the fly. Such different reactions depend on the level of hormones being secreted by the pituitary–hypothalamus.

I have noted that the hypothalamus suppresses the feeding habit of salmon once they are back in fresh water, but there may be a variation in the level of suppression so that, in a tiny proportion of salmon, the feeding habit is not fully suppressed. They may take something as an item of food, although they show a reluctance to swallow food, which is why salmon that are seen to take insects from the water so rarely have them in their stomachs. Yet one would imagine that if this suppressed feeding habit or aggression were, as some have argued, the only reasons salmon take the fly, the pattern of taking times would not be as it is but would be more constant. The main point, however, is that the aggressive or feeding habit can be manifested only when the salmon are alert – that is, in salmon straight from the sea, that are on their initial run, which may take hours or days or weeks, or that are at the start of the run, when the fish have pulled in to rest during a period of running, or just after completing a period of running. The longer the resting period, the less alert the salmon and the less likely are the feeding habit or aggression to be manifested by the fish taking fly or bait. Waken the fish up by throwing stones in the river, and they will be made alert for a short time and might respond.

Where salmon lie

It is important to know not only that there are salmon in the river or lake, which may or may not be taking fish, but also where they are lying, for salmon are never uniformly scattered throughout a river or lake, and to fish the entire water would mean that much time would be lost fishing where there are no fish. If there is a gillie, it is possible to pick the gillie's brain, or to ask someone who fishes the water frequently, if you can find one who tells the truth! Sooner or later, however, you will visit a river or lake that you have never fished before and where there is no such help. Then you will have to work out where the fish are lying by 'reading the water'.

Let me first summarize the major points made in Volume One about identifying salmon lies. Then I will add some examples that were not included in the previous volume and that might give useful pointers when you come to fish a new river or lake.

River lies

Someone who has not been salmon fishing for very long often believes that salmon lies are always in deep water, in the middle of the river or close to the opposite bank. Nothing could be further from the truth. Salmon lies are often close in, under the bank on which we are standing, and to wade into these lies will not only disturb the salmon from there but also disturb fish in deeper lies as the scared fish zoom around the pool. Always look for potential lies close to the bank you are standing on before searching the middle and further side.

Riffles or 'streamy pools' or 'runs' may vary from a few inches to several feet deep. They generally have a cross-section with a fairly uniform depth, although they are usually deepest in the middle. The river bed in a riffle consists of big boulders, together with shingle or coarse gravel, which result in a broken, popply water surface. Deeper riffles often contain excellent salmon lies, especially in low water. (In high water they are often a raging torrent and the salmon will then have to move into more sheltered high-water lies; see below.)

A true pool or 'meander pool' has a distinct neck, through which water flows into the pool, a body and a tail, through which water leaves the pool. In most salmon rivers pools and riffles alternate. As the water flows from the neck to the body of a pool, the main flow usually swings across to a cliff bank on the outside of the pool leaving a band of slacker water on the inside of the bend where shingle, gravel, sand or mud is deposited. The cross-section characteristically has deep water immediately below the cliff bank and becomes shallower towards the inside of the bend. There are likely to be back-eddies and areas of slack water in the body of the pool, with distinct lines or creases separating back-eddies, still water and the main flow.

Some parts of salmon rivers, especially in the higher rocky reaches, are not meander pools but straighter, often rock-girt pools or 'dubs'. The route of the main flow through these dubs depends on the shape of the bed, which is usually irregular and produces a turbulent, swirling current. Again there will be creases between areas of slacker water and fast water.

The best lies in pools are usually in the neck of the pool, where the water is deepening and the flow is concentrated in a fairly narrow band; at creases, where fish can lie in slacker water just off the main current; in slower-moving water off the main current where the bottom is becoming progressively deeper; and in pool tails, as long as these are not glides (see below). But look carefully for 'special fish lies', which can occur anywhere along a riffle or pool, for one feature may produce a lie of only a square yard in an area that could hold a salmon. Find these lies and there will be the fish.

Large boulders tend to deflect the flow and increase scour around themselves. These make excellent salmon lies. Where the top of the boulder is submerged and not visible, the location of large boulders can be deduced from a bulge in the water surface just downstream of the boulder's position. Fish do not usually lie behind boulders where the water is very turbulent. They tend to lie just in front, to the side or, if it is a very large submerged boulder, on top of the boulder. Putting very large boulders into a fairly featureless and moderately deep riffle is an effective way of increasing the number of lies. When many Norwegian rivers are iced over in winter, boulders are transported on to the ice and, in spring, the boulders drop to the river bed and make the lies!

The roots of large waterside trees often act like tiny groynes, producing a narrow strip of deeper, fast water close to the bank. Salmon are often found

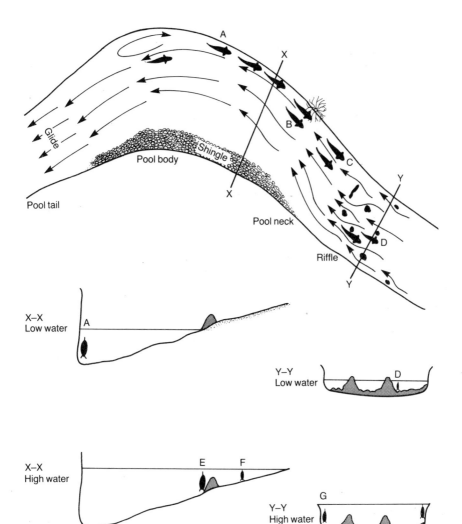

A — Steady water close to a cliff on the outside of a meander in low water

B — Under overhanging trees

C — Streamy water in a pool neck – running fish

D — By or in front on boulders in riffles

E — High water lies by boulders – normally high and dry when a river is low

F — High water lies over shingle in shallow water

G — High water lies very close to the bank in gentle flow and well away from the main current

Fig. 6 – Salmon lies in pools and riffles

113

there. One day I caught a salmon and three sea trout in such a lie, about 8 yards long and 3 yards wide, under a sycamore, on the River Wenning. At that height of water the next salmon lie was over 100 yards away.

Salmon may lie in water that is only 2–3ft deep if there is cover where they can shelter. Where tree branches trail or hang low over the water is often an excellent lie. So too are floating 'rafts', formed from twigs and branches, grass, weed and so on that have been washed downstream at high water and become trapped among trailing branches or against reed stems. In low water salmon often hide away under the bank where the flow has undercut the bank.

Sometimes the river bed is solid bedrock with a shallow, rough flow, and this is inhospitable for fish. The erosion of a weak point in the bedrock might produce a deep pothole that holds fish. Such lies are often difficult to locate. Examine the water thoroughly using Polaroid glasses at low water.

Following prolonged heavy rain or during snow-melt, river levels often rise to a point at which the fish must leave their usual lies and take up 'high-water lies'. These are usually positions off the main flow. For example:

- Where normally dry or very shallow streams or ditches join with the main river
- In meander pools, close to the bank on the inside of the bend over shingle that is normally exposed, often in less than 2ft of water
- Close to the bank (literally under the rod tip) in gaps among trees over grass that is normally far above river level

It is worth noting potential high-water lies during periods of low water for future reference. Many anglers miss a splendid opportunity to catch a lot of fish because they fail to seek high-water lies (see also page 158–63).

Weirs are often constructed across rivers to provide a head of water for old water-mills, to provide a water abstraction point or to produce well-oxygenated water below sewage works. They may be a barrier for fish moving upstream, although on salmon rivers weirs often have a 'fish-pass'. Except when the river is in maximum flood, a fine curtain of water passes over the sill or the weir (in some the sill dries up) and most flows strongly through the fish pass. Low weirs are often built by fishery owners to encourage scouring of the river bed and the formation of deeper pools in an otherwise shallow riffle. Above a weir the flow is usually fairly uniform across the river, and to protect the weir, the river is usually canalized for a short distance upstream. This part is not usually good fish-holding water, but if you can put a fly in front of a fish that has just passed over the weir and is resting for a few seconds before continuing upstream, it is likely to take. Immediately below a weir can be important fish-holding water on any river. The main flow is concentrated, and the depth is greatest usually below the fish pass. This is always a good lie, for running fish may rest here before passing upstream.

A waterfall is a natural weir, which may vary in height from a few inches to many feet. Salmon that have just passed over the fall often rest just upstream of the fall, usually in slacker water close to the banks if there is sufficient depth of water. Salmon may rest for some time below the waterfall (in the plunge pool) before attempting to leap the fall unless the fall is very small, in which case they may pass through very quickly.

Groynes (or croys) are often built out from a riverbank either to reduce erosion of the banks or, by fishery owners, to increase the flow in a long, shallow riffle so that the deflected current scours deeper lies. Groynes are often built in a series, but sometimes in pairs with a small gap in between. They are an effective means of increasing the amount of deep, fish-holding water in a river beat. The water in the angles between groyne and bank will often be slack or with slow back-eddies, and silt or gravel is more likely to be deposited there. The main fish-holding water develops along the crease between slack water and main flow or, where the current is not too strong, in the deep fast-water channel immediately downstream of the groynes, or at the edge of the main flow just upstream of the groynes.

Bridge supports often act as groynes, speeding up flow and increasing scour. The cover provided by the bridge is frequently attractive to fish, and unless the river is in flood, salmon often lie close to bridge supports where there is maximum depth and flow. Immediately downstream of a bridge there are often areas of deep, slack water close to the banks or behind midstream bridge piers: salmon rarely lie here. A great salmon lie is where the main stream has cut a deep pool immediately downstream of a bridge; the Old Bridge at Grantown-on-Spey is a classic example.

To summarize the lies found in rivers:

- Resting lies are places where a running fish may pull in for a short rest, perhaps a few seconds or minutes. Fish that are actually on the move, swimming upstream, will rarely if ever take hold of a fly or bait as they swim past it. If you find where they stop for even a brief moment, however, they are likely to take. In fact, if you can see fish running – these can be identified by their smooth, porpoise-like, upstream progress rather than splashy leaps – fish just one resting lie and you may catch fish after fish after fish.
- Pool necks often include excellent resting lies, especially if there is a very fast, shallow run immediately upstream. In high water the fish will tend to

rest out of the main flow but in deeper, slow water close to the bank. In low water the fish will rest in, or at the crease at, the edge of the popply-surfaced main flow; in high water it will choose to be tight under the bank over what may be normally dry land.

- Pool tails are good resting lies, especially if the fish have had to work hard running through fast water immediately downstream. In high water the fish will often pull in close to the bank (they will do this also on big rivers in low water if there is sufficient depth of water, say at least 3ft). In low water or in shallow pool tails, the fish will often rest by big boulders in the pool tail. However, many salmon pools terminate in a glide, a smooth-bottomed tail, where the water slides as one almost solid mass downstream. Glides are never good salmon lies. Look for a popply surface caused by an irregular river bed, for that signifies good resting water where the fish can lie in a small area of slacker water. A glide has a characteristic smooth surface because of the smooth bed and lacks areas of slower flow in which the fish can rest.
- Boulders provide suitable places, and some of the greatest resting lies on any river are by big boulders.
- Under the bank is a good resting place, even though salmon anglers are tempted to fall into two traps. First, they believe that the fish are always at or just beyond maximum casting range. Second, because they wear waders, anglers feel it essential to wade as deep as possible. Whether they are wearing wellington boots, thigh-waders or chest-waders, anglers feel they must wade to within an inch of the top. However, in the majority of rivers most of the resting lies of salmon are closer to the bank than the middle of the river. In high water or in a big, fast-flowing river, salmon cannot rest in midstream. The gentlest flows are close, very close, to the bank, and that is where they will rest, provided the water is deeper than about 2ft. So, in a fairly uniform stretch of water, when the river is high, do not wade but fish the band of water, perhaps only 5 or, at most, 10 yards wide, next to the bank. Fish will often take tight in at the side, so let the fly hang there before making the next cast. It is worth stressing the point about not wading when angling for salmon that are resting tight up to the bank. If you wade through the lies, you will disturb the fish.
- The pools inside meander bends in low water usually have a shingle beach, the water deepening to the other bank. These shingle beaches are often excellent resting lies if they are covered by a couple of feet of water when the river is falling after a spate. Again, it is essential not to wade deeper than ankle-high, because if you are standing in knee-deep water you are wading through the lies.

- Stream mouths and fords may be dry or a mere trickle in low water, but when the river is in spate they become deep, slacker areas of water just off the main current. They may then be great resting lies for running fish.
- Riffles and the bodies of pools are discussed under 'resident lies' (below).

'Resident lies' are lies used by salmon that have completed their initial run and are waiting for the breeding season. They are also used by salmon that are in the middle of their initial run but are resting for several hours or days before continuing to run. We are fishing for the latter and for fish that have only just completed their initial run. Such fish may take up resident lies that are also resting lies, but resident lies are often in deeper, steady water in riffles and pools where the fish have a good supply of oxygenated water and where they need do little work to maintain position.

I will illustrate these points with the examples shown in Figs. 7 and 8.

Lake lies

Lakes appear to be a uniform sheet of water to an angler sitting in a drifting boat, and the salmon might be anywhere. In fact, the salmon lies in a lake can be read just as easily as lies in rivers – perhaps more so.

r   – resident fish that have been in the pool for some time. We often see them leaping about, especially in summer dawns and at dusk, but we are unlikely to catch them

tr   – temporary resident fish, which may have just arrived in the pool and be preparing to move on later in the day or within a few days. They may be caught in the day in this position, but they are more likely to take just before they leave the pool when they move into the pool neck (trm)

rul   – resting, running fish in low water. These resting lies are not used when the river is high

ruh   – resting, running fish in high water. These resting lies are either dry land or are too shallow to be used when the water is low

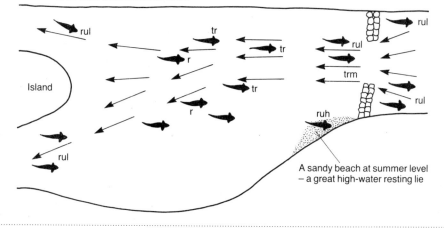

Fig. 7 – A pool on the Spey

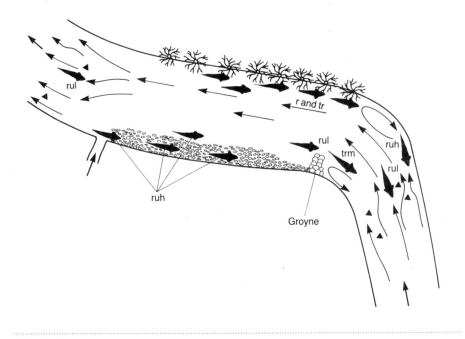

Fig. 8 – A pool and two riffles on the Lune

When salmon enter a lake via the outflowing river, they may stop for a short period near the river. They are then good takers. More often, however, they move into the lake and take up what are usually well-known, traditional lies in shallows around islands or rocky skerries, extensive shallow bays or the shallows off the mouths of feeder streams in which they will later spawn. The water can be sufficiently shallow that, if it is clear, you should be able to see the bottom. A reasonable estimate of depth range for lake salmon lies would be between 4 and 8 feet, although it is sometimes as shallow as 2ft.

I will illustrate this with two examples. When you visit a lake for the first time, look for the features illustrated in Figs 9 and 10.

Note how, in both lakes, the salmon lies are in shallow water, usually associated with reed beds, rocks and the inflowing and outflowing streams.

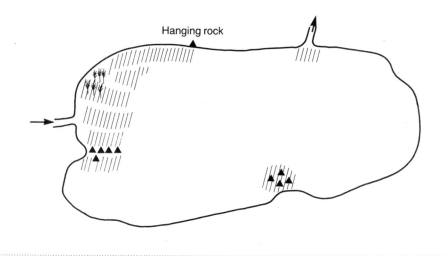

Fig. 9 – Glen Lough

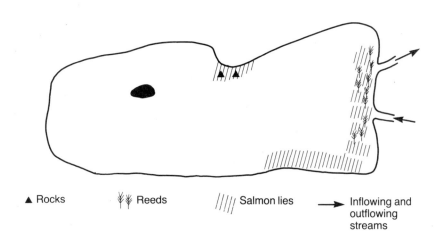

▲ Rocks   ❦❦ Reeds   ///// Salmon lies   → Inflowing and outflowing streams

Fig. 10 – Lough Fern

119

CHAPTER 6

RIVER WET FLY FISHING

. . . half the thrill is to see the swirl the fish makes as it takes the fly.
Then, of course, the wild music of the reel.

GEORGE FREDERICK CLARKE, *Six Salmon Rivers and Another*, 1960

The vast majority of fly fishing for salmon takes place in rivers and with the wet fly, which is why wet flies dominated Part One of this book and fishing these wet flies will dominate Part Two. However, many aspects of what is dealt with in this chapter apply equally to lake fishing (Chapter 7) and dry fly and nymph fishing (Chapter 8).

Before we consider fishing wet flies in rivers, it is necessary to examine the tackle we will be using, for without the tackle we cannot present the fly to the fish.

River wet fly tackle

Whenever you purchase any item of tackle, buy the best you can afford. Cheap equipment will, eventually, let you down. I was once given a cheap reel, and, like a fool, one day I went salmon fishing with it to the Ribble at Grindleton. On the third cast it broke – the spring that controlled the ratchet stopped being a spring and the reel drum revolved freely. The water was perfect . . . but I had to go home.

Fly rods

During the twentieth century there has been an increasingly rapid evolution in river salmon fly rods, from the heavy greenheart and built-cane, through the post-Second World War fibreglass – how wonderful, I thought, was my 14ft Milbro Verre! – to that most perfect of rod materials, carbon fibre (also called graphite). Today we are spoilt, for the weight of a modern carbon rod and effort needed to wield one are almost insignificant compared with these earlier materials. Moreover, in the short 20-year history of carbon fibre as a rod material, there have been great improvements that make angling even easier today, in the mid-1990s, than it was in the late 1970s. Only recently, Bruce &

Walker, which has been a pioneer throughout the development of carbon fibre rods, has incorporated into its newer models a carbon cloth that is stronger and finer than the best cloth that was available only five years ago. The current range of salmon rods is thus lighter than, but as powerful as, any previous rods.

Choosing a rod

If you look at the catalogue of any leading manufacturer of salmon fly rods you should see that several apparently identical rods are on offer. There may, for instance, be a dozen different 15ft models, all rated for line numbers 10–11. There is a reason for this apparent superfluousness. Different models have slightly different actions: some might be 'fast', others 'slow'; some might be fractionally heavier; some might have their action in the middle and tip, while in others you can feel the action going down into the rod butt through the cork handles. So there is a choice within one apparent rod specification.

We are all different. Some of us are stronger than others. Some of us are taller, with longer arms. Some of us have a perfect sense of timing; some of us do not. Different physical characteristics may mean that the ideal rod for one person is not the ideal rod for another. Then there is a psychological 'feel' – one rod might feel far better to one person than another rod that suits some-one else. Ken Walker tells of five very able anglers who went to visit his factory with the aim of buying a 15ft no. 10 salmon fly rod. Having tested all 13 models available, four different rods were finally chosen and only one rod was chosen by two of the five anglers. Five anglers selected four out of the 13 models, and each was delighted with his purchase.

I asked Ken about how any angler ought to choose a new rod.

Never buy by mail order, without trying it first. We get many anglers, who have bought a rod, untried, by mail order who have been disappointed and asked us if we will change it for them. When they test the full range, they then find the one they are best suited to.

If you are a keen salmon angler and intend to fish many rivers, big and small, throughout the long salmon season, you will need to have several rods. One will not do, for there is no such thing as an 'all round' salmon fly rod.

In big, turbulent rivers, when the water is cold (January to April, late October and November) and you will be using a sinking line and big tube flies, you need a 15–16ft rod taking a no. 11–12 line. I use the B&W 15ft 4in HF Sunk Line Special and the 15ft Powerlight HD, with no. 12 lines. In the same big, turbulent rivers, when the water is warm (April to October) and you will be using floating, sink-tip or intermediate lines and small flies, you will need a

15ft rod taking a no. 10–11 line. Such a rod is far more pleasant to fish than the heavier models for cold-water fishing. I use the B&W 15ft HF Speycaster no. 1 with a no. 11 line or the Walker 15ft with a no. 10 line.

Some anglers try to get away with using this same tackle on medium and small rivers. I have fallen into this trap, but I found that the big, heavy rods were too large. To have them working properly I would have had to cast into the fields on the other side of the river. So it is essential, if we are to enjoy fishing smaller rivers, to scale down our tackle.

In medium to small rivers, when the water is cold (in early spring and late autumn), you will be using a sinking line and big tube flies but will not be casting huge distances nor have to contend with having to start the cast with a long line, sunk deep in turbulent water. A 13–14ft rod taking a no. 10–11 line is ideal. I use the B&W 13ft HF Speycaster no. 3 with a no. 11 line.

In medium to small rivers, when the water is warm (from spring until autumn), we can take advantage of shorter or lighter rods. As a double-handed rod, something about 12ft taking line numbers 9–10 is ideal. I use the B&W 12ft 4in HF Grilse with a no. 10 line. Alternatively, use single-handed rod of 10ft to 10ft 6in with a no. 7 line; although this is basically a reservoir or sea trout rod, it is essential if you are 'working the fly' (page 154). Another alternative is a very long but light rod with a very light line, for this enables the line to be held well away from herbage. I use the B&W HF Light Line, a 15ft rod taking a no. 7 line.

Care of rods

1. If you have a carbon fibre rod, lightly wax the spigots every year. This prevents wear.
2. Always tape the joints of rods before starting to fish. After the first hour of fishing, check that the joints are tight. A loose joint will damage the rod.
3. Check rod rings for wear or cracks regularly. At the first sign of damage, have the rod re-ringed.
4. When you are travelling with your rods by car or plane, keep them safe in solid rod tubes. In a typical year my rods cross the Atlantic or visit Scandinavia by plane, fly several times to Ireland and go 8,000 miles by car. I have yet to have one break on a journey.
5. When walking along the river, carry rods pointing to the rear. More than one rod has been broken by being impaled in a stone wall or molehill.
6. If you leave a spare rod on the bank when you are fishing, make sure that it is safe from trampling cows and other anglers.
7. Insure all your fishing tackle for its replacement cost.

Reels

A good fly reel should hold the line and at least 100 yards of backing. It should have an exposed rim so that, when playing a fish, extra pressure can be put on by pressing finger or hand against this rim. Avoid 'multiplier' or 'geared' reels, on which one turn of the handle gives two or more turns of the reel drum. They are awful things with which to play a big salmon, for one fights against the gearing as well as the fish.

The best salmon reels are made by the House of Hardy (the Marquis Salmon no. 1 for no. 10–12 lines and no. 3 for no. 7 lines, or Sovereign 11–12 for big rods and heavier lines and Sovereign 8–9 for lighter lines). A good alternative is the Orvis Spey reel. For those who want a good reel at lower cost, those by J.W. Young or the B&W Expert Series are ideal.

Care of reels

1. When they are not in use, store reels in cases or cloth bags in a secure solid box.
2. Avoid dropping reels or banging them against solid objects. It is so very easy to ruin a reel this way.
3. Do not allow grit or sand to get into the reel works. If it does, wash carefully in clean water.
4. Oil and clean reels regularly (once every 10 fishing days).

Fly lines

The fly line is a specially tapered weight, and it is this weight that we use to flex the rod and propel the fly across the river. The weight of the line should match the rod rating – e.g., a no. 7 rod takes a no. 7 line. Many carbon rods are rated for more than one line weight – e.g., no. 10–12. For spey casting the ideal weight will usually be the heavier in this range – in this case no. 12.

Fly lines come in a range of densities: floating (the entire line floats), sink tip (all except the tip section floats), intermediate (the line dips slightly under the surface when being fished), sinker (the line sinks quickly under the surface as soon as it hits the water) and fast sinker (the line cuts very quickly down through the water).

For warm water, summer fishing, when the flies should be fished fairly close to the surface, a floating line will be needed for shallow lies or for very slow water; a sink-tip or intermediate line is needed for faster water. For colder water, in early spring and late autumn, both a sinker and fast sinker may be needed, the sinker for shallower lies or slower pools, the fast sinker for deeper, more turbulent water. In some slower, shallow rivers – Ireland's Finn comes to mind – the intermediate line may take the fly sufficiently deep in early spring.

Fly lines come in a range of tapers, the more usual being shooting head (SH), weight forward (WF) and double taper (DT). Shooting heads are specialist lines for extremely long-distance, overhead casting. Many anglers on very big rivers, such as the lower Tay, use them, but they are not for the novice. Weight-forward lines are the best all-round lines for long-distance overhead casting, but they cannot be used for spey casting, for which double taper lines are essential. Double-taper lines cast a fair distance in overhead casting, and they are the best all-round lines for salmon fishing.

Fly lines come in a range of colours and, although there have been many arguments as to what is the best colour, as far as salmon are concerned I do not think it makes much difference. I prefer white, if only because it helps me see the line on the water.

Each line – and we may be talking of up to eight when it comes to fishing a wide range of rivers throughout the year – should live on its own reel, so that changing lines is only a matter of changing reels.

Buy the best lines. Those by Cortland and Scientific Anglers are as good as you can get.

Backing

The best backing is Dacron – it is fine, does not stretch, does not deteriorate with age and is easy to connect to the fly line (see below). Hardy 27lb test Dacron is ideal.

Leaders

There is no need to buy tapered or braided leaders for river fishing. A length of plain monofilament is ideal. Buy the best: Maxima Chameleon in 8lb, 12lb and 18lb. The 18lb is used for big flies: tubes, Waddington shanks and singles over 2in long. The 12lb is used for smaller tubes, Waddington shanks and single, double and treble flies down to size 8. The 8lb is used for tiny flies from size 10 to 16.

For sinking lines, a leader 4ft in length is ideal. Salmon are not 'leader-shy'. One angler actually tied a big fly to the end of a sinking line and caught fish! For floating, sink-tip or intermediate line fishing a leader of 10–12ft is ideal; 10ft when using a single-handed rod and 12ft with a double-handed rod.

Putting it all together

The following illustrations and notes explain all the stages and knots needed to set up the entire salmon fishing outfit.

1. Tie a piece of thread to the end of the fly line, and then tie the fly line on to the reel drum and wind the fly line on to the reel. *Note*: If one end of the fly line is labelled 'This end' or 'Reel', use the other end.

2. Open up 2in of the end of the Dacron backing and use a knife or sandpaper to roughen 1½ in at the end of the fly line. Take a spool of strong thread (fly tying thread on a bobbin holder is ideal) and tightly whip the 2in end of the Dacron to the end 2in of fly line. I like to whip this joint with two full, tight layers of wound thread. Finish off with a 10-turn whip-finish, using a short piece of thread.

   Soak the whipping three times with fly tying cement or varnish, allowing time to dry in between each coat.

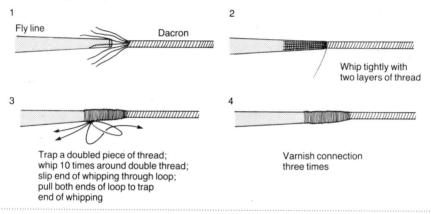

1
Fly line
Dacron

2
Whip tightly with
two layers of thread

3
Trap a doubled piece of thread;
whip 10 times around double thread;
slip end of whipping through loop;
pull both ends of loop to trap
end of whipping

4
Varnish connection
three times

Fig. 11 – Fixing fly line to the backing

3. Wind on the Dacron backing until the reel is full.

4. Go to a big field or lawn and pull the backing and fly line from the reel. Attach the backing to the reel drum with the knot shown in Fig. 12 and rewind on backing and line. You now have a full reel, with the fly line on top and the backing below.

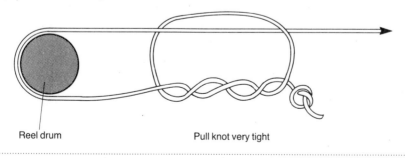

Reel drum

Pull knot very tight

Fig. 12 – Knot for connecting the backing to the reel

125

There are several ways of fixing the leader to the end of the fly line. The needle knot is as good as any and better than most.

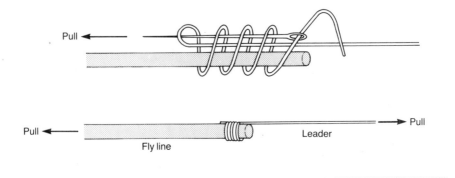

Fig. 13 – Using a needle knot

Note: I needle-knot a 3ft leader butt of about 25lb test monofilament to the end of the fly line, tie a loop at the end of this butt, and fix the leader in place with a loop-to-loop connection.

Take the monofilament leader, tie a three-turn loop knot in one end (see Fig. 14), and fix to the leader butt with a loop-to-loop connection (see Fig. 15).

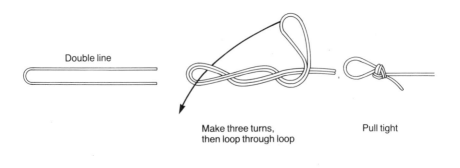

Fig. 14 – A three-turn loop to loop

Droppers can be tied to the leader using a four-turn water knot, tied 3–5ft above the end of the leader (see Fig. 16). The piece used as a dropper should be the length that points forwards towards the end of the leader. Cut off the piece that points backwards.

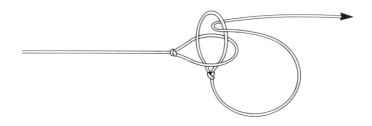

Fig. 15 – A loop-to-loop connection

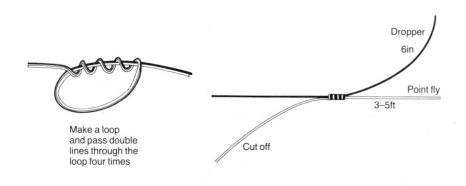

Make a loop
and pass double
lines through the
loop four times

Cut off

Dropper

6in

Point fly

3–5ft

Fig. 16 – A four-turn water knot

Droppers are most often used in lake fishing (Chapter 7). In boulder-strewn, snaggy rivers they are likely to result in a lost fish because the fly that is not attached to the fish tends to become snagged on a big boulder.

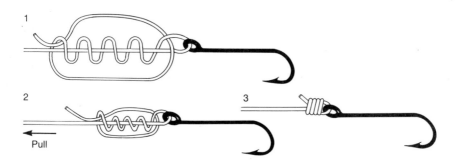

1

2

Pull

3

Fig. 17 – Tucked blood knot

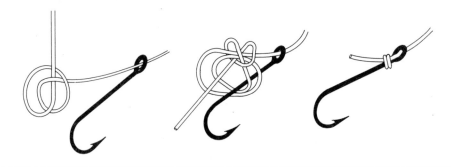

Fig. 18 – Double or two-turn turle knot

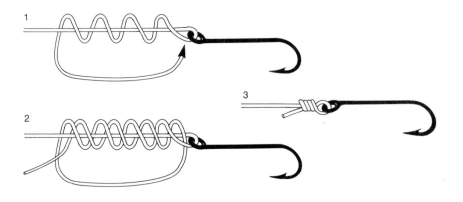

Fig. 19 – Fisherman's knot

8. Suitable knots for tying the fly to the leader are the tucked blood knot, the double turle knot (Fig. 18) and the fisherman's knot (Fig. 19). The turle knot, which holds the fly in line behind the hook eye, and the fisherman's knot, which is tightened to hold the fly on a small, articulated loop, are better than the blood knot, in which the knot may work around the eye of the hook so that the fly will fish badly at an angle to the line. Therefore, although it is the most popular, the blood knot is, perhaps, the least effective of the three.

Miscellaneous items of tackle

The following items are essential.

- Fly boxes – have a store of flies in the car and carry what you need for the day in a small fly box. The main store cannot get wet and rust, should it rain or you fall in.
- Spare monofilament – carry these in 25- or 50-yard spools.

John Todd playing a fish on the Finn, where the slow flow makes it essential to work the fly

The author dibbling the fly

Right *The Ranga River. In the clear waters of Iceland's rivers a black fly with plenty of blue in the dressing is indispensible*

Below *The Lackagh River is one of the world's greatest salmon rivers. Fish ascend it almost every day of the season, from 1 January to 30 September*

The first salmon caught on a 'What is it?'

Below *The author with a summer fish from Lapland's Alta River*

Above *Leap beat on the Bush, a great summer salmon river*

Fly fishing in the twilight of an Arctic midnight from a boat on the Alta River

Dun Fly (1496)

Wasp Fly (1816)

Glittering Fly (1694)

Spring Fly (1834)

Summer Fly (1834)

The Lady of
Mertoun (1843)

Meg with the
Muckle Mouth (1843)

Gipps (1910)

Claret (1910)

Michael Scott (1843)

White & Silver (1910)

No Name (1786)

Kinmont Willie (1843)

Meginher
Brawes (1843)

Toppy (1843)

Left *The author has hooked a fish in the sea pool on the Bush. He is keeping slightly downstream of the fish to encourage it to fight upstream. If the fish ran downstream to the sea it would certainly be lost*

Left *The advantage of a long rod – the 15ft no.7 line Hexagraph – is clearly seen here. The author has hooked a fish tight under the bank of the small river, and the length of the rod allows him to remain out of sight while casting to and playing the fish. It also prevents the line from catching on the vegetation. Only when the fish is played out will John Todd slip down the bank to net it*

Above *Playing salmon on Canada's Miramichi. Note that the rod is held high to keep as much line as possible out of the water so that the angler keeps in touch with, and can exert maximum pressure on, the salmon*

2 FLASHY STOAT'S TAILS

Tied short and sparse

Tied long and full

Yellow & Black
Artic Fox

Blue Stoat's
Tail

Willie Gunn (treble)

Silver Blue

Yellow Dog
(Arctic Fox)

Orange & Yellow
Arctic Fox

Capercallie
Shrimp

Dark Hackle

Partridge & Orange

Black & Purple

Willie Gunn (tube)

Collie Dog

Yellow Dog
(squirrel wing)

Teal, Blue &
Silver Hackle

Goldie

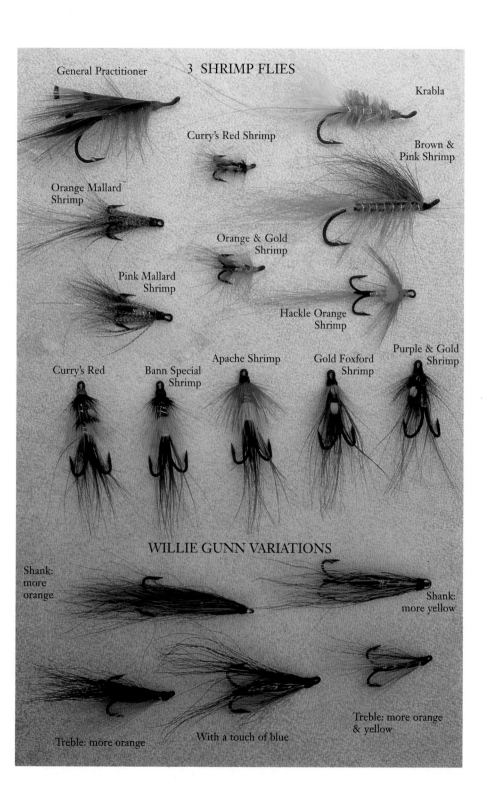

3 SHRIMP FLIES

General Practitioner

Krabla

Curry's Red Shrimp

Brown &
Pink Shrimp

Orange Mallard
Shrimp

Orange & Gold
Shrimp

Pink Mallard
Shrimp

Hackle Orange
Shrimp

Purple & Gold
Shrimp

Curry's Red

Bann Special
Shrimp

Apache Shrimp

Gold Foxford
Shrimp

WILLIE GUNN VARIATIONS

Shank:
more
orange

Shank:
more yellow

Treble: more orange
& yellow

Treble: more orange

With a touch of blue

Left and right *The mighty Spey. With the Aberdeenshire Dee, this is the most perfect of Scottish fly rivers*

Below *Mill Pool on the Aberdeenshire Dee*

Above *We often dismiss the theory 'dark day, dark fly; bright day, bright fly'. The author had fished with a black fly for an hour after sun-up on a bright morning on the Alta. He changed to a bright blue and silver tube - and caught a fish. Would it have taken the black fly that had just been taken from the leader? We will never know, but such questions make salmon fly fishing one of the greatest sports*

Above left *The author fishing the Mourne*

Above *Oliver Edwards dry fly fishing on the Dee in dreadfully low water and bright conditions. In addition to several sea trout that day, he had a grilse on the Daddy-long-legs*

Far left *A spring salmon from an Irish lough*

Left *Geoff Haslam fishing the Tweed from the bank because the salmon lies are under the bank*

This salmon was taken in the most hopeless of low water conditions in the Nith on a sparsely dress size 10 Willie Gunn (that is, a Black, Orange & Yellow hair wing). There were about a dozen black and yellow hairs in the dressing

Left *Frank Elliott fishing for spring salmon on the Finn. Even in the coldest weather a 1in tube or double fly and intermediate or sink-tip fly line will take salmon from this great spring river. In big Scottish rivers, on the other hand, a fast sinking line and a 2–3in tube would be essential*

Below *Fishing the Tweed from a boat controlled by a rope from the bank*

4 THREE BADGERS HAIRWINGS

Yellow Badger

Blue Badger

Orange Badger

Fiery Brown (hair wing)

Fiery Brown (feather wing)

Silver Doctor

Green Peter

Sooty Olive

Bibio

Black Pennel

Blue Zulu

Mallard & Claret

Golden Olive

Connemara Black

Grizzle Lure

Elver

- Snips – the best snips for cutting monofilament are nail clippers. Attach these to your jacket with a length of cord.
- Artery forceps – essential for removing a deeply embedded hook.
- Sharpening stone – a small carborundum stone is ideal for sharpening blunted hook points. Check hooks frequently, for a blunted or broken hook point often results in loss of a fish.
- Priest and landing aid – see Chapter 9.
- Wading staff – see Chapter 11.
- Torch – essential if fishing into the dark.
- Thermometer – for taking water temperature so that you can select the appropriate fly size based on this temperature plus other river conditions (page 42).
- Food and drink – salmon fishing is hard work. Have adequate food and drink with you but avoid alcohol. Rivers and lakes are dangerous places and you need a clear brain. Drink in the evening, after fishing.

Waders

If you are fishing a small river where there is no need to wade, wear boots or wellingtons. Where you need to wade, chest-waders are more versatile than thigh-waders, but do not wade into lies (see Chapter 5). For cold-water wading neoprene waders are the best. For warm water wear thin latex, PVC-coated cloth or plastic ones.

The choice of soles on waders is of major importance. Studded waders are the best on grass or mud, but they tend to slip around on smooth rock. Felt soles, which last a remarkably long time, are best on smooth, slippery rock but are treacherous on grassy or muddy slopes. A combination of the two is ideal – felt with studs. Alas, many manufacturers of otherwise excellent waders do not offer these soles, but you can buy them separately and fix them in place yourself.

Casting

Casting requires a book all by itself, and there is one currently on the market that I would recommend all salmon anglers to read and study: *Speycasting* by Hugh Falkus (1994).

The only good way to learn to cast is by having a course of lessons by a competent instructor. Fly casting is about the position of your feet and hands, timing and the correct use of controlled power. So, too, is golf, and only an idiot would take up golf without having lessons with the club professional.

To the water

Before we go to the water we choose the rod, reel, line and leader appropriate for the river and the time of the year. We might arrange to take two sets of tackle. If we are fishing in early spring, a rod taking a heavy sinking line and one taking a slow sinking line might be appropriate. In summer we might take one rod taking a sink-tip or intermediate line and one with a floating fly line. In faster or deeper water we might use the first in each pair of tackles, in slower or shallower water the second.

At the river we check the water temperature, and look at the water height gauge. We then put a marker at the water's edge to tell us whether the river is rising, falling or steady. Now we look carefully at the pool we will be fishing. Is the water clear or does it have a faint haze or a strong peat tinge or is it quite coloured? Look, too, at the sky. Is it going to be a bright, sunny day, or a dull, overcast one? Such information helps us choose the range of fly sizes and perhaps the sort of pattern that might score today (see Chapter 2).

Will we be fishing some very fast water, then some moderately fast water, and then some quite slow water? If so, we should choose three sizes of fly: a larger one for the very fast water at the top of the pool neck, one a size smaller for the fast pool neck, and a smaller one for the slowest part of the pool. In early spring or late autumn we might, in fact, start with a fast-sinking line and bigger fly in the fastest water, and change to the rod carrying the slower-sinking line in the slower body of the pool. In late spring to early autumn a sink-tip or intermediate line might be better in streamy riffles and pool necks, with the rod carrying the floating line left on the bank at an appropriate spot for fishing through the slower body of the pool.

From our store of flies we should choose flies of the sizes we will be fishing in two different patterns so that, having fished through once, we can change pattern and fish through again. If the river looks a bit snaggy, we might also take one or two spares. We will, therefore, be carrying ten flies at the most. By carrying the minimum number, we will not be tempted to be constantly changing fly pattern. We will concentrate on the presentation of the fly instead.

Presentation of the fly

Watching other anglers, one can easily be misled into believing that the presentation of the wet fly in river salmon fishing consists in nothing more than casting as long a line as possible down and across the river, making an upstream 'mend', and then, when the fly arrives downstream of the rod, taking a pace downstream and repeating the exercise. This is not the method, nor should it be. Every salmon lie and every bit of a pool or riffle may require a slightly different approach. Those 5 per cent of anglers who catch 95 per cent of the salmon are always conscious of the need to modify their presentation as water conditions vary as they fish through the lies in the ever-changing riffles, through the pool neck and body of the pool, and into the tail of the pool.

The four points to bear in mind when fishing the wet fly in rivers for salmon are:

- Is the fly fishing at the correct depth?
- Is the fly fishing at the correct speed through the water?
- From what angle should the fly approach the salmon to give the best chance of the fish grabbing the fly?
- Are there any other tricks I might use to extract a salmon from that lie?

The effective depth of the salmon fly

Except when using the riffled or dibbled fly (see page 157), most salmon anglers have no real idea of how deep their salmon wet fly is fishing once they have cast it into the water. If they are using a floating line most anglers imagine that it is 'just beneath the surface', on a sink-tip or intermediate line it is 'a bit deeper' and with a sinking line it is 'near the bottom'.

The first and most important point to consider when talking of wet fly is determining the most effective depth that will attract the salmon. However, perhaps we should initially go another step backwards and ask if depth has any importance at all in the salmon fishing equation, for if it has not, there is little to be gained from learning how best to put a fly at a particular depth.

Salmon are foolish creatures, which will take into their mouths something they do not want to eat. Because of their foolishness, whenever we decide on some general rule there will always be some fish that provides the exception to the rule. I was once fishing the Lune, casting to a lie close to some overhanging alders. I overcast by a foot or so, and the tip of the leader caught on one of those cone-like alder fruits. I pulled, and the fly plopped into the water, where it was immediately taken. That was a foolish salmon, and it would take a foolish angler to suggest that an effective way of presenting a fly to a salmon would be to hook an alder fruit deliberately. What we must do is discount the rare and exceptional incidents and look to the common, typical behaviour of salmon, and when we do this we find that depth of the fly appears to be important.

In late winter and early spring and, on some rivers and in some years, in late autumn, when water temperatures are less than 43–50°F, the fly is best fished deep. How deep we shall decide in a moment. From mid-spring, usually about the end of April but in very cold springs as late as mid-May, when water temperatures have risen above 43–50°F, the fly is best fished close to the surface. How close we shall also decide in a moment. This pattern has long been well known and has given rise to the two methods of salmon fishing: sunk-line fishing and floating line, or greased-line, fishing.

The reason for this split – cold water and deep fly, warm water and shallow fly – is a physiological one. Salmon being poikilothermic beasts, the temperature of a salmon's body is approximately that of the river water. Its energy production depends on its body temperature, which depends, in turn, on the water temperature. Thus, the colder the water the more lethargic the fish. It is well known, for example, that salmon are unable to ascend low waterfalls and white water rapids unless the water temperature is above about 42°F. They do not have the energy to do so. The bigger the waterfall, the more energy they need, so the higher must be the water temperature. This relationship between water temperature and energy level affects many aspects of salmon behaviour in fresh water. When the water is cold their eye–optic nerve–brain system is much slower than when the water is warm. To evoke a response to our fly, therefore, we must use a big fly and fish it deep, slowly and close to the salmon. By contrast, when the water is warm, the salmon are far more alert and will react strongly to a tiny fly fished more rapidly well above their heads, close to the surface.

My own researches and the information given in the vast literature on the subject suggest that the transition period between effective sinking line and deep fly and effective fly close to the surface is quite wide. Some anglers turn to the sub-surface fly as soon as the water reaches 43°F; others wait until it reaches 50°F. Some anglers ignore this general rule altogether, and fish a sinking line throughout the season, although those I have talked to generally fish big, fast rivers, such as the Spey, or autumn rivers where the water temperature will be in this transitional range when the fish are running in the back-end. Note also that I stressed 'some rivers' and 'some years' in respect of the transition from sub-surface to deep fly in autumn. In autumn in big rivers that get a good back-end run, such as the Tweed and Tay, and the Spey in September, a deep fly works better than one just below the surface at temperatures close to 50°F. But in smaller, shallower rivers, such as the Ribble, Hodder, Lune, Nith and Annan, a fly fished just beneath the surface can be effective to the end of October and into November, even at water temperatures of 41–43°F. In a very cold autumn, such as we experienced in 1993, when these small rivers were rimmed with ice from mid-October, the well-sunk fly is essential.

When in doubt during spring and autumn, take two sets of tackle so that you can alternate flies fished close to the surface with flies fished deep. One year on the Nith, with water temperature at 46–48°F, I had three fish in a week on a fly fished just beneath the surface. The same week the following year, with a water temperature of 45–46°F, my two fish came to a deeply fished fly.

How deep is deep?

For warm-water tactics, with a fly fished close to the surface, I would suggest that the fly should be within 6in of the surface but not skating in the surface unless you are deliberately riffling or dibbling it. Hugh Falkus, who is one of the very few writers to have suggested a precise depth, reckoned in his book *Salmon Fishing* on 4in as being the right depth.

For cold-water tactics it is more difficult to give a precise answer. Some have suggested that the fly should be put in front of the nose of the salmon as it lies on the bottom. To do this you must, however, have some idea of the depth of the water and know that your fly is at that depth. The answer is to alter the rig of line density and fly weight, and to vary the angle of cast and amount of slack line released into an upstream mend, to the point at which the fly occasionally touches bottom. That worked for me – it also lost me quite a lot of flies – for 20 years. The fly would stop and slowly line would be pulled from the reel as the salmon moved away with it. In recent years I have not fished that deep. Having discovered what weight of fly and density of line are necessary for the fly occasionally to touch bottom, I slightly lightened my set-up by using a lighter fly so that the fly is still fishing deep but is above the salmon. The takes are more positive because the salmon must move up to intercept the fly, and I suspect that I get a few more offers and hook and land a few more fish with the slightly less deep fly.

There are three ways of altering the depth at which a fly can be fished.

Lines of various densities

For summer warm-water salmon fishing it is usual to fish with a full-floating line. This is fine in very shallow, boulder-strewn, streamy water to, say, 3ft deep. However, I am convinced that in most fast, deeper water the intermediate density of line or sink-tip is far more effective. It is now the line I automatically use when fishing the Aberdeenshire Dee and the Ribble, Lune and Nith when the river is a foot or more above summer level. In very fast, turbulent water – as on the middle or lower Spey with 2ft on the gauge – or the bigger Norwegian rivers, such as the Namsen, and the faster lengths of the Gaula and

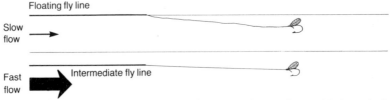

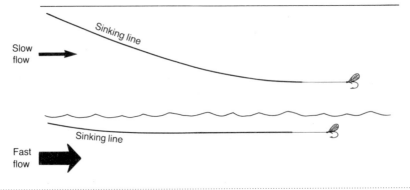

In slow, warm water a floater is fine, but in very fast water an intermediate or sink-tip may be far more effective in presenting the fly 4–6in below the surface.

In slow water a sinking line will take the fly deep, but in faster, turbulent rivers the sinker might take the fly only just below the surface.

Fig. 20

Alta, where the current tends to hold or push the line high, a medium sinker might be more appropriate, as long as a lightweight fly is being used.

For cold-water fishing a sinking line is essential. In shallow or slower pools a medium sinker may be sufficient, but on most waters a fast sinker will be essential, and on those massive, very deep brawling rivers – the lower Tweed, Tay and Spey, for example – an ultra-fast sinker is used.

Fly weight

See also page 44. For summer warm-water salmon fishing we have a wide range of fly hooks, plus tubes and Waddington shanks, each with a different weight. My personal preference is for double and treble fly hooks, when I am using flies of size 8–14, and single hooks or Waddingtons when a larger fly is required. Partridge produces three different weights of double and single fly hooks: Wilson, Low Water and High Water Heavyweight, the Wilson being the finest and lightest, the High Water being the heaviest. The Wilson is, I think, the greatest of all single and double salmon hooks and, although fine in the wire, it has landed fish well over the 20lb mark. Used in conjunction with the intermediate fly line, it catches me more summer and early autumn salmon than any other hook. By using these three weights of hook you have three weights of fly, six if you use the singles as well as the doubles. For most conditions I use the Wilson, but in faster, more turbulent water the Low Water Partridge hooks. Heavier still are treble fly hooks, including the Esmond Drury Treble and the Partridge Salmon Treble. In very fast pool necks or when there is plenty of water in the river, I tend to use these rather than the lighter doubles or singles.

For cold-water, sunk-line conditions a tube fly or Waddington shank is the answer. Tubes come in three weights: light plastic, medium heavy aluminium and heavy brass. In 95 per cent of rivers and conditions the aluminium tube has the edge over the brass tube. With a fly line dense enough to get close to the bottom, the aluminium tube fishes nicely off the bottom, and it is much easier to cast. The Waddington has a much slimmer profile than a tube and therefore sinks that bit faster, weight for weight, than the equivalent aluminium tube. It is also easy to add a little extra weight (but not bulk) to the Partridge double Waddington shank by whipping a length of lead wire in the grooves between the two arms of the shank. I would, therefore, choose a heavy line and slightly lighter fly to gain the necessary depth, rather than a moderately heavy line and very heavy tube.

A heavy brass tube is essential, however, if you are fishing very deep water from a boat or fishing very turbulent water from the bank or when wading. Conditions where this very heavy line and lure are essential include big, deep and fast rivers, such as the Tay or Tweed, sometimes the Spey, and smaller rivers, such as the Annan, Nith and Lune, when the river is fining down after a big spate and the fish are running. The fish will then be pulling in to rest in deep, slacker water, usually close to the bank, just off the main torrent. Where these fish are resting under your bank, the brass tube and heavy line are cast down and across into the main flow, an upstream mend made and, by the time the fly has come around into the slacker water, it will have sunk to the correct depth. Where the fish are lying tight under the opposite bank, with fast water between you and them, a long down and across cast with the heavy tackle, followed by a big upstream mend, in which extra slack line is shot, will allow the brass tube to sink and fish through this lie before being swept into the fishless main flow.

In still water, intermediate, medium-sink and fast-sink lines will all eventually go to the bottom. So, too, will all your salmon flies, even those being fished on a floating line. In a river it is the flow that prevents them from sinking. The speed of flow and turbulence of the flow tend to hold line and fly up in the water, so we choose a fly line density and fly weight to put the fly at the required depth. There is no one formula to give the correct answer on all rivers. Only by experience, experiment and juggling with different weights of line and fly can you come up with the correct combination on the pool you happen to be fishing – in fact, on that one part of the pool you happen to be fishing on a particular day. In a fast pool neck you may be fishing a quite heavy fly, but in the less turbulent and slower body of the pool a lighter fly may be more appropriate. I often have two rigs set up. For instance, when grilse fishing in summer, I may fish an intermediate line plus a fly tied on a treble in the pool neck, but change to a second rod set up with a floating line and the same fly tied on a Wilson double in the slower body of the pool. The following day a rise or fall in the water will probably mean that you will have to alter the fly weight and perhaps the line density. One back end on the Nith, the river fell by 3 ft in a week. I started with a fast sinker and aluminium tube; the next day I was using a medium sinker and aluminium tube; and by the end of the week I was using an intermediate line and aluminium tube in the slower pools and the medium sinker in the pool necks. I caught a fish on day one on the heavy line, two on day four on the medium sinker, and on day six had a fish in a pool neck on the medium sinker and two in a slower pool on the intermediate line.

Some readers may be wondering about the role of different densities of fly leader in controlling fly depth, for there is a wide range available, including ones with heavy lead or copper wire, which sink very quickly through the water. I have tried them and rejected them. Weighted leaders are the most dreadful things to fish with on a salmon fly rod. It is bad enough casting with a heavy fly, but a weighted leader is dangerous if you are overhead casting and, like some sink-tips, makes a hash of spey casting. Use a plain mono leader for all your salmon fishing.

Casting angle and other tricks to gain depth

I have already implied that, to some extent, one can also affect the depth of the fly by varying the angle of cast and the amount of slack line thrown into an upstream mend and by taking two or three strides downstream immediately after making a cast. Cast square across the river, do not mend, and stay put, and the belly formed in the line by the current will drag the fly round, high in the water. If you are using the floating line and a light fly, the fly may 'skate' across the surface. Cast a long line down and across the river, make a big upstream mend that involves releasing extra slack line, and then stride down the river;

the fly and line will sink deeper, and the fly will fish deeper across the river.

It is this ability to juggle fly weight, line density and fishing technique that makes some salmon anglers appear superhuman catchers of fish. The ability is one of the factors that results in 5 per cent of anglers catching 95 per cent of salmon. I hope that, if you are new to salmon fishing or thinking of taking up salmon fishing, you will be prepared to work hard at this. But persevere. Another trait of those 5 per cent of anglers who catch 95 per cent of the salmon is perseverance. Reading about it is one thing. Experience gained from long days on the river is the greatest teacher.

Speed of the salmon fly

Anglers who spend a lot of time fishing for salmon but who catch few fish tend to become automata. In fact, some of them jokingly admit that they go casting and that their casting is occasionally interrupted when a salmon takes hold. The routine of such anglers is quite characteristic. They cast as long a line as possible, in a constant direction, down and across the river. They then make a large upstream mend, and then they let the fly fish round before making one downstream stride and the next cast. By contrast, anglers who also spend a lot of time fishing for salmon and who catch a lot of salmon are anything but automata. For them, every cast is different, even if only slightly, from the one before. The length of line cast, the angle of cast, the amount of mending that is done to the line and the way in which the rod is held vary as a pool is fished through.

The reason for this variation in casting and fishing the fly is that the speed that a salmon fly fishes in a river pool is of paramount importance. Certainly, the speed of the fly through the water is far more important than the pattern of the fly, just as size is more important than pattern. Indeed, while many novice salmon anglers spend too much time on the bank debating which pattern (or, rather, colour) of fly they are going to tie on the leader, some of the most experienced and successful anglers avoid this time-wasting debate by carrying just one fly pattern. That is why earlier I recommended that you carry just two patterns with you when you are actually fishing and leave the rest in your car or rucksack or in the fishing hut. Having paid due regard to water conditions, you will have selected the appropriate sizes of two flies that will catch salmon, and you can now spend the rest of the day making sure that the fly is fished properly.

What is the correct speed? How quickly or slowly should the salmon fly be fished? This is something that has rarely, if ever, been stated with any real precision. One writer suggested the correct speed to be 1½–3 miles per hour. But how can you assess the speed of your fly in terms of miles per hour when it is travelling round, in an arc, across and below the surface of a turbulent river? Another suggested that the correct speed would be that of a small creature swimming against or across the current. But surely, all small river creatures would be carried down a stream if they tried to swim in midwater across most typical, streamy salmon lies, not against or across the river, even if they were swimming flat out? A not atypical suggestion was given by R.V. Righyni in his classic book *Advanced Salmon Fishing* (1973):

> If its [the fly's] speed of movement were judged to be such as to give a salmon just enough time to intercept it without delay, it would be considered suitable for a spell of trial fishing. On the other hand, the movement may appear to be too slow both to get the best response from the fish and to cover the water fast enough to search the pool without undue delay.

How can any novice or fairly inexperienced salmon angler begin to work out whether the speed of the fly is giving the salmon 'just enough time to intercept it' or whether it is 'too slow to get the best response from the fish' if they have not already hooked a few dozen fish?

Now, it must be remembered that the late Reg Righyni was a great salmon angler. So, too, is Arthur Oglesby, whose rod is still a threat to any salmon that dares move in a pool that he is fishing. In *Salmon* (1983), Oglesby seemingly contradicts Righyni on the subject of fly speed, for he states that: 'We do not want our fly to pass over the fish too quickly . . . hold the rod well out at right angles, so that minimum fly speed is achieved.' So, according to Oglesby, the fly should be fished as slowly as possible. But surely, minimum speed also might be taken to suggest that the optimum would be fishing with the fly stationary in the water downstream of the rod tip – in other words, 'on the dangle'. And although the salmon will take a fly on the dangle, are anglers not repeatedly told to avoid this because it usually results in an abortive pull or poor hook hold?

The one thing that all the books are agreed on is that our salmon wet flies, as distinct from riffling or dry flies (see pages 157, 180), should not be allowed to skate. Here we have a sure definition of what is certainly too fast, provided that we can see our fly skating across the surface.

Cast a fly on a floating fly line across a band of very fast water. The water will pull the fly line that lies across it quickly into a downstream belly, and this belly causes the fly to skate, head first, across the surface of the slacker water on which it landed. You can see this. Now make the same cast with an intermediate or sinking fly line. This time the fly will not skate across the surface, but it may still be dragged, head first, rapidly across the flow but under the surface by the belly in the fly line caused by that band of fast water. There is a tendency to think that, because you cannot see the fly dragging at high speed across the flow (or skating), the fly is fishing reasonably well. It might be if the salmon were prepared to take a fast-moving fly. Indeed, some intermediate fly lines were advertised as 'anti-skate' – that is, they took the fly deep enough to prevent it skating at the surface, but did not prevent it dragging at almost similar speeds just under the surface. What the eye can't see . . . but what if the salmon were more prepared to take a slow-moving fly? A fly fished across a band of fast water on an anti-skate (intermediate or sinking fly line) may not achieve minimum speed.

An important point must now be made, however. Without drag a salmon fly cannot be fished. The fly is tied to the leader that is tied to the fly line. The fly line is attached to the rod. Line, leader and fly are cast across the river, and the downstream flow pulls, or drags, the fly line across the river to below where it is fixed to the rod tip. As it is dragged across, so the line pulls the leader with it, and the leader pulls the fly. To avoid drag completely, you would have to cast a fly that is not attached to the leader and line. The fly would then drift downstream passively in the flow. We need drag – controlled drag – so that the fly flickers slowly across the lies and in front of the salmon. What we are trying to avoid is skating or excessive drag. We must control the way the fly line fishes across the flow, and this will control the fly.

Beginners have long been encouraged to prevent the fly from skating or excessively dragging by a combination of four main tricks: changing the angle of cast, moving downstream immediately after casting, manipulating the rod and mending the line. For the novice, choosing the best angle of cast is always a difficult problem, which is why so many anglers persistently make a 45 degree downstream cast for all their salmon fishing and find a more appropriate direction impossible to judge. After watching other anglers all holding their rods in the one same way – with butt shoved into the belly and rod hand and arm held out stiffly – the novice may feel that they are not 'doing it right' if they hold the rod in any other way. The majority of beginners find it much easier to take a stride downstream before making a cast than immediately after having made a cast. (Note the rule on busy Association waters: 'Step and cast', not 'Cast and step', which is a far more logical way of moving through a pool.)

Everybody likes the trick of mending the line – after all, is it not part of the aura that is special to salmon fishing? – and so we see the majority of anglers, whether they are fishing with heavy, sunk rigs or with light floating line tackle, casting in the one, constant down and across river direction and following this up with a big upstream mend. The fly swings across the river without skating at the surface – it is now up to the fish! However, the use of upstream mending on every cast is grossly excessive and is, combined with the habits of casting the line in a constant direction, holding the rod in a single way when fishing out a cast and taking a step before casting, why many anglers, I believe, do not catch their fair share of salmon. Indeed, the person most responsible for the popularity of upstream mending, A.H.E. Wood, warned anglers:

> Do not on any account acquire the habit of mechanically lifting over [i.e. mending], no matter how the current runs. Always have some reason for doing it: to prevent drag or, more often, to control the speed of the fly across the river.

In other words, if the fly is not dragging excessively and its speed is judged to be correct, do not mend! But, of course, this brings us back to the question: 'What is the correct speed of the fly?'

Speed and the salmon wet fly

The correct speed at which to fish the salmon wet fly is the speed that induces the salmon to grab it. But there is no one correct speed for all days, all rivers or all lies. Salmon are not looking for something to eat, and we are not trying to fool them into believing that our fly is an item of food, such as a small fish, or shrimp or prawn. If a salmon were prepared, when it was in a taking mood, to take small fish, then we would find parr, minnows, miller's thumbs and other small fish in their throats. We would also find that flies that closely imitate small fish would be more successful than the general run of salmon flies. But we do not. Our salmon fly is primarily a lure that evokes an aggressive response from the fish; it annoys the fish by invading its territory, and it might even make the fish curious. And the fish grabs at it.

As we saw earlier in this chapter, in cold water – say, below 41°F – the sensory system of the salmon is at its most lethargic, and in order to move the fish, we must use a big fly and fish it between mid-water and the bottom, so that it almost hits the fish on the nose. But it also pays to fish these flies as slowly as possible, to keep them moving steadily across the lies yet not so slowly that they constantly snag bottom. As the water warms up, it is standard practice to use ever-smaller flies and to fish them higher in the water. So as April turns to May, the brass and copper tubes and fast-sinking fly lines are laid aside and shorter aluminium and plastic tubes, and flies tied on salmon fly hooks, are presented to the fish on floating, intermediate or, in very fast water, slow-sink lines. Now that the water temperature is higher, the fish are more alert, and they respond better to small flies fished close to the surface rather than to big flies fished at their level. But they also often respond better to a fly that swims more quickly through the water. Yet salmon are fickle creatures, and just as a slight change of fly size may make the difference between whether or not fish are caught on one particular day or in one particular lie, so too can differences of fly speed make the difference between success and failure.

One experiment that is doubly worth carrying out is to alternate fishing the fly slowly and quickly. You can do this by fishing the fly slowly down a pool and then going through again but this time fishing it quickly, but not so quickly that it skates or drags excessively. If you agree, as I most certainly do, with Hugh Falkus's premise that it is impossible to overfish a lie, you can make two casts from each position, one with the fly fished slowly and one with it fished more quickly. On some days or parts of days, or in some lies, the faster fly will catch more than the slower fly and vice versa – as long as the fly does not skate or drag at phenomenal speed across the flow. So, both Righyni and Oglesby as quoted earlier were right after all! Sometimes we must fish the fly fairly quickly because a slower fly may 'be too slow … to get the best response from the fish'; sometimes the fly must be fished very slowly – 'minimum fly speed' – to make the salmon take it. The point is that some anglers fish the fly with one consistent technique of controlling fly speed – i.e., mending – when it pays to vary and use several techniques. The technique is used no matter how fast or slow or deep or turbulent the water. It is the automatic technique of an automaton. In addition, especially when they are fishing a very small fly close to the surface of a shallow, slowish stream, most anglers mend to such an extent that the fly is often not fished quickly enough.

Consider Fig. 21. Fish are lying in streamy water close to the far bank. Cast down and across from point A, but it is tempting also to put a big upstream mend in the line so that the fly fishes slowly over the lies. But what really happens if you do make that mend? The fly sinks and drifts inertly across the lie. It is only when the line tightens between fly and rod tip that the necessary pull (or drag) of the line makes the fly flicker with life across the flow. And by the time this has happened, the fly has moved too slowly and too inertly away from the lies. In fairly shallow streamy lies – say, up to 3ft deep – like the one illustrated, it is not unusual for a tiny fly – say, size 8–10 double iron – fished on a floating line, to snag bottom following a mended cast. Yet, in that lie, that

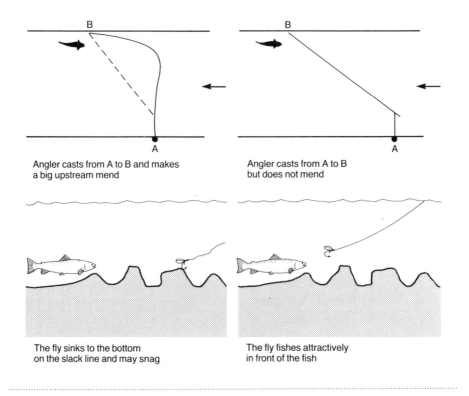

Angler casts from A to B and makes
a big upstream mend

Angler casts from A to B
but does not mend

The fly sinks to the bottom
on the slack line and may snag

The fly fishes attractively
in front of the fish

Fig. 21 – Mending a cast

little fly should be fishing only a few inches from the surface! Mending has
ruined the depth and speed of the fly. Cast but do not mend: now the fly flickers
quickly but is not dragged at excessive speed over the fish.

I know many lies and pools like the one shown here, on the Spey, Dee, Nith,
Annan, Lune, Ribble, Mourne, Finn, Bush . . . they are characteristic of many
rivers which are great water to fish from April to the end of the season with
flies fished near the surface. But a well-mended line will usually catch few fish
because the fly is not being fished at all through the lies even though it passes,
inertly, through them.

We will next examine the ways by which we can control the speed at which
our fly passes through salmon lies. But in the meantime consider this conun-
drum, which has faced salmon anglers for so many years: why do salmon fall
over themselves to take flies fished by women anglers? One theory, which
scientists have debunked, is that women secrete some sort of sex pheromone in
the water that attracts the salmon. Those who would like to read more of this
fascinating idea will find it fully explained, with copious examples, in *Salmon &*
Women: The Feminine Angle (1990) by Wilma Patterson and Peter Behan.

While not decrying entirely the possibility of some hormonal advantage, I am sure that the main reason is that women are far more careful and precise in the way that their fly fishes. The cast is not too long. Each lie within reach is carefully fished, so that every salmon sees the fly two or three times coming from slightly different angles and at slightly different speeds. In general, women are far more meticulous in the way they fish their fly, while men tend to be more concerned about how far they can cast.

Methods of control

I have suggested that each pool, each lie and, sometimes, each cast will often require a different approach or way of presenting the fly. The reason is, as that great angler the late John Ashley-Cooper put it in *A Line on Salmon* (1983): 'Control of the water-speed of the fly is one of the most important aspects of fishing, and I recommend any fisherman who has not already done so to give it careful consideration.' I touched briefly on some of the ways that can be used to control water-speed of the fly, and now I will elaborate on these.

Downstream Strides

Most anglers, when fishing down a pool, take one or two paces after fishing out their last cast and before making the next cast. They 'step and cast'. It is, however, far more effective to 'cast and step' – that is, to make the next step immediately after casting – and there are two main reasons for this.

1. When a cast has been fished out the fly usually comes to rest downstream of the angler. If the downstream step is made when the fly and line are in this position – more or less on the dangle – the step will slacken the line, the fly will sink, and, if an intermediate or sinking fly line is being used, the line will sink deeper. Unless some line is quickly stripped in, the pick-up from the next cast will not be crisp and clean, for the rod must first of all pick up this slack before it starts flexing and pulling the line from the water in the back cast or first part of the spey cast. In other words, there is the likelihood of losing casting power.

   Even worse, when a very heavy sinking line and/or fly is being used, as in early spring or late autumn, the slackening of the line by a downstream stride may be sufficient to allow the fly to sink to the river bed and snag.

2. If one or more downstream paces are made immediately following the cast, the slack resulting from the movement will:
   a) Help a sinking line and fly sink to optimal depth. The sinking line and fly tend to hold higher in the water after a straight, tight cast; they will sink

THE COMPLETE SALMON FISHER

more easily on the slack line produced by downstream pace(s).
b) Slow down the development of a belly in the fly line, which might result
in the fly skating or dragging across the flow at excessive speed.

It is important to use downstream paces carefully. The fly will fish properly –
move in an attractive, flickering manner across the flow – only when the line
between rod tip and fly is taut. On a slack line it will drift passively, like a dead
leaf. If too many paces are made or if they are too long, there may be the
tendency for the fly to drift and not fish over the lies. Each casting position
should be carefully analysed. A short pace may be enough in very slow water,
a full pace where the flow is moderate, and three or four paces where the water
is deep and fast and you want the fly to sink deep.

Angle of cast
The angle of cast is critical in all salmon fly fishing, and the most appropriate
angle should be chosen for each lie or each part of a pool. The reason for this
is that by casting at different angles from one position, the fly can be made to
fish at different speeds (see Fig. 22).

1. Cast square across the river or slightly upstream. A big belly will form in
   the fly line between fly and rod tip, and this belly will quickly pull the fly
   across the river. In fast water this belly will make the fly skate or drag at
   excessive speed. In a very slow, steady flow the speed caused by this huge
   belly may make the fly swim attractively at a perfect speed across the river.
2. Cast down and across the river. First we need to define angles. For our
   purposes, straight across is 0 degrees; straight downstream is 90 degrees.
      The larger the down and across casting angle, the slower the development
   of a belly between rod tip and fly, and thus the slower the fly will fish across
   the current. The angle of cast employed is selected according to the speed
   of flow in that lie or in that part of the pool and is modified as flow rate
   changes.
      In slower water the fly will be cast more upstream at a smaller angle. In
   faster water the fly will be cast further downstream at a larger angle. Of
   course, this does mean that to fish the same width of river, the greater the
   angle of cast, the longer the cast must be. It is, perhaps, for this reason that
   anglers of moderate casting ability try to cover as much water as possible by
   consistently casting at 45 degrees. Often, however, the master of the long
   down-and-across style will greatly outfish 45 degrees short-line casters no
   matter what tricks they may use to control fly speed. One such angler,

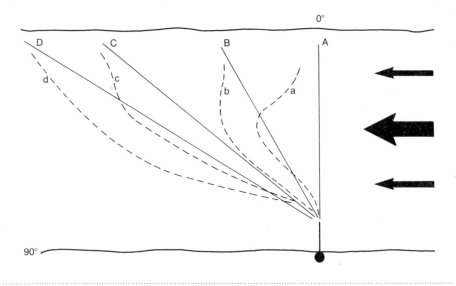

Fig. 22 – The angle of cast

who was fishing Lurg on the Spey, had two grilse and five sea trout in one
night: seven other rods had one sea trout between them.

3. Cast up and across the river, a direction to use in bright, low-water
conditions with a fairly high water temperature – e.g., 59°F. These are the
sorts of summer conditions when upstream spinning a small Mepps or
upstream worming are also effective. This is not 'conventional' fly fishing –
trout tackle is used, with a weighted shrimp- or prawn-fly or a heavy
Goldhead Stoat's Tail. Cast up and across into known or potential lies. Let
the fly sink and then strip back line so that the fly fishes through the lies a
fraction faster than the flow rate. This is an exciting way of fishing in such
difficult summer conditions, and is especially useful on rivers, such as the
Dee, or beats where the fly-only rule operates in summer or in low water.

MANIPULATION OF THE ROD
The long salmon fly rod is not just a tool for casting and playing fish – it is a
useful tool for regulating the speed of the fly through the water. The longer
the rod, the greater the advantage in this respect over shorter rods. For
instance, in the last two summers I have fished with a 15ft Bruce & Walker HF
Light Line taking a no. 7 line on small summer rivers where I would formerly
have used a 10ft single hander. This extra 5ft has been a great advantage, not in
casting or playing fish, but purely in controlling fly speed in fast, streamy water.
Suppose that there is a fairly narrow band of fast water close to the angler

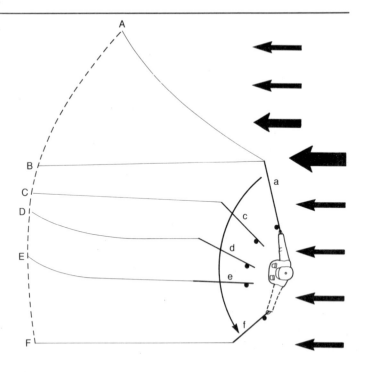

The angler casts to A and holds the rod in position a to hold line over the fast water and slow down the fly. When the fly reaches B, the rod is used to control the speed of the fly as it fishes round to F. By keeping the rod in positions c, d and e, the fly can be held stationary at C, D and E, or by moving the rod back from E to D or C or B, the fly can be fished back so that it comes across the fish from the opposite direction.

Fig. 23

and the fish are lying just beyond it in much slacker water. After making the cast, the long rod can be used to hold all the fly line off this fast water. Thus, a huge belly cannot form and the fly cannot skate uncontrollably. If necessary, because the band of fast water is that bit wider, the rod can be held high, at arm's length, to hold the fly over this patch of water (see Fig. 23).

Suppose now that the fly has fished perfectly round through streamy water and is faltering as it moves into slacker water. A salmon may have been following the fly, but as soon as it falters the fish is likely to turn away. By slowly moving the rod tip round, the fly can be led, at a steadier speed, through this slack water and the salmon encouraged to take.

Suppose that the fly is approaching 'the dangle' at the end of the cast. It is going to stop in the flow at the end of a straight line below the angler. Fish will often follow the fly and make a quick snatch at it when it is on the dangle. Usually, however, such snatches result in abortive tugs or very poor hook holds. Once more, the fly can be led around with the rod tip so that it continues to flicker across the current instead of hanging on the dangle. The hook hold, should a salmon now take the fly, to a fly that is led round is far better.

When wading deep in a productive, streamy pool at least 30 per cent of salmon will be taken while the fly is being led. This 30 per cent would not otherwise be caught.

STRIPPING IN LINE

See also 'Working the fly', page 154. As the fly fishes across the pool and is led round below the angler, so that it does not falter as it passes into slower-flowing water or end up on the dangle below the angler, there is now the temptation to pull in a few yards of line quickly and to make the next cast. But sometimes a fish will be following the moving fly. To urge a following salmon to take that fly, at the end of the lead or when the cast has been fished out, slowly draw in line, accelerating slightly as you go. A salmon will sometimes take the fly as it changes direction – i.e., begins to move upstream – especially if it accelerates as it does so. The line that you strip in slowly is that you would have pulling in prior to the next cast.

MENDING

Mending should not be a standard, automatic adjunct to casting the salmon fly. It is just one technique for controlling the speed and depth of the fly. When executed perfectly, it is a great technique. It is especially useful where there are one or more bands of very fast water between the salmon lies – that is, the bands of water through which we want the fly to swim reasonably slowly – and the rod.

Cast down and across so that the fly lands 2–3 yards upstream and a yard or so beyond the lie. As the line touches down, the rod tip is rolled up and across the stream, lifting up the belly of the line and throwing it into an upstream loop – the mend. Ideally, the fly and leader should not be affected by mending (it should not pull them out of position), just the fly line. A downstream belly in the line, which is caused by the fast flow and which causes the fly to skate or drag at great speed across the stream, cannot form until the fast water has carried that upstream mend downstream. The upstream mend therefore slows down the rate at which the fly fishes across the stream (see Fig. 24).

In very complex flows, where there are several bands of fast water, it may be necessary to carry out one or more mends to prevent big downstream bellies, which might cause the fly to skate, from forming. These mends should affect

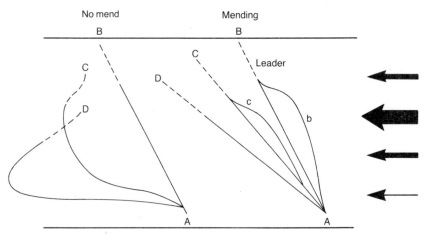

The situation when the angler does not mend is shown on the left-hand side of the figure. The angler casts from A to B and a belly forms in the fly line and drags the fly from B to C to D too quickly. The right-hand side of the figure shows what happens when the angler casts from A to B and makes an upstream mend, b. The fly fishes to C and another mend is made, c, to prevent a belly from forming in the line and thereby slowing the fly as it fishes round from C to D and then round to below the angler. Note that the leader is not affected by mending.

Fig. 24

just the part of the line with the belly so that the fly is not jerked out of position.

When you are using any sinking fly line it is possible to mend only once – that is, as the fly line touches down and before it has sunk. In very fast water, where a simple mend may not be enough to fish the fly steadily across the entire river, an even greater upstream mend is better. Have an extra 2–4 yards of fly line stripped from the reel, cast and, as the line is touching down, make as large an upstream mend as possible, shooting the extra line into the upstream mend.

There is another way of mending, which is, perhaps, especially useful when a floating line is not being used. It is simply the reach cast, which is used by trout fishers to prevent their dry or wet flies from skating across the flow. The mend is made while the fly line is in the air, and there is, therefore, no possibility of disturbing the fly or fish by pulling the fly out of position or splashing line heavily on the water in the mend.

Suppose you are casting from the right bank, with the river flowing from left to right. Have an extra 2–5 yards of line more than you intend to cast off the reel. The line is punched out to its target and, as the line extends in the air, you swing the rod tip upstream with a smooth, up-and-over action, continuing the rod swing with a swing or lean to the left with the arms and upper body.

The line now lands on the water with a distinct upstream belly, and the rod is pointing up and across the stream. As the fly fishes down and across, you can slow it down by slowly swinging the rod tip downstream. Vary the amount of reach and extra line according to the speed of the river. In a steady flow you may need just a couple of yards put into the upstream reach; in fast water a good 5 yards may be necessary (see Fig. 25).

We have discussed five methods for controlling the speed of the salmon fly: downstream strides, the angle of cast, manipulating the rod, stripping in line and mending. Sometimes it would be a mistake to use any of them. Sometimes just one of these will make the fly fish perfectly. In the fastest and most complex of pools it may be necessary to use all five methods on the one cast. It all depends on the water. And, as the water changes as you slowly fish your way down the river, almost certainly so, too, must the way you control the speed of the fly.

The neglected art of backing-up

Almost every word that is written on the subject of fly fishing in rivers for salmon is based on the assumption that the angler will be slowly working his

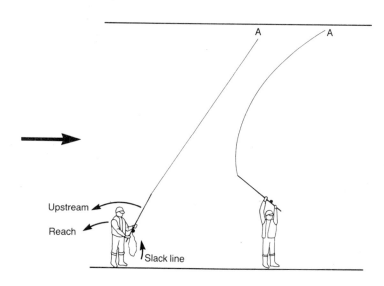

The angler casts to A and, as the line is extending but still airborne, releases slack line. At the same time, the angler swings both rod and body upstream in a sweeping arc. This puts a big upstream belly, or mend, in the line. It is an ideal technique, especially for sunk-line fishing.

Fig. 25

or her way downstream, making casts down and across the river. Backing-up, when the angler works in the opposite direction – slowly upstream – is either ignored (only 5 out of 16 books on fly fishing for salmon that I checked describe backing-up) or considered a specialized technique for certain rivers, notably the Thurso. This assumption – that it is the norm always to fish downstream – is reinforced by fishery rules. On Association waters the permit invariably insists that 'each angler must keep moving down the pool' or take 'one or two steps downstream between each cast on doing so'. On private beats, too, where anglers on one bank are sharing pools with anglers on the opposite side, the beat rules remind anglers that courtesy demands that they must start at the neck of a pool, above anglers fishing on the other side, and that they all then work downstream, taking at least a yard between casts. In heavily fished waters, some regimentation is, I suppose, essential. Imagine the chaos that would result if an angler on Lurg or Long Pool on the Grantown-on-Spey Association water decided to start at the pool tail and work upstream while 20 or more fellow anglers were stepping-and-casting their conventional way downstream. When you are sharing a pool with several other rods you have no choice: you must fish conventionally. If you have the pool to yourself, however, backing-up will often catch fish that might otherwise not be caught.

Backing-up has virtues that completely separate it from the conventional downstream method. The first is its effectiveness in very slow, almost still pools, where the flow is insufficient to make the fly swim attractively across the river, which is why the method is much exploited on a few rivers, such as the Thurso, which slowly slide their way down an almost level gradient, with very little of the streamy, bubbling riffle and pool of most salmon rivers. However, many other salmon rivers do have pools with a very steady, slow flow. These pools hold salmon yet are rarely fished by fly fishers because the conventional down-and-across method will not work, but they may well yield fish if they are backed-up. Two redeeming features of these pools are, first, that the fish in them may not have been disturbed by other anglers, although on some Association waters the rules allow worm and spinner to be used in such pools, and, second, that the angler who fishes them is likely to have the pool to him- or herself and to be in a position to attempt backing-up without invoking the wrath of a procession of anglers working downstream. At the major Association waters on the Spey, based at Grantown and Boat of Garten, for example, most fly fishers are heavily concentrated on only a few famous pools, and because of the number of anglers, the chances of the fish being disturbed by bad wading or splashy casting are high. An angler prepared to fish one of the other, more sluggish, pools will often have the water to him- or herself and

150

stands a great chance of catching undisturbed fish – both salmon and, at night, sea trout – especially if the angler is prepared to back-up the pools. For instance, I spent a late June week fishing two unpopular pools and caught 14 sea trout and one grilse, most by backing-up; three anglers fishing two of the most popular processional pools had just six sea trout between them for their week.

The second great advantage of backing-up is that the fly is presented to the fish in a completely different way from the conventional downstream cast. As the angler works slowly downstream, taking a stride between casts, the fish must see the fly coming ever closer, a yard or so at a time, and each time from the one direction. In *Advanced Salmon Fishing* (1973) the late R.V. Righyni suggested that:

> when the angler moved down the pool too slowly and made numerous further casts . . . the fish then ignored it [the fly] almost invariably. Clearly too many sightings of the fly out of range have the effect of detracting from the responsive urge by the time it is within easy reach . . . the overall policy should undoubtedly be to ensure that the fish should never be allowed to see the fly more than two or three times at the most before it is within comfortable taking range. . . . This may mean having to take as many as ten or more paces between casts on occasions.

In other words, he believed that by over-fishing a lie – by letting the fish see too much of the fly – the fish was 'switched off'. I dispute this view, for several times I have known salmon take a fly after several hours of continuous fishing of the lie. Some years ago, for instance, an angler on the opposite bank constantly fished a lie under a willow tree at Henthorn on the Ribble with a variety of 2–3in tobies from 1.30 to 4.15 p.m. He fished carefully enough so as not to frighten the fish, but he caught nothing. As soon as he departed, I fished the same lie with the fly and took a fish on, if I remember rightly, the third or fourth cast. If any lie had been over-fished, that one had. As Hugh Falkus stressed in *Salmon Fishing* (1981): 'Provided it is covered properly and the fish is not scared, a salmon lie cannot be overfished.' There are many instances of the same fly, repetitively cast down and across, taking a salmon on the umpteenth cast, and of flies held on the dangle for minutes on end over a lie eventually being grabbed. But it always pays to change your fly (a large one for a small one and vice versa) or your tactics, just in case the change triggers a response in the salmon's brain and causes it to take. Backing-up will often evoke this response. Back to Falkus. Writing of the aggressive 'crunch' take of the salmon, he noted that:

It is the sudden overhead appearance of a lure that seems to trigger off this crash-surface take: the fish has not watched the lure's gradual approach as the angler fished his way slowly down the pool. For this reason I think it is sometimes better, when conditions permit, to fish a salmon or sea trout pool by 'backing-up' rather than fishing down in the usual way.

Many experienced salmon anglers will often fish down a pool conventionally and then, provided that they have the pool to themselves, immediately back-up a pool. Although it cannot be proved, for the fish caught by backing-up might have fallen for a conventionally fished fly, the feeling is that some fish are caught by backing-up that would not have been caught by the conventional downstream cast.

BACKING-UP: THE TECHNIQUE

The angler starts at the pool tail and works upstream to the neck of the pool.

In sluggish, slow water the fly is cast at right angles, directly across the pool, and allowed to sink. In very slow, almost still, water, casting a little up, and across the river can be very effective. The angler then moves slowly 2, 3 or 4 yards up-river, so that the movement of pulling on the line makes the fly swim in an arc across the lies. The fly can be made to swim more quickly by stripping in line, which is especially important as the fly fishes round under the bank that the angler is standing on, for a following salmon will often take a fly that is accelerating as compared with one that starts to falter (see Fig. 26).

In a more typical, streamy salmon pool it is usual to fish steadily down from neck to tail. Having arrived at the pool tail and fished that completely out, it now pays to back-up this pool so that the fly is presented from a different direction, perhaps at a different (faster) speed, and, especially importantly, without the fly slowly approaching the fish through several casts made from upstream. The first time the salmon (or sea trout) will see the fly is when it is going to swim right over its head. Because the fly will be fished that bit faster when backing-up, a larger fly can be used to good effect. For instance, in spring you could try a 2in instead of a 1in tube, and in high summer, a size 4–6 instead of a size 10–12 double. It may also be an advantage to use a line of a slightly higher density when fishing a fly rapidly, backing-up after conventionally fishing down a pool. So, in summer, if you used a floater for fishing down the pool, an intermediate (alternatively a sink-tip) might be better for backing-up; or, if an intermediate was used downstream, a slow-sink might be better for backing-up. A second rod for backing-up can be left at the pool tail.

When you are backing-up these more typical streamy pools, the fly can be

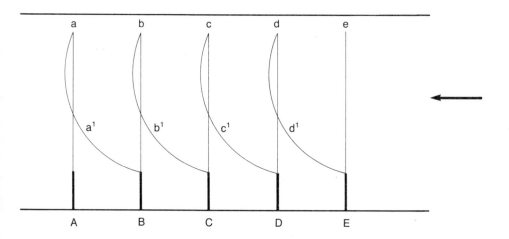

The angler begins at A, casts to a and then slowly backs upstream to B. This movement, aided by the flow (if it is significant) and stripping in of line, causes the fly to follow path a¹ and so on.

Fig. 26

cast down and across, or across the pool with or without a mend. The squarer the cast, the greater the belly that will form in the line and the faster the fly will fish. Mending will slow down this speed. Hand-lining and/or moving slowly upstream as the fly is fishing round will speed up the fly. It is worth experimenting with fly speed when you are backing-up. My own experience suggests that a slightly larger fly, fished more quickly than the fly that has just been fished down the pool, will evoke the crunchiest of crunch takes when backing-up. It is especially important to keep the fly moving, by stripping in line, until the cast has been completely fished out, for sometimes a salmon will follow the fly and take it at the last moment, just before the next cast. There is no need to give line or to wait for the reel to start running and then lift the rod to set the hook. Usually the fish takes a firm hold of the fly and hooks itself, almost wrenching the rod from your hands.

When backing-up it is important, as in all fishing, not to disturb the fish. An undisturbed salmon is hard enough to catch. One that has fled the lie is impossible. Remember, too, that when you are backing-up you are walking or wading alongside the fish that you are going to try to catch on the next cast. Keep well back from the lies, and cast carefully.

Backing-up is not superior to the conventional method of downstream fishing; it is simply an alternative method. Many anglers are quite content to change fly pattern and sometimes fly size when the fish have refused previous offerings. I would suggest that an alternative way of presenting the fly might often be more effective. Consider the approach of the more successful bait and spin fishers. Anglers float-fishing prawns and shrimps will often vary the depth of the bait, and hold back the bait so that it swings upwards or 'lifts' in the water, rather than persevere with a constant depth and rate of drift. An expert worm-fisher will vary the amount of weight on the line, the angle of cast and the speed that the worms fish. A great spin-fisher will sometimes cast the spinner down and across and fish it round without any retrieve, like a fly, but will vary it. The next time down a pool, or on the next cast if it is a major lie, he may cast directly across and retrieve slowly. The next time he or she will cast the spinner upstream and reel it back at greater speed. At least 95 per cent of the successes of great shrimp- or prawn-, worm- or spin-fishers is not the result of what they fish with but how they fish it. And the 'how' includes variety of presentation. It is exactly the same with fly fishing, and backing-up is a great way of varying the way that the fly is presented to the fish.

Working the fly

One great advantage of fishing a few new rivers every year, in different parts of the range of the salmon, is that one comes across techniques that are commonly employed in one region but rarely, if ever, used elsewhere. One, which I saw widely used in 1994 in Northern Ireland, is the 'worked' fly. I have already suggested that stripping in a few yards of line at the end of a conventional cast or during backing-up might encourage a fish to take the fly. Working the fly is an extension of that.

Many of the salmon rivers in Northern Ireland and Co. Donegal are fairly narrow and, by most British, Canadian and Scandinavian standards, fairly sluggish and sometimes also quite deep under both banks. On the lower Bush, for example, one cannot wade in most places. So fishing is from the bank and a cast of 15 yards will cover the lies under the other bank. By contrast, on parts of the Strule there are wider places where it is necessary to wade to cover the deeper water under the far bank, but other places where it is impossible to wade because the river is narrow and plunges deeply under both banks. In any case, try to wade there and you will scare the fish. Yet on the Strule, whether you are wading or fishing from the bank, there is never the need to cast more than a dozen yards to cover all the lies in this generally slow, deep river. The Ballinderry, famous for three flies that bear its name, receives its salmon from the River Bann through Lough Neagh. It is a great back-end salmon river.

Again, on many beats, the river is best fished from the bank, and some of the most important salmon lies are in deep, slowish water. The Bush, Strule and Ballinderry – and I could mention others, such as Donegal's Lennan, Lackagh and Owencarrow, all of which are outstanding but small rivers – are not the sort of water that we generally look to as being typical fly water. We look for streamy water with a popply surface, with more distinct pool necks, bodies and tails – water that will work the fly that we have cast down and across the river in traditional wet fly style. We would probably be tempted to walk past such slower, deep waters or consider them as essentially spinning or bait waters.

That is what I thought when I first saw one of these. 'I am wasting my time! This isn't fly water! Why did I not bring my spinning rod?' But my Northern Irish friend John Todd taught me how to fish these with the fly. My first mistake was to take a double-handed rod down to the water. I know John told me that a 10ft single-hander was ideal and that a 12ft double-hander was a bit big. Yet on the majority of the rivers I prefer a longer rod because, in the turbulent water with many vagaries of strong current, I can use the long rod better than a short rod to control the speed of the fly. A long rod allows me to hold fly line over particularly fast bands of flow, to mend the line, to hold the fly in the current and to lead the fly round. But in very narrow rivers these tricks are not necessary, and if they were, a shorter rod would do the trick just as well as a long rod, and when it comes to working the fly, the long rod is a hindrance.

The fly is cast across or down and across the river. In the almost still water the cast is made across; where there is a discernible flow, down and across. There is, in fact, no reason why a fly fisher in this situation should not do as a spin fisher might do – that is, fish 'round the clock' by casting in a series of angles from one place before moving a yard or so downstream or upstream. In this way the fish will see the fly approach from different angles, and this might be a better goad to take than from only one angle. The fly is allowed to sink for a couple of seconds – perhaps a few seconds more if a sinking line is being used in early spring – then it is worked across the stream by stripping in line, rather like a rainbow trout stillwater angler will fish a lure. The speed of retrieve can be varied, from a slow figure-of-eight to a rapid pulling in of the line. Summer fish, in warm water, seem to respond to an arm-wearying fast retrieve, which makes the fly fairly zoom through the water, while spring fish react to a slower fly. Whatever the speed of retrieve, it is essential not to let the line fall on the ground, for it is certain to catch up in vegetation as soon as a salmon takes hold. A line tray could be useful, as long as a smooth, coil-less fly line is being used. I compared this with fishing a lure for rainbow trout, and some writers have argued that fishing a big lure for a trout is simply spinning with a fly rod. This is exactly what this technique of working the fly for a salmon is – we can fish it slow and deep, or shallow and fast, upstream or downstream, just as we might use a Mepps or small plug.

Try doing that with a long double-handed rod. At the end of fishing out one cast, the fly is fairly close to the rod tip, with perhaps only 1–2 yards of fly line beyond the tip ring. There is not the 10 yards or more of line lying in a straight line downstream of the rod tip, as we have with conventional wet fly fishing, to provide the necessary weight to flex the rod to make the next cast. With the long rod, line must slowly be extended, and there is no current to help by pulling the line downstream through the rod rings, the trick we often use on our streamy British rivers before making our first cast. With a single-handed rod or with a very short double-handed rod, armed with a weight-forward line, it is simply a matter of a couple of false casts and out the fly goes again . . . flick . . . flick . . . bang. You cannot do that with a big rod.

So one slowly fishes the river, casting, working the fly, varying the angle of cast and the rate of retrieve, when suddenly a fish takes. When the first fish took my worked fly, my first thought was that there was no slack line, nor was I fishing off the reel, to allow the salmon to turn and hook itself firmly, as happens when we fish streamy water. I was fishing on a tight line and could give the fish no slack. Having felt a tug, I did nothing and hooked nothing. I talked to John about this. 'When you are working the fly, tighten as you would in trout fishing,' he advised. 'Don't try to give it slack . . . there's no point . . . the fish feels the tightness of the line as soon as it takes the fly, so you need to strike immediately to set the hook.'

For this reason, double and treble hooks seem the best bet, and I use them exclusively when I am working the fly. However, I noticed that John Todd also uses singles to great effect. It is true that you will get a few pulls but fail to hook the fish, yet how many of us land every salmon that has a go at the fly in streamy water, when we do give them some slack?

My thoughts now return home, across the Irish Sea. When I am fishing for sea trout through summer nights a single-handed rod is my standard choice, and, in slow or slowish water, it is normal practice to work the fly. Looking back, I can remember several grilse and, on the Spey, a 14lb summer salmon, which took a fly that was being worked for sea trout. But, and I must be slow on the uptake, I had never used this method through the day for salmon in the slower sea trout pools. There is one slow stretch of the Coquet that is magnificent at night for sea trout if the fly is worked. Why not for salmon in the day? It holds salmon. What about those slow pools on the Ribble and Hodder, the Lune and Eden, the Annan and Nith, the Aberdeenshire Dee, the

Association waters on the Spey at Grantown and Boat of Garten, pools that hold salmon, but that we fish with fly only when there is a couple of feet on the gauge? I will tell you why not: it is because, like so many anglers, I associated river fly fishing for salmon with water that will work the fly for us, other than, perhaps, water that we might back-up. Yet *Salmo salar* in Ireland is the same as *Salmo salar* in the rest of the world. And if the worked fly catches the occasional salmon at night, then it must work by day.

Dibbling and riffling

Dibbling and riffling are techniques that keep the wet fly working or skating in the water surface, something that the wet fly fisher tries usually to avoid. They are akin to dry fly fishing, at the point where salmon wet fly merges with salmon dry fly (see Chapter 8). Although it has been said that these techniques work only on some rivers and not on others, they are techniques to try on all rivers in appropriate conditions. They are tricks always to have up one's sleeve.

Dibbling is a technique to use in quite fast, turbulent water, where the salmon lie is not much further than the length of a long salmon fly rod from where the angler is standing, ideally on the bank and above the lie. A careful approach is necessary to avoid scaring the fish in the lie.

Although some anglers dibble with just one fly on the leader, I prefer two flies, the one that will be dibbled being on a dropper (see page 127) 4–5ft above the point fly. This system has two advantages over the one-fly system. First, the salmon may take the fly that is moving beneath the surface on the point as well as the fly that is being dibbled. Second, the sunk-point fly seems to hold the leader in such a way that the dibbled fly works better – rather as the point fly in lake fishing acts as an anchor that helps the fishing of the bob fly (see page 175).

The two-fly cast is pitched out on the water and the top fly worked carefully, on a tight line, through the surface of the lie. It is kept stationary, then allowed to drift downstream, then pulled across and held stationary, then pulled back a little upstream, all the while being skated and bounced to and fro, up and down the lie. In a lie where there are protruding boulders, with salmon lying alongside or in front of them, and a complex of flows and back-eddies, the fly can be dibbled to and fro from one band of water to the next, up and around boulders, held in back-eddies, and then brought a few yards upstream and dibbled back and forth as it is allowed to drift downstream. All without casting or moving, simply by manipulating the rod tip and occasionally pulling in or releasing a little line. The aim is to let the salmon see the fly, working in the surface, at a variety of speeds and from a variety of angles, and to niggle it into grabbing this object that is constantly hovering overhead and disturbing its rest. Minutes might go by. But then, suddenly, up will come a fish. You must concentrate, for if you are taken unawares it is too easy to pull the fly from the mouth of a rising fish. Let it close its mouth on the fly before you set the hook.

Riffling the fly is another technique by which we allow the fly to skate across the surface, but it is used more in water with a steadier, less turbulent flow and with conventional casts. There are two ways of making a fly riffle. First, with a fly tied on a conventional hook, tie the fly to the end of the leader and then tie a Portland hitch behind the head of the fly. The fly will be pulled partly from the side as it fishes down and across the river, and it will skate or riffle through the surface. A second way is with a plastic tube. Make a hole about a quarter of the way down a plastic tube with a hot needle. Then, when you come to riffle the tube fly, thread the leader through this hole and out of the rear of the tube (where the treble hook will be attached). On a tight line this will encourage the fly to skate or riffle through the water surface.

The riffling fly is cast across or down and across the river and fished so that it skates or riffles across through the surface. Speed of riffling is important. The fly should create a wake but not be so fast that it splashes its way across. Hand-lining can also be used to bring the riffled fly through a salmon lie. Cast it down and across the river and, as the fly nears the lie, strip in line so that the fly accelerates and moves in an upstream arc over the fish.

In both dibbling and riffling, it is essential to vary not only the speed of the fly but also the route that it takes as it passes over the lie. This is done with a combination of rod tip movement and pulling in and releasing of line by hand. Sometimes the fish will take a faster-moving fly, sometimes a slower fly. Sometimes a fish will take a fly that comes upstream, from behind it, or one that has been dibbled or riffled across to it. So, when you are dibbling or riffling a fly, make sure that you search each lie thoroughly in as varied a way as possible.

Most conventional wet flies can be used for both dibbling and riffling, but ones with a deer hair 'muddler-style' head (see page 78) have the advantage of already being buoyant.

Wet fly presentation in a spate

Throughout the summer and autumn all salmon rivers are, to some extent, spate rivers. Given a prolonged summer drought, of which we have had too many in the last twenty years, even the mighty Spey and delectable Dee, and some of Norway's mightiest rivers, will be showing their bones, with boulders

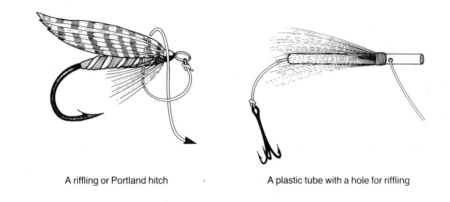

A riffling or Portland hitch · A plastic tube with a hole for riffling

Fig. 27

that are never seen by the spring anglers standing proud like sharks' teeth and with vast shingle banks on either side of the slower flow. Come a heavy downpour, however, and up will come the river, in a massive torrent. A couple of years ago I was on the Dee in such low-water conditions. On the Saturday we had heavy rain all day, and on the Sunday the river had risen 6 feet. 'Unfishable tomorrow!' was the opinion of many anglers. Even the hugest of rivers, such as the Tana and Namsen, may be at a nice level one day, but after torrential rain be 6ft and more up.

Most anglers think of spate rivers as something different, however. Mention spate rivers and immediately those small streams of the west coast of Scotland, the rivers of west Cumbria and west Wales, the super rivers of the West Country, the host of small to medium-sized streams that drain to the west Norwegian coast or the lesser rivers of New Brunswick and Quebec come to mind. Such rivers have always been traditional summer or autumn rivers and, to have a run of fresh fish, rain is essential. The bigger rivers rise quickly following heavy rain, but they fall very slowly, so the fish will run over days, if not weeks. By contrast these little spate streams are up by 5–6ft when it rains heavily but drop back to summer level within two or three days after the rain has stopped. I once saw Cumbria's River Duddon fall 6ft in 10 hours. Timing is far more critical on these little spate streams, for, certainly as far as fly is concerned, the salmon are most likely to be caught in that period when the river is falling back from its spate peak to the summer low. Sometime in this often short period the salmon will run. It may be for only a couple of hours – what Hugh Falkus called the 'magic moment' – and if you are not fishing then, you will be wasting your time, as far as fly fishing is concerned.

When the river is in full flood and heavily silt laden, with lots of rubbish –

weed, branches, plastic fertilizer bags, dead cows and the like – being washed downstream, fishing is generally a pretty futile occupation. If you find the river in such a condition, fish by all means, following the advice given in the rest of this section, and you might just winkle one out. You will, however, be constantly irritated by having to clear the fly of river-borne debris. Once the river begins to fall and most of the heavy rubbish has cleared, salmon will begin to move upstream and they can then be readily caught on fly, even though the water might be still so coloured that you cannot see your feet when you are standing ankle deep at the edge of the flow. Under such conditions the beginner is often confused – the river is still very high and fast and there is so much water, that how do you know where the fish will be? How do you get the fly to the fish? And will the salmon be able to see the fly in such murky water?

Many anglers try to solve these problems by spinning. The spinner is cast out as far as possible, so that it passes through the maximum area (or width) of river. No thought is given to how the spinner is behaving or where the fish are lying, and, as we shall see, the spinner will often not fish properly where the salmon are lying in high-water conditions. Others, encouraged by the frequent but stupid rule of permitting the method to be used only when the river is in spate (or, as it is termed on the Nith, a 'yellow flood'), turn to worm fishing. Again this bait is cast 'somewhere out there', with more hope than intent. There is no doubt that the worm is a very effective taker of salmon, but, like the shrimp and prawn, worm is most effective when the river has fallen back, almost to its summer level.

Stop and think for a moment. No self-respecting fish is going to lie out in the main flow when the river is in flood. Such positions require too much effort. The salmon will also find it uncomfortable lying in such heavy water that liberal amounts of sharp sand and silt particles are washed through their fragile gills. So, when the river is very high, the fish will tend to creep upstream in quieter water, off the main current, and very often tight under the bank. Running fish will often rest, for anything between a few seconds and many minutes, in the slower flow close to the bank, and these salmon are usually good takers. Sometimes they will rest among flooded vegetation that is well above normal river level. One lie on the Lune is a sheep-grazed grass sward, 4ft above the river's summer level. Sometimes they will rest in riverside hollows or at the entrances of normally dry ditches; sometimes they prefer the normally dry, silt-bottomed bays or very shallow water, perhaps only 1ft deep, over a normally dry shingle bank on the inside of a meander pool. One lie on the Hodder is an extensive area of shallow water, 6in deep when the river is at summer level but up to 3ft deep when the river is high, sheltered from the main flow by a limestone shelf. Another famous Hodder lie is close to a big boulder in midstream in the neck of a large pool but with the main flow immediately beyond the boulder. When the river is 18in or less above summer level the fish lie in, or at the edge of, the main flow beyond the boulder. But when the river is in spate, with more than 18in of water on, the running fish lie in the shallower, steadier flow on the inside of the boulder. One high-water lie on the Spey is in the downstream corner of a groyne. Normally dry, this is a small area of slack water where fish rest before they must fight their way through the fast water beyond the groyne when they recommence their upstream journey.

So, when the river is very high, if we are to catch salmon we must usually look to calmer water, often fairly shallow water, and water that is often tight under the bank. Now we can see why methods other than fly are not as effective as some would have us believe. When spinning the tendency is to begin to lift the spinner from the water as it slows down in the slacker, fish-holding water close to the bank, or to fish the spinner too quickly through this water – there is a great risk of snagging in such lies and spinners are expensive. The water holding the salmon is either not fished properly or is not fished at all.

Similar caveats apply to the worm unless it is fished very close in to the bank. If you know your river well and can identify the precise spots where running salmon pull in for a rest, worm can be fished to great effect. But you must know the exact spot. I know such places in seven rivers, and with perhaps just two exceptions they are quite featureless, with many other similar places that seemingly rarely, if ever, hold fish. Certainly they would be easy for the casual visitor to overlook. Because worm fishing is a much slower method of covering water than fly, fewer potential lies can be fished thoroughly in the day. With fly you can methodically work your way downstream, covering every inch of potential holding water close to the bank and fishing the fly perfectly round right into the bank.

The next concern, however, is whether the salmon can see the fly and whether, in the murky water, it will respond to the small fly. The answer to both questions is yes. Salmon look up through the water, and even in the most discoloured of water the fly is silhouetted against the light background of the sky. So the fish can see the fly. Furthermore, because the salmon you are trying to catch are running fish that have stopped for a brief rest, it is likely that they are taking fish.

So, fish the fly when the river is high. You will find resting lies when salmon grab hold. Note the positions of these and the precise height of the river, for some lies will hold fish only within a small range of depth. If you fish that beat often enough you might eventually discover two, three or even four lies that are tenanted by salmon at a particular height. When the river has fallen a little, the fish may take up different lies. Find these and again note their effective river heights. In future visits to the beat, you will be able to concentrate your efforts on those lies that are appropriate to the river height.

Two further points must be made, for they are major reasons why many anglers fail to catch salmon on fly when the river is high. The first is on the subject of casting. Too many, usually male, anglers go casting with a salmon fly rod rather than fishing with the salmon rod. These anglers will boast of their ability to cast 35 yards and more, and they do this all the time, with no regard to presenting their flies to the fish. When the river is very high, you must ignore the width of the river and fish only that strip of river that is likely to hold the fish. Only a very short line may be needed – perhaps 10 yards and sometimes less than that. Cast so that the fly pitches just beyond the potential lie and fish the fly carefully round, tight under the bank. Cast too long a line, so that the fly and a lot of line lands on the raging torrent in midstream, and the fly will not fish properly through the lies close to the bank. The difference in effectiveness between short, well-fished casts and long-distance casts can be quite astounding. One Norwegian gillie told me of two anglers fishing the same beat when the river was over 6ft above summer level. The first angler, disregarding the gillie's advice, made casts of at least 25 yards out into the fast flow but caught nothing. The second angler cast a short line of 8–12 yards so that his fly fished just the water in which the salmon were resting. He had 18 fish in the day.

The second point is about wading. One of the joys of salmon fishing is paddling in the water, preferably up to one's waist.

In many high-water lies, however, wading can contribute to an empty bag. Wade through the lies and you will disturb the fish. The great Irish angler Robert McHaffie told me of an occasion when he had taken a fish from a known lie. Later he returned to find another angler standing in the precise spot where he had hooked his fish. 'If buggers like that were forced to wear expensive leather shoes with lace holes when they went fishing they would not scare the fish and we would all catch more!' commented Robert. He was so right.

If you can cover the lies without wading, stay ashore. Stand well back from the river. Cast a line down and across so that the fly lands at the edge of the fast water, just beyond where you would expect the salmon to be lying. Hold the rod out, at right angles, and then slowly lead the fly across the lie until the rod is pointing along the bank, with the fly flickering an inch or so from the bank. Before you make the next cast, strip in some line – a fish will sometimes take a fly that is being worked upstream. In small rivers or where the potential lie is very narrow – say up to 5 yards wide – there is no need to re-cast. After fishing the fly round, swing the long rod slowly out to right angles to the bank, and the line and fly will be led out again across the lie. Sometimes a salmon will refuse a fly that is conventionally fished into the bank but will take as the fly is led in the opposite direction, away from the bank towards deeper water. When the fly and line are hanging out in the faster water, beyond a potential lie, slowly take one or two paces downstream and then lead the fly slowly into the bank and back out from the bank into the deeper, fast water. Take one or two more paces. In this way the fly is fished almost constantly through water that, if there are salmon running, might be taking lies.

A final word on fly line density and fly sizes and colour when a bank-high spate is being fished. From late April to October many anglers plump for floating fly lines. When the river is in spate an intermediate (in shallow, very slow water) or medium sinker (in deeper or slightly faster water) is usually more effective. Try also a fly size that is at least two sizes larger than the fly you would expect to be using if the river were at, or slightly above, summer level and running clear. For instance, where I would normally fish a size 10–12 double in August or early September, I would fish a size 6–8 when the river was in spate. Black flies will always catch fish, but recent observations suggest that flies with gold or copper tinsel bodies and plenty of hot orange in the dressings – some of the shrimp- and prawn-flies, for example – might have the edge over black ones.

Wet fly presentation in summer droughts

In recent years we seem to have had more summer droughts, lasting from June to September, than in the past. The river shrinks to a mere trickle, with vast areas of shingle bank exposed and large boulders, which are normally covered, standing far out of the water. Some fish, usually grilse and sea trout, will try to creep through even in these dreadful conditions in all rivers but the smallest. In July 1983, after three months of drought, I had a bright silver grilse from the Hodder a good 25 miles from the tide and, in 1993, so too did Chris Hosker from the same lie. Both fish had raw red bellies from scrambling upstream through shallow rocky riffles. In bigger rivers, such as the Spey and Dee, the fish can run easily in low water, for there is sufficient depth not to impede them. It is just that fewer fish are prepared to enter the river from the sea in very low flows.

We also have the increasing problem of land drainage in many river catchments, making summer spates much shorter and resulting in very low water only a few days after the river has been bank high. Fish move into the river during the spate, but within four or five days the river is back to a summer low, and they either stay put to the next spate or creep through, usually between dusk and dawn, further upstream.

When the river is low in summer, fly fishing for salmon is often considered largely a waste of time, but that need not be so. Two points must be borne in mind. First, the salmon will attempt to move upstream between dusk and dawn. Those that have been resting in a deep, slow pool will often move into the pool neck at dusk, and these are often good takers of the fly. Fish that are moving slowly upstream through the low water will often rest in pool necks or in boulder-strewn riffles. These, too, are usually good takers of the fly. And in many rivers there are sea trout, which will take the same flies as salmon in the dusk to dawn fishing period. So concentrate your effort from sunset to dawn and you are in with a chance.

Second, be careful not to disturb the fish. Those who fish for sea trout in low water are only too well aware that it is easy to disturb them by treading heavily on the bank, by wading clumsily and by splashing the fly line down on the water. Salmon are exactly the same. Approach and fish with care.

At dusk and at dawn, fine tackle and small flies are the order of the day – a single-handed rod taking a no. 7 floating line and a leader of 6–8lb test. Small flies are essential, until the light has fully gone, size 14–16s wee doubles and trebles being standard on all rivers. Once it is dark, I would go immediately to a line that will fish the flies close to the river bed. In shallow, boulder-strewn streams the floating line or perhaps an intermediate might be enough, but where the depth is greater than about 3ft, a sinking line that takes the fly deep is preferable. For night fishing with big flies, a heavy leader, 12–15lb test, has the advantage that you are not constantly worrying about breaking on a big fish. In the dark salmon and sea trout are not leader-shy, and the big fly fishes well on a heavy leader. The two sorts of fly to try are big singles (size 2–6) of the Falkus Medicine variety (Teal, Blue & Silver or Peter Ross or a big Stoat's Tail) or a tandem lure (see page 77).

Where the river is still streamy, despite the low water level, it may be possible to fish the fly around conventionally, letting the flow dictate its speed. At night, however, it is often necessary to keep the fly moving well by a figure-of-eight retrieve or stripping in line. My experience suggests that salmon and sea trout will respond better to a faster fly by night than they do by day. Takes are either very savage, with the rod almost wrenched from your hand, or very gentle, when you should tighten immediately to set the hook.

Other techniques to try in low water include backing-up (see page 149), working the fly (see page 154) and dibbling (see page 157). See also dry fly and weighted nymph (Chapter 8).

Boat fishing

In big rivers, such as the Tay and Tweed, Alta and Namsen, it is a common practice to fish the wet fly from a boat that is being held in place by a boatman using oars. Sometimes the boat is released slowly on a rope anchored at the top of a pool. In most rivers it is the norm for the angler to be seated, although in some Norwegian rivers the angler stands at the back of the boat, which is held prow-on to the current.

All that has been said earlier in this chapter applies as far as wet fly technique is concerned. However, a good boatman who knows his river well does a large part of the work, for he controls the boat so that each lie is brought within reach of the rod, and, by holding the boat upstream of the lies, the boatman helps to bring the fly at a reasonable speed over the fish. In addition, there is not, or should not be, any need for the angler to cast very long lines from the boat, for the boat is dropped down slowly over each lie so that the angler can concentrate on careful presentation. If only for the sake of the boatman, who is working hard on the oars, fly casting should be entirely by spey casting. No boatman is going to be diligent in controlling the boat if he has to duck every 30 seconds or so to avoid a big fly hurtling back and forth by his ear.

On many big rivers harling from a boat is common practice. Usually plugs, spoons and spinners are used, and these are fished on spinning rods. However, flies can be used also, fished on fly rods. Long, 15ft fly rods are best, with one stuck out from each side of the back of the boat, and a third pointing over the stern. To prevent a fish pulling a rod overboard, the rods are usually fixed firmly in rod-rests and the reels are arranged with the handles up and the clutches set lightly so that they can run freely should a salmon take. Having been rowed or, as sometimes happens on the Tay, motored into position, the anglers slowly release the flies downstream on, ideally, 30–35 yards of line (fly line plus leader). The boat is carefully manoeuvred to and fro across the river, dropping downstream by 2–3 yards on each 'pass' so that every fish in the pool will have seen the flies. When a fish takes the fly and is hooked (see page 198), the other rods are wound in, the boat pulled into the bank and the fish played out.

As far as the angler is concerned, this is both a pleasant and a productive way of fishing. Pleasant, because it offers half a day – surely long enough – for swapping tales with the boatman or gazing at the scenery. But it is completely lacking in skill, for it is the boatman who presents the fly to the salmon, and it is the boatman who controls the speed of the fly and the angle at which the fly flickers across the salmon. The angler's only responsibility is to do as the boatman says and to play the fish. The Overhalle Hotel, on Norway's Namsen River, acknowledges the boatman's primacy in the operation, for its record book gives pride of place to the name of the man on the oars, the name of the 'rod' being set down last.

CHAPTER 7

LOCH AND LOUGH
FISHING FOR SALMON

Let the angler devote the time and study to the loch that has been,
and is still being, given to the river, and he will soon discover that it
thoroughly deserves and amply repays all attention.

R.C. BRIDGETT, *Loch Fishing in Theory and Practice*, 1924

Although there are many lakes in Russia and Scandinavia and one or two in the English Lake District in which salmon rest on their passage upstream to their spawning becks, the only significant lake fly fishing for salmon takes place on the beautiful lochs of Scotland and great loughs of Ireland. Here the angler has the opportunity to participate in two of the most traditional ways of fly fishing, a drift with a team of wet flies and dapping. In both cases the best way of fishing is from a boat, although occasionally a salmon may fall for a fly cast by a shore-based angler – I have had a couple from Lewis's lochs when trout fishing, for example.

Conditions for lake fishing

The first prerequisite is a head of fresh fish. Some of the Irish loughs produce salmon from the opening day, 1 January, to the last day of the season, 30 September. In other Irish loughs and most Scottish salmon lochs, fish begin arriving in late spring, but it is not until summer or even autumn that good numbers are in the water. Many salmon lakes also have a good summer and early autumn run of sea trout, although many in western and northern Scotland have seen sea trout numbers collapse in recent years. The techniques of catching both species are so similar that what is said about lake fishing for salmon in this chapter applies equally to sea trout.

Weather conditions are all-important for bringing in a fresh run of salmon. If, during a long drought, the river between lake and sea is a mere trickle, the fish will remain at sea until there is rain. Within hours they may be in the lake and be in a taking mood. Because of this dependency on rain and a good river height to lift the salmon into the lake, some Hebridean estates – most famously Grimersta – have a system of sluices across lake outflows so that when a shoal of salmon appears in the estuary, an artificial spate can be created by releasing water from the sluices and the fish moved into the lakes. Such lakes, therefore, depend on the arrival of salmon offshore and not on prevailing weather conditions. There are, on the other hand, some lakes that drain to the sea via rivers that are rarely too low for salmon to pass through – Conn, Corrib and Melvin, for example. I have caught fresh-run, silver grilse in these, between June and August, when the Rivers Moy, Galway and Drowes were very low.

Weather conditions are also important for catching salmon on fly in a lake. Because the lies are usually in fairly shallow water, a ferocious gale can make the lake a dangerous place, but, because gales usually coincide with rain, fish the river between sea and lake instead for fish that are running upstream.

Never go afloat in a gale, when the lake is a mass of spume and white-crested rollers, and, at the other extreme, a flat calm and bright sunshine make fly fishing a pretty hopeless exercise. A good 'salmon wave' offers the ideal conditions, with overcast sky or sunshine broken by scudding clouds. Do not despair if there is only a slight ripple. Persevere, and the fish may oblige. In March 1995 Charlie Heggarty, John Todd and I were afloat on Glen Lough. The wind fell and the wave was reduced to the tiniest ripple. Charlie made a joke about the lack of a salmon wave and the bar being open. Whereupon a spring salmon took John's fly! You never know.

Tackle for lake fishing

Drift fishing wet fly tackle

Many, many lake salmon are caught by anglers fishing a drift for brown trout, using rods of about 11ft and lines no. 5–6, and leaders tapering to 3–5lb test. However, I would hesitate to go so fine if salmon are the intended quarry.

A rod of 10–11ft taking a no. 6–7 double-taper line is ideal. I prefer double-taper line because most casting from a boat should involve roll casting. This is by far the safest form of casting from a boat because the flies never cross the boat (as with overhead casting), and so other occupants of the boat are not endangered. Overhead casting, especially in a fair wind, can be quite dangerous and bring a premature end to a promising day. My arrival at Cloughans, on the shore of Lough Conn, for a week's fishing, once coincided with two German anglers pulling into the little jetty. They had been out for just two hours when one of them became badly hooked in the forearm by his partner's fly, which was tied on a treble hook. Two points of the treble were in round to the bend. Had they been roll casting, this could not have happened. Roll casting, down or down and across the wind, is so easy from a boat. The other point to remember is that long casting is not necessary – about 15 yards is typical, with 20 yards being a very long cast.

For most of the season a full-floating line is ideal, although in early spring an intermediate or very slow sinker might be useful to take your flies that bit deeper.

Lake salmon tend not to make very long runs, especially if they are played out in deeper water. Instead of running a long way, they usually go deep, swimming in circles. Thus a drum trout reel 3½ in wide is more than adequate, taking the fly line and 80–100 yards of backing.

There is nothing worse than having a tangled leader, especially in the confines of a small boat. For this reason it is essential that the leader 'turns over' well. Tapered monofilament leaders are ideal for this purpose. All those available on the market are ideal, the one that I use being Ken Sawada's Sussex Super Precision flat butt in 9ft and 12ft lengths (the shorter ones are for rough conditions), the 1X tapering to 9lb test and the 2X to 7½lb test. I use the 1X in cold water in spring, with flies size 6 or bigger, and the 2X with smaller flies. When the point of these leaders has become shortened by several changes of fly, I attach a new point of 9lb or 7lb monofilament to the end with a water knot (see page 127). This extends the life of these moderately expensive leaders.

It is usual to fish with more than one fly on the leader. The point fly is tied to the end of the leader and a bob fly to a dropper. For lake fishing, this is ideally about 5ft up the leader from the point. The dropper, of 7lb or 9lb monofilament, is tied to the main line by a water knot (see page 127). Start with a dropper about 6in long.

For trout fishing it is usual to have three flies on the leader. I would not recommend this for salmon fishing, the extra dropper and fly being more trouble than they are worth. In my early years I found that most salmon came either to the point fly (40 per cent) or bob fly (45 per cent), and only about 15 per cent to the middle fly of a three-fly cast. I think that, had this middle fly not been there, that 15 per cent would have taken the point or bob fly.

Chapter 3 described a range of effective lake flies and gave some pointers as to choice.

Dapping tackle

John Norris, the tackle dealer, tells me that the 17ft Shakespeare telescopic dapping rod is the most popular model available on the market, for it can be set up in the bottom of the boat, with dapping floss and reel fixed in place. Greys of Alnwick has also produced a version. However, for most salmon anglers, who will dap only occasionally, the most convenient dapping rod is a 15ft or longer salmon fly rod. I use the B&W HF Lightline 15ft, no. 7.

A piece of dapping floss, 15 yards long, is attached to a reel containing about 100 yards of backing, while a 6ft monofilament leader of 10–15lb test is attached to the end of the dapping floss. If, in strong winds, the fly is blown from the water, lengthen the leader.

Any of the flies described in Chapter 3 will score.

General boat tackle

A very big net is essential, Whitlock salmon nets being ideal (page 205). Never take a drogue on to a wild salmon lake. You will be fishing fairly shallow water, almost certainly where big rocks rise from the bottom to within a foot or so from the surface, and often in windy conditions. If a drogue snags a rock it might well result in the boat being capsized.

Fishing a drift with wet fly

Fishing a drift, or what English anglers refer to as 'loch-style fishing', is one of the most enthralling and exciting ways of fishing a Scottish loch or an Irish lough. It is also a simple technique.

The two greatest problems facing the newcomer to drift fishing are locating the fish and controlling the boat so that it drifts through the lies properly. No matter how good your flies or how great a caster you are, if there are no fish in front of the boat or the boat is swinging to and fro in the wind, you won't catch much!

Gillies and boatmen

Ireland and Scotland have some of the greatest lake fishing for salmon in the world. On their massive lakes, such as the Corrib, Mask, Conn, Melvin, Lomond, Langavat, Voshmid and Maree, bank fishing with fly is largely a waste of time. To cover the maximum amount of good water as efficiently as possible you must be afloat and have the boat drift over the rocky shoals and boulder-strewn banks where the fish are concentrated. But how can the visitor work out where these hot-spots are? They cannot be identified simply by looking at the water, for the hot-spots are hidden from view. You could use a fish-finder/echo-sounder, but that would entail many hours of searching by tracking to and fro across the lake. You could work out the position of likely hot-spots – shore margins and the areas around inflowing streams and islands – but that would still be a hit-and-miss method. And if you do happen to cross one hot-spot, how can you be sure that you have searched thoroughly the entire hot-spot? Consider the maps given in Chapter 5 and Fig. 28. You must find and then follow the lies. If you follow drifts 1 and 2 you are unlikely to catch anything. Follow drift 3 and you may be lucky enough to catch a salmon as you drift over the hot-spot at X. Ideally, to have the best chance of catching fish consistently from that hot-spot, you need to know the sinuous shape of the hot-spot and to have the ability to alter the line of drift of the boat so that it covers the maximum amount of the hot-spot. Finally, you must have on the right flies and present them properly.

No matter how perfect your choice of fly and no matter how well you present it, if you are not covering water that holds salmon you will never catch.

On the big lakes of Ireland and Scotland there is one answer: hire the services of a boatman or gillie, and preferably one who has grown up on the lake and knows it intimately in all its moods. The cost may seem high – a boat plus gillie for a day will cost at least £60 (in 1996) – but there will be two of you to share the cost, and remember that you must pay the gillie's wage for the day as well

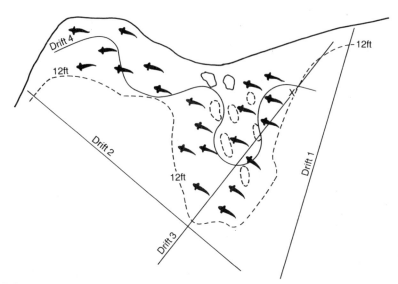

Drifts 1 and 2 are hopeless, drift 3 should produce some salmon, but drift 4, which is constantly over the fish, will catch far more. Of course, the boat is not drifting freely, but is rowed constantly as it drifts across the lies.

Fig. 28 – The angle of cast

as the hire of his boat, engine and fuel. After a few days afloat with a good gillie you will have been taught the best drifts, how to control the boat and the best flies to use and how to fish them. This information will serve you well for the remainder of your holiday, if you decide to take a boat out by yourself. Yet even when you think that you know a lake fairly well, always employ a gillie on the first day or two of the next holiday, for you will then have up-to-date information on the drifts that are fishing best and the flies that are currently most effective. For example, although I have fished Lough Conn many times, on each visit I would never forgo the pleasure and experience of at least one day with Padraig Kelly or his son, Seamus, acting as boatman. They are afloat most days of the season, and a day with them gives me the precise information I must have to catch fish for the rest of my visit. Without it I am lost.

The greatest book on fishing the great loughs of Ireland is T.C. Kingsmill Moore's *A Man may Fish* (1960). It is essential reading for any lake angler and a wonderful book to dip into time and time again, even though it concentrates on brown and sea trout fishing. Kingsmill Moore knew Corrib as well as any regular visitor, but he never set out without his favourite boatman. In his book he describes in vivid detail his Corrib boatman, Jamsie Donnellan. This was before the days of the outboard engine, and to help with the rowing the boatman employed an assistant. Jamsie's assistant was Jimmy McDonagh. Kingsmill Moore tells us:

All the Corrib boatmen were good. They knew the lake as a landowner knows his demesne. But Jamsie knew it as a blind man knows the house he lives in, with an absolute certainty. Though he could not see the bottom he could sense it, and in a shallow a mile long could smell his way to the few square yards which constituted a pet spot. Jamsie believed in pet spots, where, year in year out, trout took better than in other places. . . . A very favourite spot with him was the shelving of a bank, where the shore sloped into the water, or where a small hog's back had formed itself further out. At some level on the slope the trout would be found resting, but the level varied according to the height of the lake and the temperature. The level of Corrib may rise or fall several feet, and Jamsie knew within narrow limits at what part of a bank the trout would congregate for each level. . . . Most boatmen are only too glad to set the boat on along a straight drift and leave it so. Not Jamsie. From the bow came a continual murmur of directions to Jimmy. 'Pull a stroke now' – 'Back her a couple' – 'Pull easy, easy' – 'Back half a stroke' – and so on. This called for no particular comment. I knew that Jamsie had fished the lake for fifty years, and had an eye on him like a travelling rat.

All parts of the shallow sliding past under the keel might look equally enticing to me, one part of the bay as good as another, but to his observation, backed by experience and a most remarkable memory, there might be a significant difference.

If you ever go to fish a lake that you do not know intimately, if at all possible hire a gillie or boatman.

Once you know a lake, its dangers and its lies, then by all means go afloat yourself, although preferably with an angling friend. Most anglers free-drift in straight lines, directly downwind. However, subtle changes in direction can be made by using one oar, held by a rowlock and extending back in the water behind the boat. This acts as a rudder. When the oar is held straight back, the boat will drift in a straight line. With the handle pulled to the left and the blade to the right, the boat will swing slightly to the right, and vice versa. And if it is thought necessary to move the boat a few yards to either side of the line of drift, the boat can be sculled into the new line by that one oar. With a little practice it is possible to manoeuvre the boat along an irregular lake margin or through a group of islets or rocky shoals without having to stop fishing and waste time rowing, provided that the lake is not too rough.

However, fishing a drift is hard work – a 10-hour day involving a thousand or more casts. What I like to do, therefore, is take it in turns on the oars with my boat partner. On the first drift I may take the oars and manoeuvre the boat carefully so that my companion is constantly covering the best spots. When a hot-spot is reached, the boat is held in position so that he can make several casts. If a salmon moves at the surface, a couple of pulls on the oar brings his flies over it. Then, when that drift has been thoroughly fished, we swap places and he controls the boat as I fish. Such a system may appear less effective than both of us fishing simultaneously, yet I think it has several advantages. First, you do not tire as quickly, and, when it comes to your turn on the rod, you fish much harder; second, the lies are fished much more effectively; and third, when a salmon takes, the boat is already under control and not drifting freely across the surface nor is there another rod and line to be packed away before the oars can be picked up.

Such a system of gillieing for each other promotes a feeling of teamwork, every fish coming to the boat being a joint effort. If one of you manages to catch three fish, the other nothing, the accolades go equally to the fishless angler, who controlled the boat so well for his companion, and to the one who did the casting and playing of the fish.

Before you go lake fishing for salmon with a good friend, read that last paragraph together. For friendships have been broken when one angler fails to catch and the other succeeds with a big bag of fish.

The standard way of fishing from a boat on most lakes is to row or motor upwind to the start of the drift and then to turn so that the boat drifts side-on to the wind. The engine is switched off and raised so that the propeller cannot snag the line when a fish is being played, and the angler fishes 'over the front' of the boat as it drifts across the water. It is quite usual for two anglers to share a boat when they are over-the-front drift fishing, with a boatman on the oars between them. Etiquette demands that each angler fishes the water on his side of the boat, keeping his flies out of the path of the flies of the other angler – imagine that there is an invisible barrier across the boat and the water in front of the boat separating you from your boat partner.

Mention must also be made of safety. With two teams of flies being whipped to and fro over the confines of a small boat, serious accidents might happen. For this reason learn to roll cast so that the flies are never 'back-cast' overhead.

Presenting and fishing the flies from a drifting boat

You are now at the head of a drift. You have a floating fly line, or an intermediate, on your long loch rod, and at the end of the line a leader carrying two lake flies. You are in the right side of the boat, as it drifts side-on with the wind, and your friend is in the left side. You can cast, with due regard to your friend, over an approximately 90 degree arc, from directly downwind round to directly across wind (i.e., to your right). Where do you cast within this arc? Do you cast a long line (say, 20 yards or more) or a short line (say, up to 10 yards)? You might, in fact, cast in any direction and with any length of line.

Short-lining

After a few days on a lake, one thing that you quickly learn is that fish have little fear of drifting boats, provided that you are sitting down and not banging about on the boat timbers. On numerous occasions fish, whether trout, sea trout and salmon, have taken my fly within 1 yard of the boat and several times when I was dangling my flies over the side of the boat and wondering whether to change flies or tactics. Short-lining takes advantage of this boldness.

Cast about three rod-lengths of fly line downwind, finishing off with the rod pointing low over the side of the boat. Wait a few seconds for the point fly to

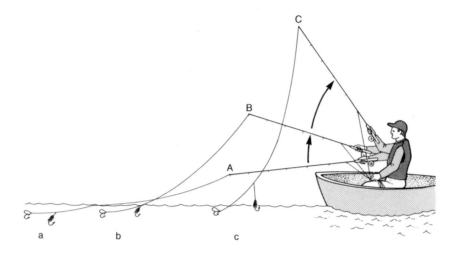

Flies are roll cast to a, with the rod low at A. The rod is raised slowly, with the non-rod hand retrieving the slack line, as the flies are brought closer to the boat. At b the bob fly breaks surface and by c is being dibbled or bobbed on the surface. A flick of the rod, and out rolls the flies on the next cast.

Fig. 29 – Short-lining

sink. Then pull in any slack line and at the same time slowly raise the rod so that the flies are brought towards the boat, a little faster than the rate of drift of the boat. You will – or should – see the top-dropper bob fly cutting a wake through the surface during this part of the retrieve. Now, with the flies close to the side of the boat, pull in line and keep the rod high so that the bob fly splutters and bobs on the surface and the point fly is making a wake in the surface film. If a fish does not rise, simply roll cast the flies out, shooting the loose line. Should a fish take at any time, firmly but not violently lift the rod point and simultaneously pull down the line that is held in the left (non-rod hand) to set the hook.

Short-lining is one continuous smooth process: cast, raise the rod and pull in some line to make the bob fly work, dibble the bob fly, re-cast. And if you can spey cast (roll cast with a change of direction) it is possible to fish round the entire 90 degree arc quickly, efficiently and without having your flies or line tangling with your boat partner's or catching him or the boatman in the flesh.

Long-lining

Long-lining is often considered to be exactly the same as short-lining but with longer casts. Simply cast out a long line, hold your rod low over the water and

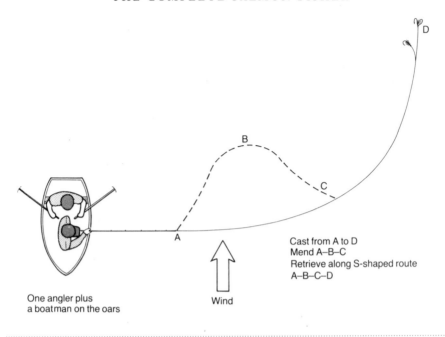

One angler plus
a boatman on the oars

Wind

Cast from A to D
Mend A–B–C
Retrieve along S-shaped route
A–B–C–D

Fig. 30 – Long-lining

pull in line at least a little faster than the boat is drifting, to impart life to the flies. Then, as the flies come closer, raise the rod to dibble the bob fly in the surface film at the side of the boat before making the next cast.

Often a more effective method of long-lining is the S-cast and retrieve. Cast the flies on a long line across the wind, at right angles to the line of drift. Do not be too forceful in the final forward flick. The fly line will land on the water, with the leader and flies curved around in a downwind direction.

Immediately, throw a downwind mend in the line close to the boat. Do *not* disturb the end of the line or leader. The line and leader are now on the water in an S-shaped curve. Hold the rod point low and pull in line. Because of the S-shaped line arrangement, when you retrieve by pulling in line, the flies do not travel in a straight line back towards the rod tip, but in an S-shaped route. As the flies come close to the boat, speed up the retrieve by raising the rod tip and stripping in more line. Then, before making the next cast, dibble the bob fly on the surface.

Sometimes the catch rate between straight long-lining and the S-cast and retrieve are insignificant. But on others the S-cast and retrieve greatly outscore the straight line method.

Usually fishing a drift is just that – while the boat is drifting, you simply fish the water in the hope that you can entice a fish to rise to the flies. But what happens if you see a salmon move at the surface? It is then imperative that you cover that fish as quickly as possible with your flies. This may be difficult to do. If short-lining, you may need extra line to reach that fish. It pays to be prepared by having some extra line arranged in careful coils on the bottom of the boat or in a line tray. Then it is simply a matter of gauging distance, a quick false cast – this is the only time for an overhead cast – and final delivery. Within a couple of seconds your flies can be in the ring made by the rise of the salmon. If you are long-lining, you will already have sufficient line off the reel. Immediately you see a rise, quickly pull in sufficient line so that you can deliver the flies into the ring of the rise. And as soon as your flies land in the ring of the rise, play them back quickly towards the boat by stripping in line. If the salmon does not take, re-cast beyond where you saw the rise and retrieve the flies through the rise position.

Dapping

Dapping is a form of 'dry fly fishing', in which the fly is allowed to flutter, down the wind, from wave to wave, spluttering and flickering on the surface as it travels across the water. A good wave and fairly brisk breeze are essential for

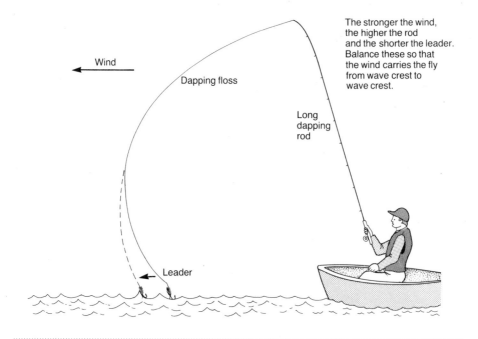

Fig. 31 – Dapping

dapping, for without the wind the dapping floss would not work the fly, and in a light ripple or flat calm the bushy dapping fly would lie, like a dead mouse, on the water.

Dapping involves fishing on a drift, so what has been said earlier about boat handling applies. What is different is the way the dapping tackle is handled and the way the fly is fished.

At the head of a drift, the fly is released and dapping floss is stripped from the reel so that the line and fly billow downwind of the boat. Line is released until, with the rod held at an angle of about 70 degrees from the horizontal, the fly bounces across the water in front of the boat, hitting a wave crest. Then, as the boat drifts forwards and the dapping line responds to the wind, the fly is pulled from the water surface and bounces on to the next wave. The main thing is to make sure that the combination of rod angle, length of dapping floss and length of leader are adjusted to make the dapping fly work correctly. Once this has been achieved, it is up to the wind and the salmon. Should the wind freshen or die a little, the angle at which the rod is held and length of dapping floss out are modified to keep the fly working across the water.

Otherwise dapping is quite a passive pastime. Some anglers never dap because they find it a most boring exercise. A few will dap often, even in conditions that are far too calm. Personally, I use the technique simply as a break from the repetitive casting of a team of wet flies. It is a relaxing way to spend an hour or so, especially on lakes that are the home of dapping, such as Maree and Conn. But when conditions are right for dapping, they are perfect for the more effective wet fly techniques.

CHAPTER 8

DRY FLY AND WEIGHTED NYMPH FISHING FOR SALMON

. . . after refusing everything else, the salmon took the bug. If this indicates anything it may point up the fact that, when the going is tough, the name of the game is experimentation.

JOSEPH D. BATES, *Atlantic Salmon Flies & Fishing*, 1970

Almost 100 per cent of river salmon fishing involves the wet fly. Although dry fly was found to be effective under certain conditions in the 1920s, and weighted nymph in the 1950s, even today few anglers bother to give them a try. They stick with their wet flies. However, a dry fly or a weighted nymph might catch a fish that has refused a wet fly and, if only for these occasions, the all-round salmon angler ought to have dry fly and weighted nymph in his or her repertoire.

Conditions for dry fly and weighted nymph

The ideal conditions are warm weather, fairly high river temperatures with the level at or about summer low, and a population of fairly fresh-run salmon. In such conditions the best chance with wet fly comes from about dawn to late morning and as the sun falls to well into the dark. However, dry fly and nymph can pick up fish throughout the hours of daylight, and dry fly can certainly be effective in the brightest of conditions, when most wet fly anglers would be sunbathing on the bank with a gin and tonic.

Incidentally, for anglers fishing the salmon rivers of the eastern side of the Atlantic, dry fly and weighted nymph will also score highly throughout the brightest of days and lowest of water for sea trout. In a week of abysmally low water and swelteringly bright weather on the Aberdeen Dee in August 1994 Oliver Edwards and I both rose salmon; Oliver had a very red grisle, which he returned, and we had a big bag of sea trout to dry fly. If only we had had a few fresh salmon in the river as well! On another similar July week on the Spey, my day-time bag to dry fly was two grilse hooked, but one lost, and 17 sea trout. Altogether I have had sea trout on dry fly from 23 European rivers, on weighted nymph from 11. The techniques for sea trout are the same as for salmon described here.

Tackle for dry fly and weighted nymph fishing

Basic trout tackle will do – a rod of 8–9ft, taking a no. 5–6 floating line. However, I prefer a slightly longer rod, of 10ft to 10ft 6in, taking a no. 6–7 line. There are four reasons for that choice. First, on the back cast the slightly longer rod helps lift the line higher, above obstructions behind. Second, the longer rod allows for greater control of the line on the water. It is easier to mend the line or to hold it over bands of fast or slow water, which may otherwise cause the fly to drag. Third, the slightly heavier rig handles weighted flies and weighted leaders better than the shorter rod and lighter line. Fourth, this basically single-handed salmon rod (see page 122) can later be used, from dusk onwards, to fish conventional wet flies for salmon and sea trout. I need only the one set of tackle to serve for nymph, dry fly and wet fly.

For dry fly and weighted nymph, overhead casting is, on balance, far better than spey casting in these conditions, so I favour a weight-forward line. However, if I am going to be wet fly fishing into the darkness, and spey casting, I use a double taper line.

We will consider leaders later, when appropriate.

The approach to dry fly and weighted nymph fishing

In low, clear water and bright, sunny weather, salmon are very easy to disturb. It is essential to locate either the fish or the lies in which there are likely to be fish. This is usually fairly straightforward, if you know the river beat that you are fishing well. If you do not, seek precise information from a guide, gillie or a local angler who tells the truth.

Keep well back from these lies or fish. Wade carefully, if at all. Be prepared to approach and cast on your hands and knees or sit down to the job. Such advice should not need giving, for this is standard practice in trout fishing. However, some anglers believe that, because they cannot see the salmon, the salmon cannot see them. This is especially not the case in clear, low water and strong light.

Dry fly fishing

Technically dry fly fishing is the easiest of all forms of fly fishing, simply because you can always see the fly and when the fish takes the fly. The rig is also simple: a tapered monofilament leader 9–12ft in length, or a floating braided leader with a 3–4ft tippet of 6–8lb test monofilament to which the fly is tied. I would be reluctant to go finer, partly because salmon seem to be not particularly shy of leaders, but mainly because to go finer runs the risk of the salmon breaking free. To risk leaving a hook and trailing length of line in the mouth of a fish is crass stupidity.

Your choice of dry fly is up to you. All those described in Chapter 4 have caught salmon. Choose a really buoyant fly with deer hair for fast riffles, hackled sedge-like patterns or the Daddy-long-legs for slower water. The deeper or faster the water, the bigger the fly, and vice versa.

Angle of cast

The first question to answer, before you start fishing, is where to stand and cast from in relation to the fish or lie. There are five possibilities (see Fig. 32).

1. Directly upstream. The major problem is that you are casting over the fish; the fly line and/or leader will fall on to the water over the fish with the usual

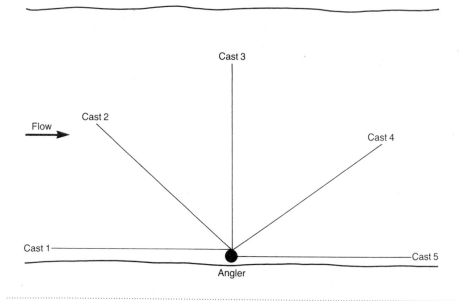

Fig. 32 – The angle of cast

straight line cast and might possibly – in clear water, almost certainly – scare the salmon. A salmon that has been frightened is unlikely to take the fly. This can be avoided if you can make a hook cast, where the line and leader fall to the side of the fish but the fly hooks around and falls immediately upstream of the fish (we will look at these casting modifications later). I restrict the direct upstream cast, first, and second, to very narrow rivers, where the only chance of concealment is by creeping up the stream behind the fish, and second, to positions where the salmon lie is tight under my bank, often close to tall reeds or trees, and I must wade the river below them.

2. Up and across the stream.
3. Across the stream. Casts 2 and 3 are, in the majority of cases, the best line of attack with the dry fly. In cast 2 the fish have less chance of spotting you, or the rod and line, but there is a chance of the leader and tip of the fly line passing over the fish before the fly. In streamy water this does not matter, but in very low, clear water conditions and very slow flow these might put off the fish from taking the dry fly. It certainly does in dry fly fishing for trout. In the across-stream cast, cast 3, accurate casting can put the fly over the fish before the leader and tip of the fly line come into the fish's line of vision, and it is perhaps the cast to make on very clear or slow water. But, because you are opposite the fish, it is essential to keep as low as possible and false cast behind or downstream of the fish so that the fly line is not zooming to and fro over its head.

In casts 1, 2 and 3, when the fish takes the fly, slowly raise the rod to set the hook. The fish will be moving away from the rod so that a firm tightening will pull the fly into the mouth of the fish.

4. Down and across the stream.
5. Directly downstream. You must accept that hooking power in casts 4 and 5 is not as great as in casts 1, 2 and 3 because you will be striking with the fish downstream and tending to pull the fly away from the mouth of the fish. If, however, you give the fish a second or two to move down with the fly – shout out, 'A salmon has taken my dry fly! – and tighten, the hook is likely to take a good hold in the roof the fish's mouth.

When you are casting downstream you must take great care not to disturb the fish or the lie. If you are fairly close, the salmon will be able to see you, so keep a low profile. Also, false cast as little as possible so that the line does not flash to and fro over the salmon.

Sometimes you may have no option but to cast in these directions. A fish lying under overhanging trees, for instance, prevents any other approach, and you must cast the fly downstream to it. You could cast so that your fly pitches right on the salmon's nose. This sometimes works, and takes are usually dramatically violent. Alternatively, you could cast with a slack line or reach cast so that the fly alights just upstream of the fish and the fly drifts down on the slack line. Where a long drift is essential, extra slack line can be fed through the rod rings.

Drag and casting modifications

Perhaps the greatest problem facing a dry fly angler is drag, a phenomenon that can result in the fly performing quite a remarkable skating display across the surface of the water in directions and at speeds that bear no relation to the river flow.

Before we can think about coping with drag, however, we need to answer the following questions: 'What is drag?' and 'Why does drag occur?'

Tie on a well-oiled dry fly, stand on one side of the river and cast a straight line squarely across the fast water so that the fly lands on the slow water beyond. Look carefully at what happens to the fly line and fly. The floating line that lies across the fast water is carried downstream more quickly than the fly line, leader and fly lying in the far band of slow water. A downstream belly forms in the fast water, and this pulls the dry fly quickly down and across the slow flow. The fly skates or 'drags' from A to B to C (see Fig. 33). It moves faster than the natural objects that are drifting downstream in the slow flow. It moves across the flow, instead of directly downstream on the flow.

When dry fly fishing for feeding trout and grayling we must avoid drag at all costs, for it makes the imitation dry fly behave differently from a real insect. This is not so in salmon dry fly fishing. Rarely, if ever, will we be imitating what the salmon is eating. Sometimes a salmon will take a dry fly that passively drifts down the flow, but sometimes it will not take a passively drifting fly but one that is moving slightly across and down the river (slight drag), sometimes one dragging greatly. So, when we are fishing to a salmon that we can see or are fishing into a lie that we are pretty sure holds a salmon, we should vary the approach with a combination of dead drift, slight drag and skating dry fly, letting the fish see the fly coming past it at a variety of speeds and from slightly different directions. We might start off with 30 or more dead drifts, and then try 30 casts where the fly drags ever so slightly above the salmon's nose. We might, if we have so far failed to rise him, try a couple of casts where the fly zooms over or past the fish with a great deal of drag. And we keep on until either the salmon takes the fly or we decide to move to another fish or lie.

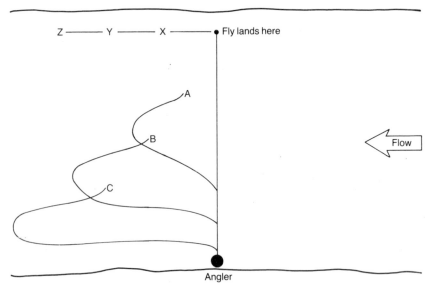

A 'natural' fly would drift down to X, Y or Z. Drag causes a dry fly to travel unnaturally across the strong flow.

Fig. 33

It is, therefore, essential that we can fish the fly without drag, so that it floats passively down the flow. In the simplest of cases, where there is just one band of fast water between us and the fish, this is not too difficult. But often the problem is far more complex, especially in rough, boulder-strewn streams where several bands of water, all moving at different speeds and sometimes at different angles, lie between salmon and angler. Consider this situation, where there are three bands of fast water between you and the fish, together with two back-eddies behind the two big boulders. The bands of fast flow quickly put downstream bellies in the fly line, but in between the back-eddies hold firmly on to the line. The combination of these results in the fly skating at a phenomenal speed as soon as it hits the water.

After making one or two tentative casts, most anglers would give up on that fish and walk upstream to find easier ones. However, low-water salmon lies are often very tricky lies.

There are two major ways of avoiding drag or, at least, postponing drag so that it does not affect the fly until it has drifted naturally over the salmon. First, by working out and then taking up the best position before casting; or second, by modifying casting technique.

In simple situations, such as shown in Fig. 33, one of these will overcome the problem. In more complicated situations, such as shown in Fig. 34, you will have to use both. I would recommend that, after reading the water and deciding to cast to a certain lie or fish, you ask yourself: 'If I put the fly there from here, will it drag?' If it will – and the answer will often be 'Yes' – ask yourself: 'Where is the best place to stand or kneel?' and 'What cast should I use?'

Often, drag can be eliminated by casting directly upstream. Wade below the salmon so that you stand and cast in the band of flow in which the salmon is lying. Then you have no bands of different flow speed between you and the salmon. However, casting directly over the fish may scare the fish, especially if the heavy fly line and not just the fine leader lands, with a splash, over the fish. So if you want to take such a position either cast so that only the leader tippet lands on the water over the fish or learn to make a 'hook cast'.

To make a hook cast, cast upstream about 1 yard to the side of where the salmon is lying. As you make the forward stroke, flick the wrist round towards the fish so that the rod point also flicks around. The line will land to the side of the fish, out of harm's way, but the leader and fly will hook round, if you have judged distance correctly, so that the fly lands immediately upstream of the fish. Raise the rod tip to 11 o'clock and strip in line as it is carried downstream. The fly will float downstream, without drag, over the fish. Note that,

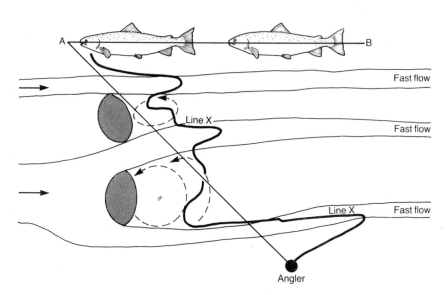

The angler casts to A, hoping to drift the fly to B, over the heads of the two salmon. Instead, the two back-eddies and bands of fast flow grab hold of the line, which drags the fly on a crazy route, line X.

Fig. 34

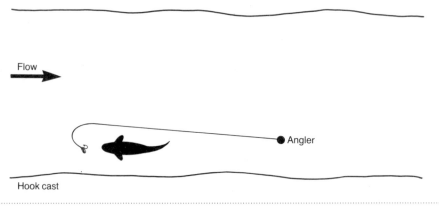

Fig. 35 – The hook cast

for a right-handed angler, it is easier to cast to the right of the fish and hook the fly and leader towards the left. Practise this cast. It is very useful.

It is often impossible to wade directly below the fish. It may be too deep, there may be bushes in the way, or there may be other fish there that you do not wish to disturb. So you will be looking to cast up and across or across the stream, or even, if obstacles prevent one of these, down and across. Remember that it is more difficult to hook fish on a downstream cast and that the fish is more likely to see you. Two other casting techniques are invaluable here: a 'slack-line cast' or a 'reach cast'. Both are outstanding casting modifications and, to judge from conversations with and observations of great dry fly and nymph anglers, probably account for over 80 per cent of all the casts they make, especially on rivers with complex flows. It is the ability to make this sort of cast that separates the great angler from the mediocre on rivers – not the fly nor the ability to cast great distances.

The slack-line cast is the easier to master. If you make a forward cast and, as the line is extending out over the water, wiggle the rod tip from side to side, the line lands in a snake-like way on the water. Before the current can form a belly in the fly line and cause the fly to drag, it must first of all take up all these wiggles. And until all these wiggles have been taken up, the fly will drift downstream naturally. Of course, if a fish lies 10 yards away, you will be casting not just the 10 yards of line, but 10 yards plus the extra length taken up by the wiggles you will put into the slack-line cast. Again, judging this is a matter of practice and experience. The easiest way to judge the correct distance is to make a short slack-line cast so that the fly lands short of the fish, and then to estimate how much extra line you will have to shoot on the next cast to cover the fish.

This cast can be modified to suit the particular lie. For instance, suppose

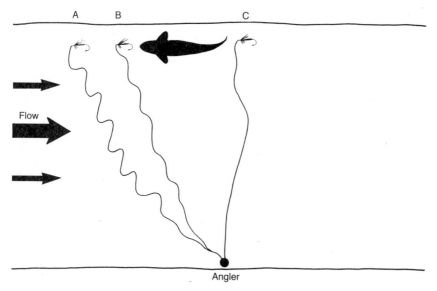

A slack-line cast made to A guarantees that the dry fly is not dragging when it floats over the salmon at B. Drag commences when all slack has been taken up by the flow, well downstream of the fish at C.

Fig. 36 – The slack-line cast

that there are two bands of fast water between you and the fish. On the forward cast you make two series of wiggles with the rod tip, with a gap in between. If you get it right, you will have the fly landing just upstream of the fish, wiggles in the line over each of the two fast bands, which would usually be the cause of drag in a normal straight-line cast, and a straight line over the intervening bands of slower water.

In a reach cast the aim is to put the fly just upstream of the fish and to put a big upstream belly in the line over bands of fast water. The fly will then drift downstream naturally, with the flow, until the faster water has carried the upstream belly downstream of the fly. Again, because you are not casting a straight line, extra must be shot to put the fly over the fish plus the amount in the belly you create. So, if the river is flowing from left to right, you will need a 'left reach cast'. Make a first, ordinary straight-line cast that lands short of the target and then strip off extra line so that, on the next delivery, the length of line beyond the rod tip will put the flies on target. Now strip off extra line – perhaps 2–3 yards – and trap this under the index finger of the rod hand or by the other hand. You now lift off in the back cast, keeping the extra line trapped, and then, as soon as you have punched the forward cast out and the line is extending in the air, you release the extra line and at the same time swing

187

the rod point upstream, extending the arm and leaning upstream and to the left, to increase your 'reach', as you do so. The flies will continue to the target, but a massive upstream belly will have been formed. As this belly drifts downstream so you follow round with the rod point, arm and body, holding the rod at arm's length and leaning or reaching out, to keep that upstream belly for as long as possible to delay drag.

You may, and often will, find that vagaries of current move parts of the upstream belly faster than others, and that you need to slow this down to enable a long, drag-free drift. If, for instance, a faster band of flow close to the rod tip is destroying the belly and causing drag, make an upstream mend. Flick the offending length of line back upstream with a circular, upstream movement of the rod tip, but make sure that the rest of the line on the water is not disturbed or you may pull the fly out of position.

Where the flow is a complex of fast and slow currents, it is perhaps worth wiggling the rod from side to side to add extra slack in the line immediately after the upstream reach has been made and as the line is still shooting out. This will add a series of wiggles in the fly line that, with the upstream reach, will further postpone drag. This modification is really a 'slack-line reach cast'.

If the river is flowing from right to left you will need a 'right reach cast'. This is exactly the same as the left reach cast to execute, except that as you

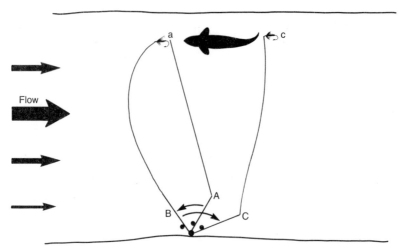

The reach cast: the fly is cast with overhead cast A to a, but, as the line is extending, extra line is shot and, at the same time, the rod is swept upstream with a reach of the body and arm (B). This puts a big upstream belly in the line. The fly now drifts downstream, over the salmon. As it does so, the angler follows it down with the rod and reach of arm and body (C), until the fly reaches c without dragging.

Fig. 37 – The reach cast

make the forward cast and as the line is extended in the air over the water, you swing the rod point, arm and body smoothly round in an upstream arc to the right. This, again, will make the upstream belly you need with the fly landing just upstream of the fish, and as the fly and belly in the line move downstream you follow round, with the rod point and with reach of the rod arm and swing or lean of the body to the left.

Just to show how effective the slack-line cast and reach cast are in delaying drag, some measurements were made on a pool with a steady flow down the middle. The flies were cast across this flow into slower water beyond.

- On an ordinary straight line cast the fly dragged after 2½ in of apparently drag-free drift.
- With a slack-line cast the fly dragged after 4ft–4ft 6in of apparently drag-free drift.
- With a right reach cast the fly dragged after 7ft–7ft 6in of apparently drag-free drift.
- With a right reach cast, with the addition of slack line and mending, the fly dragged after 7ft 6in–8ft 3in of apparently drag-free drift.

The measurements were made to illustrate the value of these casting modifications. In practice, on some faster pools and riffles where a straight line cast drags after about 1 yard, apparently drag-free drifts of around 30ft are easily possible. Again, a little practice will soon make any competent angler adept at the reach cast.

Which cast do you use in any particular situation? The reach casts are ideal when you are casting to a fish or into a lie that is just a little way upstream, directly across the stream or downstream of the angler. It is especially useful on very clear waters, where the fish may be leader-shy, because, when distances are accurately judged and the cast perfectly executed, the fly will drift over the fish while the leader and fly line are still upstream. By contrast, the slack-line cast is the one to use when casting to fish well up and across the stream or to fish lying at the far side of very complex flows.

So you can now fish the dry fly so that it floats downstream without dragging. Always start by fishing the dry fly in this way. Then, after fishing several casts over the salmon or lie, repeat the dead drift, but twitch the dry fly as is drifts downstream by pulling in short lengths of line or raising and then lowering the rod tip. The twitched dead drift will sometimes score after a series of plain dead drifts.

If that does not succeed in raising the fish, introduce drag, so that the fly skates a little across the surface over and in front of the salmon. Make a straight line cast across the river flow so that drag sets in as the fly moves downstream, and then try two or three casts where you cast a straight line across the lie, or upstream of the fish, and skate the fly across the surface by raising the rod and, if necessary, pulling in line.

The process of dead drift, dead drift with twitch, dragging and skating dry fly can be repeated from several positions, so that the fly crosses the fish from different angles.

Sometimes a salmon may boil at a dry fly without taking it into the mouth. Do not re-cast immediately. Go and fish another lie, and return later. From my research and my conversations with other dry fly anglers, a salmon that has boiled at a dry fly will usually sulk on the bottom if casting over it is continued. However, an hour or so later, the same salmon may take boldly.

Another approach, which was suggested by J.D. Bates, is to cast the dry fly upstream of the fish and allow it to drift down passively, without drag. But, just before the fly reaches the salmon, but at a time when it is certainly inside the salmon's window – i.e., the fish can see it – lift the fly from the water and re-cast. Repeat this several times, lifting the fly off the water in the same place, just upstream of the salmon. Then allow the fly to drift down to the fish. This sometimes triggers the salmon to take. It is as though the salmon, having grown accustomed to the fly disappearing before it reaches him, reacts to the fly not taking off but drifting that bit further.

The weighted nymph

The weighted nymph is meant to fish deep, in front of the nose of the resting salmon. Simply tying a leaded fly to a plain leader and casting it into the water may not be enough. The fact that our heavy fly sinks so that we cannot see it does not necessarily mean that the fly is deep enough. Weighted nymph tactics for salmon mean getting the fly so that it fishes only a few inches from the river bed, and not simply 'well below the surface'. If the river is 6ft deep, we mean at least 5ft below the surface; if it is 3ft deep, at least 2ft below the surface. In both cases, no more than 1ft from the bottom.

But, some of you might protest, did not the great Frank Sawyer catch salmon solely with Killer Bugs on de-greased, plain monofilament leaders? He did, but in the fairly even flow of chalkstreams. In the deeper, turbulent-water salmon lies of many northern British, Canadian and Scandinavian rivers, the Sawyer system of using a weighted fly and de-greased leader with an upstream cast may not be enough. It is essential to add weight, which is conventionally achieved by wrapping lead wire round and down the hook shank in either close turns (heavyweight fly) or open turns (middleweight fly). Alternatively, lead heads, gold heads and silver heads, with or without lead wire wrapped on the hook shank, can be used. Such added weight to the fly will take the fly down.

Rivers flow, however, and a weighted fly that is not tied to a leader will, when it is thrown into the water, tend to move in two directions: downstream with the flow and vertically down through the water. In a very slow pool the fly might reach the bottom a couple of yards downstream; in a faster flow the same weighted fly might reach the bottom 10 yards or more downstream; in very fast, turbulent water even the heaviest of flies may not touch the bottom but be swept far downstream. In other words, the more rapid and turbulent the flow, the longer, and further the drift downstream, before a weighted fly will reach the bottom. So, if you are trying to catch a salmon in a precisely known position, the faster and more turbulent the water the further upstream of the fish you must cast the fly.

But it is not that easy! Because we want to catch the fish that take our weighted flies and do not want to lose the entire contents of our fly boxes by just throwing them in the water, we tie our flies on the end of monofilament leaders. As soon as we do this, we greatly slow down the rate at which weighted flies sink. There are two reasons for this. First, monofilament leaders tend to float and retard the fly's sinking rate. To overcome this, always treat leaders with a good sinkant or rub them down with a piece of dock leaf. Second, the turbulence of the river flow tends to push the leader, and with it the fly, upwards and/or sideways. Summer salmon anglers, fishing wet fly on a floating line, know this only too well (see Chapter 6). They may want their quite heavy fly, sparsely dressed on low-water doubles, cast across or down and across the river, to fish within 6in of the surface. And in fast, turbulent water they will commonly fish a fly two sizes larger than they would in a steadier flow, simply to take the fly to the correct depth and to prevent it skating across the surface. In very fast, turbulent water they may have to resort to intermediate or sink-tip lines to take their fly down the necessary few inches. What chance the nymph salmon angler, fishing flies of comparable weight, who wants his fly to fish much deeper, along the river bed?

The answer is, no chance – unless the the leader and casting techniques are modified.

Leaders for bottom tactics

A weighted fly tied to the end of a fine (say 5lb) tippet will sink more quickly than one tied to the end of a heavier leader (10lb or more). The finer leader has less surface area on which turbulence can act. But how fine a leader point can we fish for salmon? I would hesitate going less than 6–8lb test, for I consider it wrong to risk fishing so fine that breakages are likely. Another solution is to put extra weight on the leader. Nip a piece of split shot on the leader or, as some American anglers do, add quite huge amounts of lead strip coiled around the leader. These are dreadful things to cast. In fact, you cannot really 'cast' them in the normal fly fishing style. The cast must be more of a lob that can be effectively made only over very short distances. Thankfully, there is a better solution: specially designed high-density sinking leaders.

Anglers who wish to fish weighted nymphs, close to the river bed, should have a complete set of the relatively new braided leaders, which will include a full-floating leader, an intermediate (very slow sink) leader, and two or more faster-sinking leaders, including a very heavy 'bottom bouncer'. Both of the brands readily available, by Fly Fishing Technology of Wales, marketed under the brand name Airflo, and by Roman Moser of Austria, offer such a range. Both are attached to the end of the fly line in the same way:

1. A braided mini-connection is fixed to the end of the floating fly line. This involves sliding the last 1in of fly line inside the core of the braided mini-connection and fixing it in place with a sliding plastic sleeve. Always use superglue to fix the connection. It is possible to buy special flexible and waterproof superglue for the Moser leaders. I once lost a large fish and leader when an unglued link slipped from the fly line. This mini-connection thus stays permanently on the fly line.

2. The appropriately weighted leader is fixed, loop to loop, with the mini-connection. Thus, in the course of one day when fairly slow, moderately fast, and very fast and turbulent waters may be fished, the leader can quickly be changed to one of a more appropriate density. And if I want to try dry fly after fishing the nymph through a lie, I can change to a floating leader for dry fly fishing. If I want to try a conventional wet fly, the floating leader is removed and a monofilament leader or a braided intermediate or slow-sink leader slipped in place instead. So, with a packet of leaders of different density and a box of dry flies, nymphs and wet flies, I can fish these three techniques on my 10ft 6in rod and no. 7 line in one day quite simply.

3. A length of tippet material is tied to the end of the leader – 3–4ft is usually adequate.

Casting for bottom tactics

First of all, we must consider casting direction in relation to the river flow. The most effective directions are upstream, up and across or across. This is because if you cast in any downstream direction, the flow will tend to push up on the leader and retard its sinking rate. If you cast across or upstream the flow will often increase sinking rate by pushing down on the leader. This is easy to demonstrate with a simple bait fishing rig. Tie a baited hook to the end of the reel line, with swan shot pinched on to the line a couple of feet above the hook to take the bait to the bottom. Stand below a fast run and cast up and across, adding swan shot until the weight and baited hook hit the bottom. You might need two shot. Now move upstream to the head of the run. Cast down and across the flow. You will find that the same weight will not go to the bottom, and you may need four or five shot to achieve the same depth. It is precisely the same with a weighted fly rig. To reach the bottom you will need a heavier rig if you cast down and across than if you cast up and across the flow.

Most proficient casters consistently cast a tight line – that is, after the final delivery, the fly line and leader are extended on to the water in a perfectly straight line. Although this looks good, it is, in fact, a hindrance when it comes to fishing the weighted nymph deep, close to the bottom. As soon as the fly line and leader hit the water, the flow will pull on them, keeping them so tight that there is not the slack for the weighted fly/braided leader to sink freely to depth. In very turbulent water even a very heavy fly may skate across the surface as the flow drags on the fly line. Again, consider the floating line wet fly salmon angler: to prevent this from happening, he deliberately mends the line by putting a loose loop of line upstream of the fly – and he wants the fly to fish only a few inches deep, not close to the bottom!

There are many casting modifications that can be used to aid sinking of the weighted fly and leader; slack line and reach casts were described earlier in this chapter. One other that is useful for getting the nymph deep is the tuck cast.

As you make the forward delivery stroke, make it with more power than you would normally and stop the cast early and abruptly, aiming high, with the rod at between 11 and 12 o'clock. The line shoots out high, but the extra power causes the leader and nymph to flick or tuck around, under the extended fly line. Nymph and leader fall in a heap on the water below the end of the fly line and start to sink before the fly line lands on the water. They thus sink quickly without the constraints of the tight line.

These casting tricks are essential for deep-water tactics, and anyone who cannot perform them should seek out a proficient teacher of casting. Books and videos can help. But there is nothing like personal tuition. They can be taught and learned easily in a day; but they must be taught, practised and learned on a river, in the situations for which they were designed. I find is amazing that,

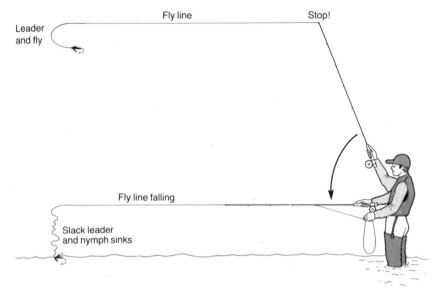

Fly line

Stop!

Leader
and fly

Fly line falling

Slack leader
and nymph sinks

The rod is stopped early and abruptly. The line extends, and the fly and leader tuck under the fly line. The rod is then lowered. The weighted nymph and leader reach the water before the fly line and sink quickly.

Fig. 38 – The tuck cast

while the average club golfer is prepared to pay for professional instruction to improve his or her game, the average fly fisher is not!

If you cannot execute these casts there is another little trick that might help. Immediately after having made a cast, quickly raise and lower the rod in one movement. As you lower the rod you will be putting slack into the line, which will help the weighted fly to sink.

Putting it all together

You can see a salmon lying deep in the pool or know a lie in which there is usually a salmon lying. You fancy trying a weighted nymph. You must now choose a nymph. Any one of those listed in Chapter 4 will do – I would start with the Hare's Ear Goldhead or a big Killer Bug, but it is up to you. You must then decide on the appropriate weight of leader and a casting style that will take the fly to the bottom. If the water is so clear that you can see both the fish and the fly in the water, you can see if your fly is reaching the fish. This is not possible in most rivers, so a few trial casts and changes of leader density are appropriate until you get it right. The clue that you have got it right is that occasionally the fly will hit the bottom, catch in weed or water moss, or snag up. Expect to lose a few flies on the bottom in the course of a day. So start light, with a weighted fly on a floating or intermediate leader, and go progressively heavier until you can feel the fly touch bottom; the tip of the fly line will also show this (see below). And, as you move from lie to lie, or through a large lie that might hold several fish, be aware that the terminal rig might have to be lightened or made heavier as water conditions change, or that your casting techniques may have to be slightly altered.

Bite indicators and the induced take

You cast the fly and leader up and across to where you think that a salmon should be lying, and then, as the fly drifts freely and deeply along the bottom, slowly follow it round with the rod point. By holding the rod out at arm's length you may be able to extend the length of the fly's drift by an extra few yards. A salmon may take the fly at any time in the course of its downstream drift, but it will usually do so quickly, and immediately it feels the hard, artificial object in its mouth, it will spit it out. Remember, however, that, from the few accounts available and very limited personal experience, salmon tend to hold on to a weighted fly longer than a trout does. Rarely do fish on deeply fished flies hook themselves.

How do you know when a salmon has taken hold? Many anglers fix a bite indicator (a sort of float) on the line, close to the end of the fly line or in the leader butt. If the float stops or bobs under, the rod is raised immediately. Other anglers, and I am one, consider that the use of a float is not fly fishing – if you need to use a float, why not go the whole hog and use coarse float fishing equipment? Instead, the tip of the floating fly line is used, and for that reason the tip of the fly line is heavily greased, with Mucelin. If that stops, twitches, jerks to one side or dips under, assume that a fish has taken the fly and tighten immediately. Often it will be the bottom. Check that the fly is not carrying a bit of weed or detritus before making the next cast. But it may be a fish. A trout, maybe a sea trout, perhaps a salmon, for all three will take these deeply fished nymphs. But do not hesitate. As soon as any indication comes, tighten.

If a heavily weighted nymph is cast and allowed to drift without drag downstream, the fish may ignore it. The same fish might take the same nymph if, as it passes the fish, the nymph suddenly rises through the water. It is as though an inanimate object suddenly becomes animate, a living creature worthy of being attacked. Controlled drag, involving careful manipulation of the rod point, produces this lift or rise of the artificial. The late Oliver Kite referred to the technique, when he used it in trout fishing, as the 'induced take'; in North America it is called the Leisenring lift after James Leisenring.

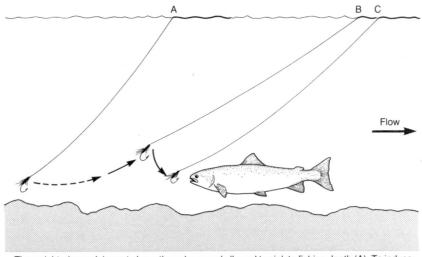

The weighted nymph is cast above the salmon and allowed to sink to fishing depth (A). To induce a take, when the nymph approaches the fish, raise the rod tip. This pulls on the line and causes the nymph to rise (B). If you lower the rod tip immediately, the nymph will fall (C). This is an attractive way of presenting weighted nymphs.

Fig. 39 – The induced take

There are two ways of causing the nymph to rise through the water in a way that the salmon might find attractive.

First, cast upstream or up and across so that the nymph lands 1–3 yards upstream of the salmon or lie. Distance depends on depth and speed of current, for it is essential that the nymph has sunk close to the river bed before it reaches the fish (see above). Quickly strip in any slack line that develops as the nymph sinks close to the river bed. Then, as the nymph passes in front of the fish or through the lie, lift, then lower the rod tip smoothly. The drag imparted by this movement will cause the nymph to rise and then fall through the water.

Second, reach cast up and across or across the stream so that the nymph lands at least 2 yards (further in deeper or faster water) upstream of the salmon or lie. While the nymph is sinking as it drifts downstream, follow the fly around with the rod point. As the nymph reaches a little upstream of the salmon or lie, swing the rod point around downstream towards the bank. This will create a belly in the line, which will immediately cause the nymph to drag in an up and across direction in front of the fish's nose.

You can modify this method in an attempt to induce salmon that are lying downstream of you to take a moving nymph – for instance, in positions where an across or up and across cast is impossible, perhaps because of an obstructing tree. Cast down and across with a slack-line cast, far enough upstream of the fish or lie so that the nymph will have sunk deeply by the time it has drifted down to the fish or lie. The squiggles in the line, resulting from the slack-line cast, will aid this sinking by preventing drag. However, it is worth having some loops of slack line in the left hand – that is, the hand that is not holding the rod – and feeding some of this quickly through the rod rings should the line between rod tip and line tip become tight. A tight line on a downstream cast will prevent the leaded fly sinking properly. Just before the fly reaches the fish or lie, swing the rod point smoothly around to tighten the line. This will immediately result in the inertly drifting nymph stopping moving downstream and instead it will rise and swing round in front of the salmon's nose.

The induced-take method does work for salmon. Sawyer used it in the 1950s to catch salmon on the Avon. If a fish has not taken after, say, 10 dead drifts, as the fly drifts through the lie or in front of the salmon's nose, make the nymph rise up through the water. This sudden coming to life of a drifting nymph often goads trout and sea trout into action. It has also been shown to work, on occasion, for salmon too.

Although it is almost fifty years since the first salmon was caught deliberately on a leaded nymph, we still have much to learn on the subject of catching salmon on nymphs. So, when you catch one, please give us all as much information as you can in a note to the angling press.

And I hope you catch one by this fascinating method.

CHAPTER 9

HOOKING, PLAYING AND LANDING SALMON

Ten times more fish are lost from striking too quickly
than by striking too slowly.

FRANCIS FRANCIS, *A Book on Angling*, 1867

Getting the salmon to take the fly is only the start of catching the fish. You have to set the hook. Then you must play the powerful fish. And then you must land the fish.

Hooking salmon

Many, many years ago I was invited to fish one of the best beats on the Lune. This was in the days when the river was full of salmon. Although I had never fished fly for salmon before, I was highly optimistic for, as I tackled up on the bank, fish were showing throughout the pool. I tied on the size 10 Jeannie that Mr Gough, the Lancaster tackle dealer, had insisted that I use, waded into the neck of the pool and lengthened line. After only a few minutes there was an almighty swirl and tug. I struck hard, in true trout fisher style, and, in what seemed to be slow motion, a silver salmon leapt from the water, my fly left its mouth and the line sprang back like elastic and coiled itself around my neck and shoulders. 'You fool!' I told myself. 'Don't strike when a salmon takes.' I can still see that fish clearly. I can still remember feeling an idiot.

You see, I had done my homework, and I knew the theory, or at least the theory laid down by the writers of that age. I had read Antony Bridges, who wrote, in *Modern Salmon Fishing* (1939): 'If you had seen the rise [of the salmon taking the fly], I would have advised you not to strike at once, but to give the fish time to go down with the fly and close his mouth on it.' And Richard Waddington's *Fly Fishing for Salmon* (1951):

Immediately you become aware of a fish, drop the point of the rod, let go any

198

loose line in your hand, pull more line off the reel, step forward – do in short anything that will help create a good big belly in the line well downstream of the fish. When all this is done you may now strike or not as fancy pleases you. It will make no difference, for by now the fish is hooked!

In subsequent years most leading writers on the sport of salmon fishing reinforced these views. R.V. Righyni, in *Advanced Salmon Fishing* (1973), wrote:

With the rod held reasonably high, when the line is seen to be tightening, it is enough to lower the rod instantly and release a yard or so of slack line from the left hand. A few seconds later, the strain will gradually be felt to build up and then as the rod begins to respond, very firm pressure should be applied until the fish sets off to commence the fight.

More recently, in *Salmon Fishing* (1981), Hugh Falkus wrote:

I feel we have a better chance of hooking a fish if we avoid tightening the line too soon: if we let the speed of the water set the hook for us.

So – you can chalk me up as one of the loose-liners.

Whether fishing with sunk or floating line, I keep a yard of slack line trapped in the crook of my rod-hand forefinger. This is held so lightly that the slightest nudge, even a floating leaf, will draw the line away.

This advice is fine, and many successful anglers still abide by it. Indeed, have not all these writers caught many hundreds if not thousands of fish in their life-times? The problem, however, is that many anglers, especially those who do relatively little salmon fishing and much trout fishing, find it difficult to overcome their inbuilt reflex actions to strike at the first sign that a salmon has taken the fly. There is the loop of line trapped by the forefinger against the rod handle. As soon as anything happens at the other end of the line, instead of letting that loop of line go, the forefinger tightens on the loop as an involuntary strike is made. And, because just enough salmon grab hold and hook themselves instantly to keep some of these anglers happy, they are unaware that anything is wrong. The fish that were not hooked because of the precipitate striking, such anglers argue, simply did not take the fly properly. They 'came short'.

Some anglers have tried to overcome the reflex strike by holding the loop of line in a completely different way. Instead of trapping it with the forefinger of the rod hand on the underside of the rod handle, they trap it loosely under the thumb on the top of the handle. The idea is that, when they lift into a fish, using the fingers and palm of the upper rod hand, the pressure of the thumb on the line loop, which is on top of the handle, is relaxed, and thus the essential loop of slack line is released immediately, giving the salmon the necessary slack line for it to hook itself. This system works, but no better than the traditional method.

In the matter of how and when to strike, and whether slack line should be given when a salmon takes the fly, it is instructive to describe how salmon are hooked when harling, with fly rod, fly line and flies, on Norway's mighty River Namsen (harling is discussed on page 165).

On the Namsen two, sometimes three, rods are used, the line from each being slowly fed out once the boatman has rowed into the start position. One rod extends to either side of the boat and, if used, the third points back over the stern. Each rod is clipped in a holder so that, in the event of a salmon taking, the rod is not pulled overboard. Great care must be taken in ensuring that the reel handle is facing skywards, so that, when a fish takes, the reel can revolve unimpeded. It is also important to ensure that the reel check is just sufficient that the movement of boat and river flow will not pull line from the reel. Because the rod points more or less down the line and is held fairly low, there is very little slack in the system, and certainly no large loop between rod tip and water or between reel and first rod ring. After setting up the rods the angler sits back, admires the scenery and chats with the boatman or reads a book. Slowly the boat is rowed across the river, searching every lie, and is allowed to drop downstream after each pass so that new lies are constantly being fished until all the pool has been thoroughly fished. Suddenly a reel screams as a salmon takes. The rod point cannot be dropped. There is no loose line to feed out. Stepping forward is impossible, unless the angler wishes to take a dip. It is difficult to strip more line from the reel, for the salmon is doing that itself. And there is not a good big belly in the line downstream of the fish. The salmon has hooked itself already without the angler doing anything. It is now a matter of having the other line(s) reeled in and of playing the fish. But note one important point: with the angler sitting back in the boat and with the rods firmly clipped down, a few seconds elapse between the reel indicating that a salmon has taken the fly and the angler lifting up the rod. It is thus impossible for the angler to strike as the salmon takes.

It seems, therefore, that letting the salmon hook themselves from the reel is the most foolproof way of hooking them when you are salmon fishing in rivers. The reel check is tightened or slackened just to the point where the reel spool will not revolve when a big mend is made, otherwise, instead of mending the cast line, further line is released. The fly is then cast out and mend(s) are made as appropriate (see page 140). The rod hand grasps the handle with all the fingers and the thumb on the cork so that the fingers are kept well away from the line. It is important also to ensure that the reel handle and exposed rim are not held against the arm or clothing – they must be able to revolve without any obstruction – and the rod tip is kept moderately low as the fly is being fished round so that there is minimum friction between the reel drum and fly. If you are fishing a floating line you might see a swirl at the surface, or the line may stop or move away. No matter what, the sole indicator of a salmon taking the fly is an auditory one – the reel check. As soon as the reel goes 'Zzzzzzzzz' lift slowly but positively into the fish. And as soon as you have heard that 'Zzzzzzzzz' and lifted the rod firmly, the fish will already be hooked, so it is impossible to strike prematurely.

I stress, do not strike violently. Lift the rod firmly or, as Richard Franck put it in 1694, 'that secret art of striking, which ought never at any time to be used with violence'.

It is possible that newcomers to the sport of salmon fishing might still be tempted to strike when they see a salmon boil to the fly fished on floating line and not wait for the reel to go. One further tip is to keep your eyes on the rod tip and first few yards of line and to ignore the water in the vicinity of the fly. After all, provided that the cast has been made and fished properly, there is no need to watch for salmon taking the fly. We do not, indeed often cannot, do this when fishing the sinking or intermediate lines. I recall one instance to illustrate this. After a long night testing the wine of Scotland, I was feeling very rough as I fished down the first pool. Suddenly a small flock of golden plover flew over. I looked up and watched them flighting on to some stubble. The ornithological alcoholic haze was shattered by the 'Zzzzzzzzz' of the reel, and I found myself playing a 14lb salmon that had hooked itself.

Hooking a fish from the reel is a great advantage when backing-up a pool (see page 149). With the traditional loop system, pressure must be sufficient to prevent extra line being fed out from the loop as you move upstream, otherwise there will be no slack loop. And if you do not do a lot of backing-up salmon fishing, there is the temptation to hold on to the loop too tightly and have a 'snatch take' when a salmon grabs hold. When backing-up and fishing directly from the reel, tighten, or slacken, the reel check to the minimum that will not allow the reel drum to give extra line as you fish the fly round. Again, hold the rod by the handle, with nothing touching the line or reel. When the reel sings, lift the rod and play the fish. You need do no more.

The only time it is impossible to have the fish hook themselves from the reel is when you are working the fly by stripping in line or by figure-of-eighting.

The same is also true of fishing a slack loop or giving the fish a lot of slack line. You are working the line back and bang! The salmon is or is not hooked. You feel the salmon take and, at the same time, the salmon will have felt the resistance of you pulling on the line as you worked the fly back. Let this salmon have 1 yard or 10 yards of line – it is already hooked or it is not. But there is another side to hooking salmon when working line. They tend to take more fiercely, with a crunch. Indeed, sometimes the fly will have been engulfed by the salmon at the back of its throat or will, at least, be so firmly embedded in the scissors that the hook must be cut out.

Happily, nothing that we can do will prevent some fish not being hooked properly. If there were, we would miss out on so many great tales about gargantuan salmon that were never landed. But, for the novice at least, by letting the fish hook themselves from the reel and by using the sound of the reel check as indicator of an offer, more fish will be hooked than would be by the slack-line, loop method.

When we are fishing wet fly in lakes, things are slightly different. We are working the flies through the water and perhaps dibbling the bob fly on the surface. When the salmon takes, slowly lift the rod to set the hook. It is not really a strike, more a tightening, just to see if the salmon really has taken the fly and is hooked. No violence is involved at all. Forget the word 'strike'. Tighten is a more appropriate term. It is exactly the same when you are dry fly fishing or dibbling for salmon. The dry fly disappears in a swirl. Lift the rod point, and as the salmon moves down with the fly the combined forces of rod movement and salmon movement drive the hook into the jaw of the fish. No violence, and no real strike, in the sense that a deep sea cod fisher would strike.

When we are dapping we must be a little slower. Some anglers shout, as soon as the salmon breaks the surface and takes the dap, 'God Save the Queen!' or 'Hello there Mister Salmon!' I have used the latter and find it quite effective. Tighten on the 'n' of 'Queen' or 'Salmon'.

Hooking a salmon on a nymph requires a much faster response. You will be watching the floating tip of the fly line and leader butt (see page 195) if you cannot see the fish in the water. The sudden dipping under or jerking forward of those indicators signifies that a fish has taken the nymph. Tighten with a firm, but not violent, sideways movement of the rod tip.

Playing salmon

A salmon is hooked. At this point many wading river anglers immediately try to leave the water. Don't. The first thing to do in all circumstances when a salmon is hooked is to make sure that it is well hooked. Hold the rod point high and bent solidly into the fish, but allow the fish to take line from the reel if, as is likely, it is moving away from you. If the hook comes out, the hook hold was a bad one and you would probably have lost the fish anyway, even if you had been very gentle on it. Initially, however, the salmon usually move away from you on this very tight line. By being firm with the fish when it does this there is more chance of the hook sinking further in or, if the initial hook hold fails, the hook may take purchase more securely elsewhere in the mouth of the fish. I suspect that the latter happened twice last year with fish that I had hooked, for in both cases there were signs of the hook having partly penetrated the front of the salmons' mouths although both had the fly in the scissors when landed.

The fish is well hooked. If you are wading in a river, leave the water, keeping a well-bent rod pulling on the fish all the time. If you are right-handed, hold the rod in your right hand and use the wading staff in your left hand. If, as you are leaving the water, the fish turns and starts to come towards you, stop. Let go of the wading staff and use the reel to keep everything tight. Then leave the water. If you are fishing a river from a boat, have the boatman row you ashore while you keep everything tight.

Never, ever, let a salmon that you are playing have slack line. When you are fishing from a boat on a lake there is much to be said for having the boat move slowly out into deeper water. This reduces the chances of the line or the other fly on the leader snagging in weed or boulders.

No matter where you are fishing, from the time the fish is hooked to when it is landed, keep as much as possible of the line between rod tip and the fish out of the water. This reduces the chance of the line being 'drowned' if it extends in a big curve under the water. If the fish turned back on this curve of drowned line, slack line would develop and the hook hold may fail. Get as high on the bank as you can or hold the rod as high as you can if you are in a boat.

If you are on a river, after leaving the water try to keep opposite or slightly downstream of the fish. By pulling the fish sideways or from slightly upstream the fish must fight not only the power you are exerting through the rod but also the river. Try also to get the fish to your side of the river, away from the main flow. Should the fish get downstream of you and tire there, you have a deadweight on the end of the line which, in a strong current, you are likely to lose.

One of the main faults with anglers playing their first few salmon is being too soft with them. Bully the fish. If the fish is not pulling away hard, then you pull on it. Don't let it control things. In this respect, whenever the fish makes a run, increase the reel pressure by pressing against the exposed rim of the reel with a finger or palm of the hand. Make the fish work hard for every yard of line it takes.

If you are in a boat on a lake, keep everything tight. Give the fish line when it makes a run, but put pressure on and retrieve line when it is not running away from you. One of the most important aspects when playing a salmon from a boat is to try to prevent it swimming under the boat, for the line may catch up on the underside of the boat and you will lose the fish; always pull up the outboard when fishing to remove this potential snag. Teamwork between you and the person on the oars is essential here.

The fish is now tiring. It rolls on the surface and attempts to make another run, but is running out of steam. It is almost ready to be landed. This is when utmost care should be taken. The sight of a net, tailer, the boat or the angler (stand well back on the riverbank) or feeling the bottom in the shallows invariably gives a fish an extra rush of adrenalin. It will zoom off once more and, if you are not prepared for this last dash, the hook is likely to be pulled out.

It is coming in, faltering and turning on its side. It is now ready to be landed.

Sometimes salmon and often sea trout, once they are hooked, can be 'walked' upstream. This is an ideal way of getting the fish upstream away from possible hazards such as a heavily treed section of the river or a weir or waterfall just downstream of where you hooked it. After the fish has taken, clamp the reel and walk slowly upstream. The fish will usually follow. If it does not, do not force it, but play it out where you are. 'Walking' is a useful trick, however, and it is a method I used when fishing Lower Bend pool on the Spey, below which is the fast neck of Tarrig Mor pool and some obstructing alders. Fish, both sea trout and salmon, that have just passed through the shallow fast neck of Tarrig Mor rest at the tail of Lower Bend, close to the bank. They are invariably good takers of the fly, and whenever I hooked one there I would walk it upstream for up to 30 yards and then play it out, well away from the overhanging alders and fast water.

Landing salmon

You should plan where and how you will land your salmon before you even start fishing for them. On rivers look for good places to land fish by every pool. In a boat work out, with the boatman or your fishing partner, where the boat will be rowed when a fish is hooked and how any fish will be landed.

There are several ways of landing salmon.

- Gaffs, which are illegal in many areas, are, in fact, the worst thing to use. Never use one.

- Tailers are wire snares on the end of solid handles. As the played-out fish comes in and turns on its side, the tailer is slipped over its tail and lifted firmly. The snare holds the fish by the wrist at the base of its tail fin. In the hands of someone who knows how to use it, a tailer is a great implement. I would be happy for Roy Brierley or Geoff Haslam to land a fish for me with their tailers any time, but in some hands tailers are a good way of losing fish (see page 206).

- A large net – and I stress 'large' (see page 208) – is essential if you are fishing from a boat or in some deep and awkward river pools (page 207). Once in the net the fish is yours. But check the mesh regularly for holes (page 208). As the fish comes in, the sight of floating mesh will often scare it and result in another run, during which the hook hold may fail. So, before you start fishing, put a stone into the net bag or have some lead strip fixed permanently in the bottom of the net bag to sink the mesh. Hold the net deep under the water, pull the fish over the net and lift so that the fish is trapped. Then, instead of lifting the net high out of the water, slide it up the bank or into the boat. Even the most robust net may collapse under the weight of a big salmon. Never make swipes at a salmon with the net, rather as a lepidopterist might do with his or her butterfly net. The landing net is a trap. Spring the trap by lifting the net when the fish is over it, and do not let the fish see the net   until it is too late.

- Hand-tailing. Play the fish out into a bit of very slack water or, better, to a point where there is a shelving beach or patch of waterside mud. As the fish comes over on its side, bring its head round and on to to the beach or mud, making sure you are behind the fish. Bend down and grasp the fish firmly around the wrist of its tail base, with the back of your hand facing the head of the fish and your palm encircling its tail. Lift the fish and carry it to the safety of dry land.

- Beaching. Play the fish towards a shelving beach or a patch of mud. Guide its head on to the land and, usually, the fish will make one or two feeble flips with its tail. Keep on the pressure and it will flip itself out of the water to a point where it is high and dry. Walk round behind the fish and lift it by its tail.

Kill or return

If, for some reason, you want to return the fish to the water, quickly unhook it and hold it in the river, head pointing upstream so that water can flow easily into its mouth and out through the gills. When you were playing the fish, it accumulated a considerable amount of lactic acid, the stuff that gives us cramp or the 'stitch', in its muscles. It must be rested until it has got rid of all that lactic acid, and this may take 10, sometimes 15, minutes. So hold the fish there, quietly. Keep holding it until it swims away strongly.

Otherwise, kill the fish immediately it has been landed. Tap it firmly on the top of the head, between the eyes, two or three times with a priest. Then remove the fly and wash the fish in the river. Put the fish in a rush salmon bass or place it among some cool grass. Keep it cool and flat for about eight hours before freezing it.

Lessons from lost fish

'Nay, the trout is not lost; for pray take notice, no man can lose what he never had.' Izaak Walton's advice is as relevant today as it was over three hundred years ago. For despite the great advances in fishing tackle technology, the weak link still remains the same: the bungling angler who will blame anything and anybody but himself when a fish is lost.

Two friends went to fish for salmon in a weir pool on the Ribble. One had just bought a tailer, and he wore it in macho-professional style over his shoulder. It was not long before a nice bright grilse seized the other angler's toby.

'I will tail it for you!' announced the proud owner of the new tailer.

The fish was played quickly and skilfully into deep, slack water. The proud owner of the new tailer reached out and, with one well-executed sweep of his weapon, neatly tailed the toby and wrenched it from the jaw of the fish. The salmon flicked its tail and vanished into the dark depths.

'Hell!' apologized the less proud owner of the new tailer. 'How did that happen?'

The unfortunate angler mumbled something about accidents happening. They started fishing once more, and within minutes the same angler hooked another nice, bright grilse on the same toby.

'I will tail it for you!' announced the less proud owner of the new tailer, obviously determined to show that misfortune was responsible for the earlier loss and not him or his new tailer. This fish too was played quickly and skilfully into deep, slack water. The less proud owner of the new tailer reached out and, with one well-executed sweep of his weapon, again neatly tailed the toby. Again the salmon flicked its tail and vanished into the dark depths.

'What can I say!' protested the owner of the offending tailer. 'I cannot understand it.'

I will leave you to imagine what the unfortunate angler said. Those two anglers never fished together after that day nor did they acknowledge each other when they passed on the riverbank.

The moral of that true story (I watched and listened from the other bank) is that friends should not land each other's fish or that a previous agreement should be made that, if an accident should happen, no blame should be attached to the one helping land the fish. If friendships are not to be broken this is essential, for incompetence in the landing of salmon is one of the main reasons for the fish not being landed.

M and R are great salmon anglers and good friends. What is more, they are great fun on the riverbank. Recently R hooked a grilse on a spoon and M offered to net it for him. R agreed. Whereupon, M made a complete mess of things by getting the spoon treble tangled with the outside of the net, whereupon the grilse wriggled to freedom. M said he was sorry. R questioned M's parentage. And the matter was dropped. That is how it should be between friends.

A few years ago I was fishing the Dee beat that Oliver Edwards, John Woods and I share. Both Oliver and John had several fish in the freezer by the time Wednesday evening arrived; I had just one sea trout to show for my efforts. That evening I chose to fish a tricky pool with a sheer rock face bank, and I decided to take the big net to make the landing of fish easy. But the net was so cumbersome that, at the last minute, I decided to leave it on top of the bank rather than clamber about in the river with it and my wading staff. 'After all,' I told myself, 'Yvonne is in the car, and I can always shout if I need the net.' I did hook a fish, a good-sized grilse, and I played it out and drew it into less turbulent but still fast water under the rock face. I reached down to hand-tail it, but it regained sufficient energy to make another short run.

'Yvonne, Yvonne!' I shouted, but in vain.

I brought the fish in again. If only there were somewhere to beach it, or slack water that would make hand-tailing a bit easier. I bent down and put my hand around its wrist. But it flicked its tail and set off into the deeper, fast water.

'Yvonne, Yvonne!' I screamed, but in vain.

I brought the fish in again and bent down to tail it. Just as my grip was about to take a firm hold, the fly slipped from its jaw and the fish drifted downstream for about 8 yards, righted itself and disappeared from view.

Of course, it was all Yvonne's fault for not hearing my shouts.

I arrived in Speyside one Saturday for the start of my long summer fishing holiday. After a quick supper and rest I decided to have a couple of hours with the sea trout. 'Just take the little net,' I told myself.

At 25 minutes to midnight (at midnight all fishing must cease for Sunday) a fish took the fly. It did not seem that big when I walked it about 10 yards upstream away from fast water in the pool tail. 'Stay here and net it. And then there will be time for another,' I told myself.

So I stayed put about waist deep in quite fast water, some 15 yards from the bank. The sea trout then began to fight for its freedom, and as it did so its size grew from the two to three pounder I had initially estimated. Now it was a good-sized grilse. I continued to play the fish without moving position. The fish continued to grow. It swirled in the failing light. 'My God!' I exclaimed. 'If this salmon is a pound it is twenty!'

Having played out the fish upstream of me I brought it back to the net, a net that had once landed a 13lb pike. But the net was hopelessly too small. I hurled the net to the shore. 'Try hand-tailing!' I told myself.

Once more I persuaded the fish to swim upstream before drawing it back towards me. Its deep, silver form came downstream, inertly, side on to the current. I reached for its tail, but missed. The fish bounced into my midriff and I saw clearly, in slow motion, the fly fall from its jaw. I made another grab for its tail but missed again. And the fish slid around my waist, righted itself and swam away.

How many gross errors did I make on this occasion? I can think of two or perhaps three!

Some years ago I was fortunate to spend some time salmon fishing the Namsen with Norway's Thorbjorn Tufte. Thorbjorn makes a most disarming commentary whenever somebody is playing a salmon: 'You will lose it . . . you will lose it . . . you will lose it . . . if you are not very careful!'

And to get back at him I would say: 'No I won't . . . no I won't . . . no I won't!'

When the fish was successfully landed, Thorbjorn would announce: 'You are very lucky you did not lose it!'

One evening I hooked a grilse and the usual conversation commenced. 'You will lose it.' 'No I won't.' And so on, and on.

I had the fish played out in deep, slow water when Thorbjorn interrupted his usual commentary with, 'Here, use my net!' I slipped the net under the fish and lifted. Nothing? Then I realized that in Thorbjorn's net was a big hole! I lost that fish.

'I told you that you would lose it!' responded Thorbjorn.

I have stressed the importance of keeping opposite or slightly downstream of a fish when it is being played. One angler hooked a fish in the neck of a big pool but, instead of getting out of the pool and opposite the fish, he stayed there like a statue. The fish behaved itself by running to and fro around the big pool for perhaps 10 minutes, but eventually came round to the pool tail. For about 200 yards below the pool tail is a tree-girt series of rocky rapids at the end of which is another nice pool. It is essential, if a fish threatens to leave the pool tail, to get opposite and exert as much side pressure as possible to turn its head and force it back upstream. But this angler stayed firmly rooted in the one place. So downstream went the fish.

A quick check showed that the fish had reached the pool below and was still hooked – always have plenty of line on the reel! – so I organized a passing of the rod around the trees, downstream. Alas, just before we reached the pool, I noticed that the line was slack. The fish had gone. But from the corner of my eye I saw an angler on the opposite bank carrying a big salmon and hiding it under some tree roots. Strange, I thought!

What we later discovered had happened was this. The salmon, weighing just over 20lb, arrived, played out, at his feet. He had lifted it out, bitten through the line and tried to hide his booty before we arrived. He refused to hand over the fish. We could not cross the river to discuss the matter further. And our angler thus lost more than a fish.

Happily, most anglers are ladies or gentlemen.

Sometimes the fish never get as far as the landing stage, other blunders causing fish and angler to part company early on in their acquaintanceship.

I was sitting on the riverbank, wondering what to try next, when I noticed two anglers approaching the pool from opposite directions. The one walking downstream spotted the one walking upstream and increased his pace so that he would have prior claim to go through the pool. As he rushed along the bank, so he snipped off his old fly, chose a new one from the fly box and tied it to his leader.

The other angler joined me on the bank and we watched as the rusher strode purposefully into the pool neck and began to lengthen line. He had made only about a dozen casts when a large back-end salmon took a firm hold. He backed out of the river and started to give the fish some stick. But then everything went slack. He reeled in and, you've guessed it, instead of a fly at the end of the leader was a curly-twirly bit of nylon!

There are, too, some anglers who announce that they have lost fish when, in fact, a fish has been nowhere near the hook!

One chap I knew was a notorious loser of big salmon. 'Fish on!' he shouted. And the other three of us reeled in and waded from the river. There he stood, in statuesque pose, with rod bent double.

'It's a big one!' he proclaimed. 'I can't do anything with it!'

We noticed that there was something there, for his rod tip knocked up and down. But if it was a fish, it wasn't going very far slowly.

'Are you sure it is a fish?'

'Yes. Definitely. Look, it has just taken a yard of line and moved upstream.'

We took his word for it. But then it moved downstream, but only for a yard or so. Minutes past. We three watchers had coffee. But still that big salmon stayed put.

'Could it be an eel that has gone under the boulders?' we suggested.

'No!' came the response. 'The take was definitely a salmon, and it has moved up and down the lie several times since I hooked it.'

All of a sudden the fish moved downstream, fast. The angler put on side strain, and the fish kited across to our bank. The angler sped off down the shingle, reeling in the slack as he went, in an attempt to keep opposite the fish. And then, the angler skilfully beached a bright orange fertilizer bag.

It reminds me of that time when an English angler called to a Dee gillie to help land a big spring salmon that he had been playing for quite some time.

'Och!' exclaimed the gillie. 'That's nae salmon. 'Tis a wee bit o' Scotland ye've hooked.'

CHAPTER 10

THE IMPORTANCE OF PERSEVERANCE IN SALMON FISHING

They went forth, and entered into a ship immediately;
and that night they caught nothing.

The Gospel According to St John 21:3

The man who first said that you will not catch salmon if the fly is not in the water was absolutely correct, but after many hours of hard fishing, with not a sight of a fish, disillusionment can tend to take over. There are no fish. What is the point of carrying on? But you never know. There may be fish, and, if you do carry on, you might just catch one.

I went down to the river at first light on what seemed to be a perfect September day. In addition to my salmon gear, I also took my grayling rod, for I had some new grayling flies I wanted to test. My plan was to fish for and catch some salmon in the morning and then, when the afternoon hatch of pale wateries began, to fish for grayling.

Everything went according to plan up to one o'clock, apart from the fact that I had not seen, never mind caught, a single salmon. And I had fished all the lies carefully. So I sat on the bank of the biggest pool, had lunch and set up the grayling rod. As I was tying on the first experimental fly, old Harry Hargreaves appeared carrying his single-handed salmon fly rod. We chatted. Apparently Harry had been unable to fish for some considerable time.

'I'll go and give it a try!' said Harry, as he made his way cautiously into the pool neck.

Just then I saw a big tail in the premier lie by the big boulder. I shouted to Harry and pointed. Within what was probably only half a dozen casts the salmon took Harry's Peter Ross, and a few minutes later I tailed out a fish of about 12lb for him. I can honestly say that I was delighted for him, and having congratulated him, I went upstream to catch some grayling.

211

At three o'clock I returned to the big pool. There was Harry, still sitting, in the sun, on the bank next to his salmon.

'Why don't you have another go?' I asked.

Harry slowly waded back in to the neck of the pool, and as he started to lengthen line I saw a big tail move in the same lie by the big boulder. I shouted to Harry and pointed. That fish may have taken Harry's Peter Ross on the first cast, though perhaps it was the second. A few minutes later I tailed the fish for him – a fine salmon of about 10lb. I can honestly say that I was not quite as delighted for Harry as I was when he caught the first!

In some rivers the salmon rarely show themselves, and it is easy to convince oneself that there are none in the river. One day last season I had caught a fish in a favourite pool and laid it on the grass next to my seat while I tried to catch another. I heard a clatter from upstream and a voice proclaim: 'There are no fish in the river!' It was an old friend. As he slowly walked along the bank to the seat, he continued: 'I have fished the entire length and seen nothing. I have fished since first light. Not one fish has moved. We need some more water to get the salmon running. There are no fish in the river. Oh! I do feel such a fool!'

Roy did me in much the same way. We had fished hard all day and, feeling a bit weary, I decided to give up an hour before dark.

'You are a fool!' Roy warned. 'It will soon be the taking time!'

'But we have seen nothing,' I exclaimed. 'There are no fish in the river, other than old potted ones.'

I went. Later Roy telephoned. He had caught his first just as I disappeared from view, and his second a few minutes after landing his first!

With Roy and me it is a matter of swings and roundabouts. One day a couple of seasons ago, when the river was indeed dour, Roy and I had fished several times through the 'dream pool' without even seeing a fish.

'I'm going down to Limekiln!' said Roy. And away he went. About two hours later he returned, fishless, and for another hour we fished the 'dream pool' together. But to no avail.

'Look, Malcolm,' suggested Roy. 'Why don't you sod off to Limekiln for a couple of hours and leave me alone!' I sodded off to Limekiln Pool.

On the fifth cast a fish grabbed hold and a few minutes later I slid a 10lb cock fish up the limestone slab bank. Two casts later another fish took. This was a hen fish, which, according to my Little Samson scales, weighted a fraction over 15lb, so I called her 16lb. As she was on the red side I put her back to spawn. Then I returned to the 'dream pool' with my 10lb fish behind my back. I had been away no more than 20 minutes.

'I thought I told you to sod off for two hours!' exclaimed Roy. I held up my fish. 'Where do you want me to sod off to now?' I asked.

Often anglers give up fishing for salmon because they have not seen any, turn to lesser quarry and find themselves attached to a salmon.

One angler had arrived on the riverbank to find the water hopelessly low and out of condition. He fished hard, for several hours, but then the afternoon sun made him feel drowsy. So he decided to fish a worm for chub or trout or eels or whatever else came along. He cast in, lay back in the sun and went to sleep. The chill of dusk woke him. He looked; the line from his rod tip lay lethargically across the water. Clearly nothing had bitten in the four hours of his slumber. So he reeled in, only to find a 17lb salmon sleeping on the bottom with his hook in its mouth.

Another angler had been on the river since dawn. It was now close to sunset. He had fished the entire beat thoroughly with a variety of salmon flies but had not seen a single fish. Now the trout were rising to the evening hatch of blue-winged olives. He put away his long salmon rod and set up a light trout rod with a three wet fly cast. On the second cast a salmon took his size 14 Orange Partridge point fly. He played it carefully, for his point was only 3lb test, and eventually managed to land a silver 12lb fish, fresh from the sea.

Some years ago, when the Nith had a fairly reasonable spring run of salmon, two anglers booked in for the week. They fished, with large spinners and heavy flies, Monday (for nothing), Tuesday (for nothing), Wednesday (they saw a fish but caught nothing) and Thursday (for nothing). Each afternoon there had been a good hatch of fly and great rise of trout. So, at lunchtime on Friday they set up their trout rods, separated and proceeded to extract lesser fry on wet flies.

Not long after starting, one of the pair found himself attached to a salmon that had taken a size 12 March Brown Spider. He played the fish for almost an hour before landing it. The fish scaled 11½lb and the tiny trout fly was buried in the fish's scissors. He walked – nay, skipped, for he was so elated – upstream to find his friend. He spotted his friend sitting on the bank.

'Look what I've caught!' he shouted with glee, holding up his prize.

'And look what I've caught!' his friend replied, holding up a silver 9lb fish. 'It took a size 14 Greenwell!'

Such incidents are not rare. Tiny spider trout flies, notably Orange Partridge, Greenwell's Glory and Black Pennell, catch too many salmon for these to be exceptional occurrences (see page 60). Perhaps we should fish these tiny flies more often. Especially when the salmon are being very dour.

Salmon are complex animals. Oliver Edwards put it this way. Salmon eggs hatch in the gravel, become parr and live in the river for a couple of years. Then they swim off to Greenland and a year or two later they swim all the way back. Some fish have had your name stamped on them from the start. And you will only catch those fish that bear your name, and then only if you are fishing for them. So you must fish as hard and for as long as you can just in case a fish carrying your name is in the river. Of course, your fish may not have run or it may have run through by the time you reach the river, and in that case you won't catch any. Other rods may be more fortunate, simply because the salmon bearing their names are there, waiting for their rightful owners to catch them.

One Friday afternoon in October many years ago, when I was still manacled to the education profession, I interviewed a student teacher who was to spend a few weeks on 'teaching practice' in the college. He said that his hobby was carp fishing, whereupon I invited him to come and watch me salmon fishing the next day. It being the last Saturday of the season, several members were down on the water at first light, most of them carrying bottles of Scotch.

'This beats carp fishing!' said the student, as he downed yet another coffee and whisky.

Now, the surest way of failing to catch a salmon is to take someone to watch you salmon fishing. But that day was an exception. Despite the fact that we saw no salmon moving throughout the day, at 10.30, when the other rods were having an early elevenses, I took my first. And at 12 o'clock, when the other rods were having an early lunch, I took my second.

I explained to my companion that all the other anglers were great salmon anglers and that the reason that they had not caught had nothing to do with their ability. It was simply a matter of those two salmon having my name on them.

We all fished hard through the afternoon, but to no avail, until, at four o'clock, we gathered on the bank. A new rod, Tony Hindle, then appeared.

'I thought that I would pop down for the last hour,' he said, pulling a bottle of Sheep Dip from his bag.

'Waste of time! Malcolm got two this morning, but we haven't seen a fish move all day!'

Tony walked to the waterside, cast a tiny Mepps into the river and immediately hooked a bright silver fish of 14lb.

Nobody else could have caught that fish, for it had Tony's name written indelibly on it.

Those few tales illustrate one essential side of successful salmon fishing: perseverance. There are many wealthy anglers today who will fish only the top rivers when they are at their most prolific and most hideously expensive, and, if conditions are not quite perfect, they will ignore the fishing and instead sip champagne until things are spot on. That's fine. But making a big bag of fish when the river is full of them is easy. Anyone can do it given the chance. The greater challenge is catching a fish or two in the lesser rivers or lakes, or in a river where fish are few and far between, where you have to work for your fish and try as many tricks as possible until you succeed.

In the second part of this book I have suggested some tricks that are worth trying. But it is now up to you. Take every opportunity of going salmon fishing and, if late in the day or towards the end of the week you have not caught a single fish, keep going to the bitter end. Tell yourself, 'I won't be here tomorrow!' or 'I won't be here next week!' And keep plugging away.

For anyone who has just taken up the sport, let me say that the hardest salmon to catch is your first one. After that they seem to be far more cooperative. Don't be persuaded to do what you see other anglers doing or to use only the flies that they recommend. Keep thinking about what you are trying to do – catch salmon – and be prepared to try many flies and many methods in your quest. Persevere, for that salmon is not too far away, and be thankful for blank days, for each blank day's fishing brings you one nearer the day you will catch your first fish!

CHAPTER 11

SAFETY

Most accidents happen because of some elementary mistake.

HUGH FALKUS, *Sea Trout Fishing*, 2nd edition, 1975

Angling is one of the most dangerous sports, judging from the statistics, simply because so many anglers make an elementary mistake and drown. It is essential that, if you are going to enjoy fishing to a ripe old age, you do not make one single elementary mistake. Ever!

The most important thing is to learn to swim if you cannot do so already.

River safety

Wading up to one's waist in deep, turbulent water is one of the joys of salmon fly fishing. But it is too easy, in a seemingly easy wading pool, to trip over a boulder and find oneself floundering in deep water, or to find oneself in an impossible position, marooned on a tongue of gravel with deep water all around and unable, because of the force of water behind, to get back into safer water upstream. The majority of accidents would never happen if all anglers, wherever they were wading, used a good wading staff and learned how to use it effectively.

Wading staff

Many anglers make their own. Don't. The wading staff is a life preserver, and needs to be top quality. Life is too short to skimp on safety. A good wading staff will:

- be rigid throughout;
- be long enough so that the handle is out of the water when you are wading deep – there is nothing worse than groping about underwater for the wading staff; the handle should be there, close to your hand, all the time;
- have a quick-release lanyard that fits over the shoulder comfortably and that is of a length that holds the wading staff handle at just the right distance

from the body – not too tight in and not 3 yards downstream;
- have sufficient weight at the bottom to hold the river bed in the fastest of flows.

The wading staff is a third leg and a probe. When wading down the river, use it to find the perfect stance for casting. Make a cast and take hold of the wading staff while you fish out the cast. If you think that there is a hole or big boulder in front of you, check with the wading staff first. Always keep both feet or one foot and the wading staff on the bottom. Never raise one foot and the wading staff off the bottom simultaneously.

Ask advice before wading a new beat of river, or watch other anglers and the line that they take. If the gillie says, 'Don't wade past that boulder,' heed the advice.

What to do if you fall in

First of all, do not panic.

If you can swim – and you should not be wading a river if you cannot – you should emerge safely but wet.

There is a misconception that, if you are wearing waders, the air in the waders will lift your feet high in the water and force your head under. Another misconception is that water will rush into your waders and the weight will pull you down. Both these beliefs are wholly fallacious.

As long ago as the early years of this century A.H. Chaytor wrote, in *Letters to a Salmon Fisher's Sons*:

> Great controversy rages in the smoking-rooms of fishing inns as to whether you should or should not wear a strap round your waist when wading in dangerous waters. Many anglers assert that if you do use a belt, and do not allow the water to get freely into your waders, if you should have to swim for your life the buoyancy of your legs will drown you by causing your head to go under water and your feet to bob about on the surface like corks. I have even met men who avowed that they had seen this happen. Well, that is utter nonsense. A salmon fisher who has been swept away by the stream may be stunned or numbed by having his head or his limbs struck hard against a boulder, or he may be dazed by the knocking about that he gets when he is trying to struggle to his feet in a swift current that is tumbling him along down the stream, but he has no need to fear the result of having air in his waders. His feet will not bob about on the surface or sink his head. I have tried it more than once . . . and the result is nothing of the sort. The buoyancy is enough to keep your legs well up, but it does not bother you at all, and you

swim quite easily, although the clumsiness of the waders makes you very slow, and the weight of water in the waders makes it difficult to get out if the bank is high. Indeed, when the legs of the waders do fill with water it becomes much harder to swim, although you can do it well enough if you swim carefully and keep calm and go with the stream. The real danger is that when you slip in heavy water you struggle to recover yourself and get greatly knocked about and flustered in the attempt to regain your footing or to reach the bank at the point where you fell in.

In other words, it is panic and a patently futile attempt to stand up when an angler has fallen in that causes drowning. Having air in the waders is an advantage because it helps the angler to float as he or she swims down and across the river to safety.

The Americans are great waders. Rarely do you see them wearing thigh boots; chest-waders (body waders) are usual, and they commonly wade as deep as possible in the big, roaring, turbulent rivers draining the Rockies. Ernest Schweibert, in *Trout* (1978), defined the American attitude to the air-in-waders problem as follows:

There is a popular mythology about waders and wading accidents. It holds that waders will trap air that balloons upwards when you fall, riding your legs to the surface and holding your head submerged. It is a dangerous mythology that has killed some men, because they believed the waders would drown them unless they could get them off, and they wasted precious energy and time trying to jettison them. They cannot balloon your legs to the surface and drown you, and if you want proof, try it yourself in shallow water sometimes.

In recent years Hugh Falkus has patently, and patiently, demonstrated in his books *Sea Trout Fishing*, *Salmon Fishing*, *Speycasting* and *Falkus & Buller's Freshwater Fishing*, and in his classic documentary film, *Salmo the Leaper*:

- that having air trapped in waders and clothing helps an angler who has fallen in to float and swim ashore;
- that panic is the cause of drowning in most instances;
- how to swim safely ashore, by taking a backstroke position, which Falkus calls the 'crucifix' or 'safe position', in the water with the feet downstream, so that the feet, not the head, will hit boulders. This is almost always the position in which a salmon angler will find him- or herself after being swept off his or her feet. Then, by extending both arms sideways and using the flow, steering with legs and hands, the angler can swim down and across to the shore, and then crawl out on hands and knees.

Voices of doom occasionally repeat the misconceptions that I quoted earlier. A typical one was voiced in the November 1991 issue of the magazine *Salmon, Trout & Sea-Trout*:

> The prudent angler who does a lot of deep wading should . . . also carry a sharp instrument where it is readily to hand. Then, if he loses his balance and falls in, and air is trapped in his waders, forcing his legs up, he can puncture or cut them to release it immediately. This is a small but essential precaution, but it has saved many lives.

Such a ridiculous – indeed dangerously stupid – statement makes liars of Chaytor, Schweibert and Falkus and implies that the photographs in Falkus's books and the sequence in his film where he throws himself into 15 feet of cold, turbulent, fast-flowing river were rigged. But they are not liars. Think about what was being suggested.

- 'A sharp instrument' – what sort of instrument? A penknife that will have to be opened by the angler as he is swept downstream? A sheath knife, fixed to a belt, which must be grappled for? A little, pointed, open-bladed knife that is kept in the little pocket of the chest-waders (together with the fly box and packet of mints)? Or a pair of pointed scissors, kept on a lanyard clipped to the fishing jacket? Oh! and the lanyard must be long enough to reach to at least the knees so that the waders can be cut there to release air from the feet.
- 'Where it is readily to hand' – so, having fallen in and while you are being swept downstream, you are expected to rummage in your pockets or find the scissors at the end of the long lanyard or unclip the sheath knife and remove it from your scabbard? Where is your body while this is going on? Feet floating on the top with your body submerged in the boulder-strewn current?
- 'He can puncture or cut them' – you are being swept down the river, arms reaching for the offending waders (your arms are down, therefore, forcing your body underwater) and trying to stab them or make a neat job with the scissors! What about the type of waders you are wearing? I use Red Ball, which are incredibly tough and strong and would be the very devil to cut if I were floating, supposedly feet up, down the river. Come now. The outcome, certainly in the sorts of rivers where an angler is likely to be swept off his feet in the current, will be a corpse that has both drowned and bled to death. The manoeuvres may work in a swimming bath, but not in a real river.
- 'It has saved many lives' – I know that Hugh Falkus has received messages from many anglers who have followed his advice and whose lives have been

saved by reading his books and watching *Salmo the Leaper*. I know of no one whose life has been saved by cutting open a pair of waders while they were being washed down the river.

Safety afloat

When you are fishing a big lake from a boat, especially one that you do not know well, there are several potential hazards that must be avoided. This is especially true with salmon fishing, for the wild lakes of Ireland and Scotland often have dangerous rocks just beneath the surface. Hit one of those with the outboard going full tilt, and, at best, you will knock off the propeller and have to row home. At worst, the boat will either be rolled over or be split asunder. Remember, too, that the best salmon lies are usually in shallow water, where big boulders are close to the surface.

- If you are going on a lake you have never seen before, go with someone who knows the lake well, such as a professional gillie. He will teach you the safe passages and best lines of drift.
- If the lake appears rough, check the weather forecast. Will it become rougher? If so, do not go afloat. High winds, big waves and small boats do not go together. I know that the best salmon fly fishing conditions on lakes are a fair wave and stiff breeze, but not a hurricane and white water! Err on the side of caution and take local advice.
- Wear a buoyancy aid. If you do finish up in the water and have to make a long swim, you will be able to rest at intervals as you swim out. Remember that a buoyancy aid is not a life-jacket. It helps to keep you afloat, that is all.
- Learn how to use the outboard motor before you go out on the lake. Also find out how to clean and change the spark-plug, which from my experience is the main cause of engine failure. Does the engine you are using take petrol or a petrol/oil mix? You ought to know that. Recently, in Ireland, Alastair Thorne and I were on hand to tow a boat over 2 miles to safety because the occupants, whose boat it was, had broken down because they forgot to put oil in their fuel!

  Motor very slowly in shallow water, so that if you do hit a rock the boat will receive a gentle rap, not an almighty, rib-crushing wallop. Pull up the engine when you are fishing a drift, which obviates the possibility of the propeller hitting a rock or of the line tangling round the propeller.

  If you own your own outboard motor, have it serviced before the start of each fishing season.

- Sooner or later the engine will fail. Then you will have to row for it. I have had to do this three times in the last year, hired engines letting me down. Learn to row, therefore, and, when the outboard motor has let you down, if you cannot make headway back to base, carefully land the boat and walk back. You can always retrieve the boat when the wind and waves subside.
- When you are getting into and out of a small boat, put your feet in the middle.
- Take great care when changing places with someone else. Plan the move first, or don't change places at all.
- Carry a torch and whistle to attract attention if you get into difficulties.
- If someone falls in, they should get back into the boat over the front or back, not the sides, of the boat. If they try to clamber in over the sides they are likely to turn the boat over.
- Do not take alcohol on the boat. It dulls the mind, encourages bravado and chills the body.
- Stow everything carefully in the boat and make sure that you know where everything is so that you can reach it easily. An untidy boat is often a dangerous boat!

I am sorry to have finished this book with such a sad short chapter, but salmon fly fishing is a potentially dangerous sport unless you are sensible. Be sensible. Take precautions and it is 100 per cent safe.

INDEX

Allen, Farrow 57
Ally's Shrimp 76
Anderson, Gary 105
Apache 73
artery forceps 129
Ashley-Cooper, John 143

B&P Silver Head 99
backing 124, 125
backing-up 149–54, 201
Badger 83
Badger and Red 88
Bainbridge, George C. 19
bank lies 111, 116, 135
Bann Special Shrimp 73
Barker, Thomas 14, 15
Bates, J.D. 190
beaching 205
Behan, Peter 142
Bibio 85
bite indicators 195
Bivisible series 88, 94
Black Dog 23
Black, Orange and Yellow 66
Black and Peacock 58–9
Black Pennell 59, 87
Black Pennell Dap 88
Black and Purple 59–60
Black and White Dap 88
Blacker, William 26
Blue and Purple Shrimp 74
Blue and Yellow 68
Blue Zulu 84–5
boat fishing 165–6, 170, 173–7, 220–1
bob flies 81, 84–7
Bomber series 95
boulders 112, 116
Bowkler, Richard 18–19
bridge supports 115
Bridges, Antony 198
Brookes, Richard 18
Brown and Pink Shrimp 68–9
Brown Shrimp 49
Brown Turkey 45
Buck Bugs series 95–6
Buckland, John 57
Butcher 83–4

Capercaillie Shrimp 63
casting 129
  angle 139, 144–5, 181–3
  for bottom tactics 192–4
  and downstream strides 143–4
  and gaining depth 136–7

hook cast 185–6
length 162
reach cast 187–9
roll casting 169
S-cast 176
slack line cast 186–7, 189
spey casting 124
tuck cast 193, 194
Chaytor, A.H. 24–5, 217–18
Chetham, James 18
Chilimps 76
Claret Bumble 85
Claret Dabbler 86
Collie Dog 36, 44, 49, 70–1
colour of flies 40, 44–6, 48, 50, 57–8, 80, 163
Connemara Black 81
Cotton, Charles 16
Curry's Red Shrimp 72

dabblers 86
dapping 177–8, 202
  flies 87–9, 90
  tackle 169–70
Dark Hackles 61
Deer Hair Daddy 94–5
Deer Hair Dibbler and Riffler 78
Dennys, John 51
depth of fly 131–3
dibbling 78, 90, 157–8
donne flye 13
double-hackled patterns 61–4
downstream strides 143–4
drag 139, 183–5, 189
dragonfly 18, 19
drake flye 13
dressing 43, 44
drift fishing 168–9, 170, 173
droppers 126–7, 169
droughts 163–4
Drury, Colonel Esmond 33–4, 75
dry flies 36–8, 90–6
dry fly fishing
  casting angle 181–3
  drag 183–5, 189
  hook cast 185–6
  reach cast 187–9
  slack line cast 186–7, 189
  and water temperature 42
  and weather conditions 179–80
dubbes 12
dubs 112

Edwards, Oliver 213–14
Elver 87

222